Parsippany-Troy Hills Library
Main Library
449 Halsey RD
Parsippany NJ 07054
973-887-5150

NOV 2 8 2017

Cheap Sex

The Transformation of Men, Marriage, and Monogamy

MARK REGNERUS

OXFORD

UNIVERSITY PRESS

OXFORD
UNIVERSITY PRESS

Oxford University Press is a department of the University of Oxford. It furthers
the University's objective of excellence in research, scholarship, and education
by publishing worldwide. Oxford is a registered trade mark of Oxford University
Press in the UK and certain other countries.

Published in the United States of America by Oxford University Press
198 Madison Avenue, New York, NY 10016, United States of America.

© Oxford University Press 2017

CIP data is on file at the Library of Congress
ISBN 978-0-19-067361-1

3 5 7 9 8 6 4
Printed by Sheridan Books, Inc., United States of America

Those who meant well behaved in the same way
as those who meant badly.

—ALDOUS HUXLEY, *Brave New World*

Contents

Acknowledgments

THANKS ESPECIALLY TO Ellyn Arevalo Steidl for her exceptional interviewing skills and particular talent at summarizing and contextualizing her conversations. Dorothy Morgan came alongside as a capable research assistant after David Gordon left for graduate school. My editor at Oxford, Cynthia Read, remains a pleasure to work with; I appreciate her fairness and advocacy, as well as good judgment in selecting two excellent reviewers whose suggestions improved the manuscript. Terry Cole, Kevin and DeAnn Stuart, Meg McDonnell, Laura Wittmann, Nick McCann, Joe Price, Jason Carroll, Glenn Stanton, Matt Breuninger, Brad Wilcox, Mary Catherine Huffines, Jeremy Uecker, Johann Huleatt, J. P. De Gance, Andrew Litschi, Kurt and Lisa Schroder, Bill Hogan, Chris Smith, Bob and Barbara Sleet, Greg Grooms, Bryan Richardson, and Guli Fager all played various intellectual or supportive roles along the way. Conversations with Helen Alvare and Catherine Pakaluk motivated me at the right times. Thanks also to my department chair Rob Crosnoe for being flexible, fair, and courteous to me as a colleague and scholar. I am grateful to the Chiaroscuro and Witherspoon Institutes for early support of the interview project, as well as the GFC and Bradley Foundations for support of the Austin Institute and the *Relationships in America* data collection project. Eric and Keri Stumberg's support—on numerous levels—is unmatched. A particular word of appreciation is in order for Luis Tellez, whose confidence in my work never wavered when nearly everything else did. My family—Deeann, Sam, Libby, and Ruthie—remains the reason I write (even if it doesn't always feel that way to them).

Cheap Sex

I

Introduction

SARAH IS 32 years old and recently moved to Texas from New York, looking for a new start—in more ways than one. Brooklyn had grown too expensive for her hipster pocketbook. A relationship she had hoped would blossom and mature there had instead withered. So to Austin she came, hoping she could improve upon her modest $22,000 annual earnings the previous year. Like many young Americans, Sarah's cash flow is not in step with her expectations or her education. She finds the gap "very embarrassing." Ten years removed from most of her college education, she still has about $20,000 in educational debt to pay off. The failed relationship, however, was the last straw. It was time to move.

Her most recent sexual partner—Daniel—was not actually a relationship per se. He was not the reason she moved. Rather, he was a 23-year-old American she had met in China four years before during a three-week language immersion program. The acquaintance and the sex were not that unusual for her, historically: "I meet people in strange places. . . . It just happens." When they first met, and slept together, Sarah was in a relationship with David, the man for which she had moved to, and then away from, New York. She ended up "cheating on him," that is, David, several times. She felt guilty, because "I'd be heartbroken if someone was cheating on me, you know." So she would stop.

If you're having trouble keeping times, dates, and boyfriends straight, it's understandable. Sarah herself laughs at the drama of it all. Relational reality for very many young adults is not easily mapped today. There are fits and starts, flames and flame-outs. Sarah conveyed an account replete with honest attempts at working it out with David, a musician who seemed more committed to making it in the industry than to making it work with her:

> I'm like, "I want to get married. I want to have kids." And you know, he basically told me that I shouldn't waste my time on him because he didn't know. And I said, "All right then, I'm not gonna waste my time."

David and Sarah were finally through. She plotted her move in part to make her decision stick. But then Daniel reappeared. He was not actually living in New York; he was in Rhode Island. But that did not matter so much, especially when on the rebound: "from then until three weeks ago we had this (arrangement), basically like whenever he came to town, we got together and dated and, like, slept with each other." Getting serious was never much of an option. He was 23, and she was 32: "We both knew ... he was graduating from college and, you know, like we both, at least I knew it was never gonna work out. I think he kind of felt the same way." Why? "He's 23 and I didn't want to be in New York ... we had fun and everything but I was like, I don't wanna marry the guy." Her mental age range for a mate is between 32 and 40.

Daniel and David were not Sarah's only partners. She recounted "probably about 20" partners when asked about it. Most of them were during a several-year stint in Baltimore, before her time in New York. Four were one-night stands, the rest longer. Abstinence advocates, and their opponents, have long fought over the territory of teenage sex and how to curb it and its consequences, but that was not Sarah's problem. Her first sexual relationship did not happen until she was 22. But the comparative delay in her case did not spell success in romance, as some social conservatives claim. Indeed, concern has largely shifted away from adolescent sexual behavior, which has dipped in the past decade, to the full-blown "failure to launch" that has quickly materialized and now characterizes many Americans in their mid-twenties to mid-thirties.

When asked how rapidly her relationships tend to become sexual, Sarah replied, "the first or second date." That account did not stand out from those of many other interviewees. The numbers are on her side, too. In the 2014 *Relationships in America* survey, sex before the relationship begins was the modal—meaning the most common—point at which Americans report having first had sex in their current relationships. Is her timing of sex intentional? No. "It just happens," she reasoned. Trained to detect unlikely passivity, I responded skeptically with a "Nothing just happens. Tell me how this works."

Well, it happens if there's really strong physical chemistry. If there's physical chemistry then usually it's gonna, the date's gonna end with some kind of, like, physical (activity), at least for me in my experience. [*Even date number one?*] Oh yeah, (laughs). Date number one, like, kissing, and then I feel like the kissing always leads to something else. [*You feel like it, or you make it, or ...?*] It just does, I don't know. I don't think it's me, I think it's more the guy, and then I'm just OK with it. And then a lot of times, though, I will say, like, there are times when I feel comfortable with having sex on the first date, and other times I don't feel comfortable. [*How do you discern those?*] Depending on if I like the guy more or not. [*So if you like the guy more which one happens?*] I don't want to have sex with him. [*OK. Can you explicate that a little bit?*] (Laughs) ... Because I wanna see him again, and I don't want it to just be about something physical.

She nevertheless often finds herself regretting "first-date sex," she admits, but finds it difficult to predict beforehand: during the date itself "I feel like I get (sighs) . . . caught up in the moment." So waiting for the second or third date, she asserts, is a better strategy than first-date sex, because "he's going to stay interested." This, she claims, is the standard approach to dating among her peers, if not necessarily the most optimal: "I don't think it's unusual, but I think that for a lasting relationship, it's not the best approach." What is? "Um, to take things very slow physically." How slow, I wondered.

I don't know, like waiting to have sex maybe, like, one or two months. In theory that always sounds great to me. I'm always like, "OK, cool, I'm going to (wait) this time," and then I meet the guy and there's chemistry and the next thing I know I'm sleeping with them and I'm like, "Shit." [*So you often start out with the intention of waiting?*] Oh, I always do.

Subsequent dates predictably expect sex.

That pattern is the way that most of my, maybe all, I don't know, almost all relationships start, is that they start ... really intense and passionate and they become like, it becomes like, you know. Like I go out with a guy. We really like each other and we have sex and then it's like you see him every day and they're just, like, they become your world. And then all of a sudden it's been like, I don't know, months and you like come to (your senses) and you're like, "What the hell just happened?" [*What happened? Like what do you mean?*] Like, where have I been the last two months? All I've been doing is hanging out with this guy. [*And that bothers you?*] Yeah, it bothers me because it's just, that's not, I don't think, that's not healthy. [*What's healthy?*] (Laughs and claps hands) For me, it's um, maintaining my own life and not ... have the guy become my life. [*Has that happened?*] Oh, all the time. That's what happens.

The move to Austin was intended to turn over a new leaf in several ways, including relationships. When asked about her ideal scenario for how a future romantic relationship would develop, she paused for a few moments, then responded:

I guess for me I feel like the way that I always felt like it was gonna happen was it would be, like, it would start out slower (laughs) than I've done in the past and then, like, we become friends, and then you know become romantic and, um, and then the engagement, and marriage coming within a year or two.

Her ideal and her reality almost couldn't be more different. Her self-criticism around relationships has nothing to do with religious faith because she has none. A few experiences with more devout men on eHarmony reinforced that religion was not for her. OKCupid was a better match, and not just because it was free. OKCupid users were more likely to fit her "independent, Bohemian" style and interests. Does online dating work for her? "Um, I mean, I met people. I, uh, it's not like I'm with them, but (laughs) I think it's, uh, yeah." I asked if dating was more challenging in New York than in Baltimore. She thought it was:

I feel like New York men, not all of them, the ones ... some that I've dated, it's very about, they're so them-focused and career-focused and like, I feel like the last thing on their mind is family and getting married. ... Whereas, um, I don't know, in Baltimore it's a little bit different. I feel like here (Austin) it's probably a little bit different as well.

Whether the drama around relationships contributes to her ongoing battle with depression is unclear. She does not make a connection. They certainly do not seem responsible for its onset at least, which occurred when she was 18. She has seen a psychiatrist and has been on antidepressants ever since.

As noted above, Sarah was 32 years old when we spoke with her. The thirties are notorious for their association with women's "ticking biological clock." Sarah was well aware of her age and the fertility challenges it might soon present, but had grown ambivalent on the matter. Did she want children, as she noted in passing when discussing the end of her relationship with Daniel?

> I don't know. I've always wanted, it's interesting because I've always wanted children. It was like, "Oh, I'm gonna be a great mom," and, and umm, the last couple years, I, I don't know. I definitely want to get married, like that, I definitely wanna get married and do that deal, but I don't know if I wanna have kids or not. . . . [*But you used to want them?*] I used to want them.

Three years later, now 35, Sarah continues to live in Austin and continues to find commitment elusive. She does not dislike her life, but it is not the one she envisioned a decade earlier.

Her account is not unusual. In fact, the relationship histories that young Americans tell us about are growing increasingly predictable: plenty of sex, starting early (before expressions of love but not necessarily before feelings of and hopes about it), underdeveloped interest in sacrificing on behalf of the other (especially but not exclusively discernable in men), accounts of "overlapping" partners, much drama, and in the end nothing but mixed memories and expired time. Valuable "experience," many call it. Some have fulfilling careers to focus on, steering their attention away from other, less-successful areas of their lives. Others, like Sarah, find themselves frustrated there as well. Some are becoming jaded, skeptical. Others hold out hope or redirect themselves toward a different vision of the good life. While some observers are adamant that we are making progress in sex, sexuality, and relationships, others aptly wonder about the state of our unions.

This book takes readers on a tour of the romantic and sexual relationships Americans are forming—with a particular (but not exclusive) focus on the ones they form in their mid-twenties through their mid-thirties. Mine is not an elegy for a lost era, though critics will try to convince you that it is so. No—it is an explanation of the present, occasionally with reference to the past and hints about the future. It is an account of how young Americans relate today: what they think about relationships, how they interact sexually with their partners (and without them), what they hope for romantically, and my best efforts at explaining why. I draw on several large, population-based surveys to provide a representative overview of what Americans think and do, while sharing stories from the 100 people my research team sat down with in person in five different parts of the country.

What emerges is a story about desired social change, yet with mixed results, about technological breakthroughs, but with unintended consequences. In the end, many find themselves ambivalent about it all. There are personal and relational freedoms for which many fought hard. And there are certainly technologies that seem to boost equality and simplify our lives—including how people meet and evaluate each other—but somehow they have not spelled notably greater happiness and relationship contentment. In fact, the harm and dissatisfaction is palpable. Young Americans appear to be having more sexual experiences, more partners, and more time to "try them on," but seem less stable in, and less content with, the relationship in front of them. Why?

Part of the reason, I assert, is because most of us fail to recognize the underlying market forces at work around coupled sexual behavior, how those forces have shifted, and the reasons for that. You might think basic economics doesn't or shouldn't have anything to do with this most intimate and private of actions, replete as it often is with romance or the pangs of desire. But it does. It must. And it always has. Mating market dynamics continue to be consequential for the options people are afforded, the choices they make, even what they claim to want—as Sarah demonstrates when asked about children. I discuss modern mating market dynamics at length in the next chapter, but what preceded them—and perhaps brought them about—is a dramatic shift in how men and women relate to each other. It did not, however, appear out of the blue.

The Transformation of Intimacy

In part, this is also a book about a book. British social theorist Anthony Giddens—a leading public intellectual in England and one of the most famous sociologists alive today—offered what turned out to be a prescient introduction to shifting sexual norms in his 1992 book entitled The Transformation of Intimacy. Although not chock-full of statistics or interviews, Giddens nevertheless aided us immensely by beginning to name things that those of us who traffic in data on sex and sexuality now perceive with a good deal of regularity. For example, the wide uptake of contraception, Giddens wrote,

> meant more than an increased capability of limiting pregnancy. In combination with the other influences affecting family size ... it signaled a deep transition in personal life. For women—and, in a partly different sense, for men also—sexuality became malleable, open to being shaped in diverse ways, and a potential "property" of the individual. Sexuality came into being as part of a progressive differentiation of sex from the exigencies of reproduction. With the further elaboration of reproductive technologies, that differentiation has today become complete. Now that conception can be artificially produced, rather than only artificially inhibited, sexuality is at last fully autonomous.[1]

Fully autonomous. That is, not only separated from its long-standing association with marriage and baby-making but free from even being embedded in relationships—the malleable property of the individual. Almost all Americans take birth control for granted, and most of us alive today never inhabited a world before it. How did it change things? Giddens asserts that its uptake has, among other things, fostered the idea of sex as an "art form" and injected that into the heart of the "conjugal relationship," which then made the

> achievement of reciprocal sexual pleasure a key element in whether the relationship is sustained or dissolved. The cultivation of sexual skills, the capability of giving and experiencing sexual satisfaction, on the part of both sexes, [has] become organized reflexively via a multitude of sources of sexual information, advice and training.[2]

Sarah could be a case study. Despite all the sex and relationships she has had, she has never pursued pregnancy or become pregnant. The prospect of mutual sexual pleasure animates her dating life, even first dates. Sexual interest or its absence commonly dictates what happens next, even though her ideal relationship, she claims, would develop and mature before sex, not because of it.

And all of these comparatively new achievements, Giddens asserts, have been sealed in language—how we talk about sex and relationships. And that is significant: "Once there is a new terminology for understanding sexuality, ideas, concepts and theories couched in these terms seep into social life itself, and help reorder it."[3] What he means is that when we name something in the social world—unlike in the natural world—we are not only mentally mapping it, but we are also providing the idea with a reality that allows it to then act back upon us (and the wider social world), altering how we then must subsequently navigate it. Thus the world after something has been named is not as malleable as it was before it. To identify something socially is to give it life and power, not just a name. It's been occurring for decades already in the study of sexuality, Giddens holds:

> The Kinsey Reports, like others following on, aimed to analyze what was going on in a particular region of social activity, as all social research seeks to do. Yet as they disclosed, they also influenced, initiating cycles of debate, reinvestigation and further debate. These debates became part of a wide public domain, but also served to alter lay views of sexual actions and involvements themselves. No doubt the "scientific" cast of such investigations helps neutralize moral uneasiness about the propriety of particular sexual practices.[4]

Sociologist James Davison Hunter asserts similarly when he defines culture as the power of *legitimate naming*.[5] That is, to classify something in the social world is to penetrate the imagination, to alter our frameworks of knowledge and discussion, and to shift the perception of everyday reality. In the domain of sexuality—fraught as it is with great moral valence—this can make all the difference. It's why there is often poignant and bitter struggle over words and terms around sex, and the politics of using them or avoiding them. We tend to move, albeit slowly, from the "urban dictionary" to the everyday lexicon. But what is very unlikely is a return to the patterns witnessed prior to the "sexual revolution." As Giddens asserts:

> We are dealing here with much more deep-lying, and irreversible, changes than were brought about by such movements, important although they were in facilitating more unfettered discussion of sexuality than previously was possible.[6]

Giddens makes this claim because he holds that what emerged in the domain of sex and relationships is not simply different norms or values among subgroups but new (or restructured) realities around the intimate life of the vast majority of Westerners. We now value and express what he calls the *pure relationship*. This is

> where a social relation is entered into for its own sake, for what can be derived by each person from a sustained association with another; and which is continued only insofar as it is thought by both parties to deliver enough satisfactions for each individual to stay within it.[7]

Or, as sociologist Eva Illouz describes it, it is "the contractual assumption that two individuals with equal rights unite for emotional and individualistic purposes."[8] The pure relationship is not just distinctive from the older regime of institutionalized matrimony. It is also unlike the more recent romantic love model, which seeks relationship fulfillment and is the stuff of "soul mates." In the pure relationship model, Giddens holds, love is "confluent."

> Confluent love is active, contingent love, and therefore jars with the "for-ever," "one-and-only" qualities of the romantic love complex. The "separating and divorcing society" of today here appears as an effect of the emergence of confluent love rather than its cause.[9]

Confused? That's understandable. These are not terms we use every day. In a nutshell, in romantic love there may be stops and starts, but the quest is for settled-ness, the destination is a family, and the assumption is distinctiveness (and magnetism) between men and women. Its type of love is not "liquid," to use social theorist Zygmunt Bauman's term, but instead seeks to solidly preserve the object of care and add to the world, to expand by giving itself away to the object of love.[10]

With confluent love in the "pure" relationship, contingency is its foundation, equality is its organizing principle, taste and emotion are its barometers, discovery is a key goal, and while the dyad—the couple—is the basic structure to the union, it is never to usurp the individual's primacy and will. Indeed, "in lasting commitments, liquid modern reason spies out oppression."[11] Bonds make human relations "impure," and children are expensive, they complicate things, and are for much, much later in a relationship.

The realities I document herein suggest the "transformations" in intimacy that Giddens detected back in 1992—just before the Internet era— are blossoming today. In a time wherein childbearing can be avoided, thus making possible an extensive and diverse sexual life, what he claimed would result is what has materialized, now almost 25 years later:

- Strong norms about emotional and physical satisfaction in relationships
- Expectations of paired sexual activity emerge quickly in budding relationships.
- Sexual exclusivity is no longer assumed but rather the subject of negotiation.
- Shorter-term relationships, together with perceptions of commitment "phobia"
- Plastic sexuality—interests and directions are shaped and remodeled
- The flourishing of non-heterosexual identities and expressions
- Obsession with romance among many, and yet stability seems increasingly elusive

To most young Americans, these are all self-obvious realities—the way things are. To write them down here seems almost an unnecessary exercise for them. They are that obvious. And yet each is a profound social accomplishment. They are far from a historic certainty, and not the product of some sort of social or sexual "evolution." Not all of them are universally welcomed by everyone, as ought to be obvious. And plenty of people are fond of some of the changes more than others.

In tandem with these transformations in intimacy, sexual acts themselves can be said to have become comparatively "cheaper" or less expensive, economically and socially speaking. That statement may throw some for a loop, but it is not a very controversial one. What I mean by it is that coupled sexual activity has become more widely accessible, at lower "cost" to everyone than ever before in human history. Pregnancy, childbearing, and childrearing are, after all, extremely expensive in terms of time, investment, lost (paid) labor and income. (They have their rewards, no doubt.) But infertile sex is surely "cheaper" than sex that risks—and occasionally entails—pregnancy. Sexual intercourse also costs men less today than ever before, on average. (And paying for sex is becoming rarer.[12]) If Giddens's claims are true—and few would suggest he is wrong—then it means that men have to do less wooing (fewer dates, less costly indicators of commitment, etc.) in order to access real sex. Hence, sex is cheaper. Additionally, solitary sex—masturbation—is now able, by use of digital pornography, to mimic coupled sex more realistically than ever before. That, too, is a source of cheap sex. You may prefer I not speak about sex in this way. That's fine. But your preference for a different lingo about sex does not make any of this untrue.

While cheaper sex is a straightforward result of several significant technological developments, some of which were desired by men, some by women—and some by both—the ramifications of cheaper sex are just beginning to unfold on a panoramic scale. Greater sexual access is no longer just the purview of the most attractive, the wealthiest, the most discreet, or the biggest risk-takers. No—coupled and uncoupled sexual experiences of wider variety and novelty are now democratized. They're more accessible to everyone. The supply has increased dramatically while the cost has diminished, but not necessarily because all the participants wish for that to be so. Even Sarah expressed ideals that were out of step with her own choices.

Cheaper sex has been facilitated by three distinctive technological achievements: (1) the wide uptake of the Pill as well as a mentality stemming from it that sex is "naturally" infertile, (2) mass-produced high-quality pornography, and (3) the advent and evolution of online dating/meeting services. All three are price "suppressors" that have significantly altered mating market dynamics, often in ways invisible to the individuals in the market. They have created a massive slow-down in the development of committed relationships, especially marriage, have put the fertility of increasing numbers of women at risk—subsequently driving up demand for infertility treatments—and have arguably even taken a toll on men's economic and relational productivity, prompting fewer of them to be considered marriage material than ever before.

Certainly men are languishing when compared with women. There are 2.4 million more women in college than men.[13] In 2015, 39 percent of 25- to 34-year-old women, but only 33 percent of men, had earned at least a bachelor's degree. There are now more women than men in the paid labor force. Documentation of the dismal state of men almost constitutes a genre of literature today. Where exactly are all these missing men? As recently as October 2016, the Bureau of Labor Statistics revealed that over 11 percent of men between the ages of 25 and 54—about seven million people—were neither employed nor seeking work. What are they doing, and why have they come to languish? How, if at all, does some men's failure to thrive shape not only their own relationship behavior and sexual and marital decision-making but also those of their more successful male counterparts? There are, of course, a variety of reasons that have been floated to explain the plight of men, and the state of marriage and relationships. But few if any have wrestled with the possible sexual sources of these significant shifts. Basically, does cheap sex undermine men's motivation to achieve? Perhaps. I will explore the evidence for it.

What the West has witnessed over the past several decades may not simply be the social construction of sexuality or marriage or family forms toward different plausible ends as a product of political will, but the reality of technology-driven social change. Recognizing this counters the simple and reductionist explanations like "social construction," "the right side of history," "liberation," "enlightenment," or "the triumph of rights and freedom over ignorance and bigotry" for the new variations in socially sanctioned intimate relationships, including the decoupling of sex from committed relationships and the altered meaning and now altered structure of marriage. These technological developments helped spawn a series of social changes in human sexual behavior and the wider world of relationships that remain commonly misunderstood. Various authors have noted, praised, or lamented aspects of these shifts, but an explication of the big picture is overdue.

The story about how exactly technological uptake has made sex cheaper and relationships more challenging is nevertheless not straightforward. They don't change things overnight. Or even over a decade. Or for everyone in an identical fashion. But this is how "sea change" works—slowly but surely. And once such change happens, undoing things is pretty much impossible, and by then perhaps even undesirable to most since they will have calibrated much about their lives in light of the new realities.

A Guide to the Rest of the Book

This book not only assesses the modern mating market and its dynamics, it also explicates the sexual ideas, habits, and relationships of Americans, with a recurrent focus on those in their mid- to late twenties and thirties. They are out of college, if they ever went at all, and coming face-to-face with what it has historically meant (in America, at least) to be an adult: living apart from your parents, working, earning financial independence, marrying, and having children. But for many, that pathway is no longer obvious, direct, quick, or even desired. In particular, I am after answers to several important questions, including:

- How common is non-monogamy—the practice of overlapping sexual partners—today?
- How exactly have contraception, porn, and online dating affected the mating market?
- Do women think men are afraid of commitment, and do men genuinely fear it?
- Is marriage still perceived as a key goal, or is it increasingly perceived as optional?

I tackle questions like these using nationally representative survey data as well as in-person interviews. Both are necessary. The one offers a 30,000-foot view that enables us to effectively compare lots of different people at once and to speak authoritatively to what is going on with young Americans. The other offers illumination of the dynamics at work in real relationships themselves—how people actually think and act when asked about such matters.

I lean on a variety of data sources here, but I privilege one survey in particular—the *Relationships in America* survey project, which interviewed just under 15,000 Americans between the ages of 18 and 60 in 2014. The large sample size enables me to analyze particular subgroups of respondents that smaller data-collection efforts often cannot. Most of the time I concern myself with those young adults under the age of 40, but occasionally it is helpful to look at the 40- to 60-year-olds for comparison purposes. And this survey enables that. The data collection was conducted by Knowledge Networks (or KN), a research firm with a very strong record of generating high-quality data for academic projects.[14]

Other datasets provide assistance as well. The National Survey of Family Growth (NSFG) is a nationally representative survey of Americans ages 15–44 that concentrates on fertility, health, and parenting. It is not a longitudinal study, but rather asks detailed questions to a different group of people over time. It includes thousands of men and women, and is now in the process of near-continuous administration. The New Family Structures Study (NFSS) is a survey of just under 3,000 young adults administered in 2011 and early 2012. The NFSS asked numerous questions about respondents' social behaviors, health behaviors, and relationships, including numerous questions about their sex and sexuality. It is cross-sectional in nature, having collected data from respondents at only one point in time, when they were between the ages of 18 and 39. I oversaw both the NFSS and *Relationships in America* projects, and so was enabled to ask the sorts of survey questions to which I sought answers, rather than rely on the judgment of others' data-collection interests and efforts.

The combination of these three surveys—plus discussions of numerous other studies drawing upon still other data and a few statistics from the Census and from the longitudinal Add Health project—gave me more than enough numbers to think through, crunch, and present. More complicated regression models are sometimes helpful, and they appear in Appendix A.

I supplement these survey statistics with in-person interviews with adults between the ages of 24 and 32 who live or work in or near five different metropolitan areas: Austin, Denver, Milwaukee, Washington, DC, and the Tri-Cities region of Tennessee (Bristol, Johnson City, and Kingsport). I selected these areas for a variety of reasons: convenience, diversity, rural/ urban mix (especially in Tennessee), regional variation, and information vs. industrial economies. My interview team and I conducted in-depth, semi-structured interviews that ranged from 90 to 120 minutes in length. Such interviews allowed me to inquire about attitudes, processes, and relationship dynamics in ways just not suited to surveys. Survey participants were compensated $30 for their time. Considerably more than 100 people indicated a willingness to be interviewed, but I limited the interviews to 100 overall. My selection criteria primarily concerned getting ample representation on gender, age, relationship status, and employment status— that is, ensuring we spoke with men and women who were unemployed, underemployed, those working blue-collar jobs, and those in professional positions. The participants in this current study were an average age of 27 years old. Half were men and half were women. Sixty-three percent of the sample was working full time, 19 percent were working part-time, and 18 percent reported that they were currently unemployed.[15] I have changed their names to protect their identity and ensure their confidentiality.

Critics will no doubt be quick to point out that a self-selective sample is hardly representative of the American population. I agree, and will not portray the interviewees as more generalizable than I ought to. And yet such a sample may actually be very fitting for this book. Given the focus of books like Hanna Rosin's *The End of Men* on underemployed and underachieving men, perhaps this interviewee pool is ideally poised to help answer my research questions, for my claims have less to do with lawyers, doctors, and executives than they do with regular people farther down the socioeconomic ladder—the kinds of men and women social scientists often claim to represent but frequently overlook in their own research methods.

Additional information on the data collection processes, including the in-person interview questionnaire and survey instruments, is available upon request.

In the following chapters, readers will be offered my best understanding of what is happening in American relationships and my attempt to answer the questions I have posed. It is not a dry presentation of academic facts and theories, one in which the fascinating is made dull, but rather will explore several narratives and answer a variety of questions about contemporary sexual behavior patterns, including these: How often do Americans have sex? Has masturbation actually increased, and if so, why? How frequently are men using porn today? Is there an uptick among women? Who cheats on a spouse or partner?

I spend time outlining the contemporary mating market and its dynamics, detailing how the sexual behavior patterns witnessed today both favor men's interests and yet subtly undermine them, drawing upon men's and women's own words as well as the assertions of scholars ranging from evolutionary psychologists to gender theorists. Virtually no one, it seems, is happy with the state of maleness today, and yet the male behavior we witness today seems a rational, if short-sighted, response to their circumstances.

Chapter 2 wrestles first with conceptual questions of "What happened?" and "How did we get here?" It offers my best explanation for why young Americans' relationships look the way they do today, and why they do not readily resemble the patterns as recently as 40 to 50 years ago. It is here where I elaborate more extensively on the subject of "sexual economics," an increasingly popular set of general conceptual tools that enables us to better understand the exchange behavior we continue to see in romantic relationships around us. The theory's explanatory fit is extensive, and reaches into Americans' minds, bedrooms, and marriages, even though many ignore it, deny it, or actively resist it. It is also here that I define cheap sex and describe the modern mating market, how it has changed and in particular how it has become imbalanced, and how such sex-ratio imbalances have had profound consequences for how men and women form relationships today. That is, I detail how the thing so many Americans now take for granted—the Pill—ironically created new barriers in the mating market for those who seek long-term relational security. Contraception, which is firmly embedded in Western relational systems and practice now, was more of a "grand bargain," or a trade-off than a magic pill. This and other technological innovations have functioned to lower the cost of real sex, access to which women control. And again, all this is largely invisible to casual observers, who commonly assert that men have become afraid to commit. I just don't see it. Men are not afraid to "man up" and commit. They simply don't need to. We should not be surprised in the least, except at our remarkable failure to anticipate it. Men, I argue, work best under pressure—from women—but social constraints upon what motivates men are rapidly disappearing today, with little sign of a return. And yet many eventually fall in love and commit, but later than in previous eras.

Anthony Giddens, whose observations and predictions shape the flow of this book, held that the revolution in sexual autonomy also ushered in an era of plastic sexuality and paved the way for the flourishing of non-heterosexual identities. I hold that Giddens's observations actually fit (albeit imperfectly) expectations of exchange behavior in a domain—non-heterosexual relationships—that has long been presumed to operate independently of male and female exchange relationship preferences. I consistently find a key source of influence upon straight and gay relationship behavior is sex (that is, male/female) differences, not orientation.

Chapter 3 revisits the "cheap sex" motif of the book in an overview of Americans' sexual behavior patterns. There I develop the conceptual claim that online dating makes sex cheaper simply by doing what it does best—making the search process more efficient. No wonder the online dating sphere is so attractive, yet so maddening, to so many. I also spend time documenting the latest estimates of sexual behavior of both unmarried and married young adults, again with a particular (but not exclusive) interest in those no older than 35. I highlight sexual partner numbers—and test a popular theory about them—before exploring sexual inactivity rates, the strange politics of expressed sexual desire, and the emergence of "monogamish," the overlapping of partners. I also explore a key piece of evidence about the falling price of sex—the timing of its addition in relationships—and conclude with a discussion of satisfaction with sexual unions in the era of the "pure" relationship.

The topic of Chapter 4 is the cheapest forms of sex—pornography and masturbation—sibling subjects that are seldom given the scholarly treatment they deserve. I use new data and new methods of inquiry to generate the most up-to-date information yet on their patterns in the wider population. They signal still more compelling evidence for the robust nature of sexual exchange and economic insight into intimate (and in this case solitary) sexual behavior. Questions about gender and orientation effects on pornography use are considered, as is the claim that a share of men are exiting the mating market altogether, choosing porn over the pursuit of the real thing. Masturbation, the subject of speculation but little hard data, is given more space than it typically receives, including questions of its rising prevalence in the era of digital porn.

Chapter 5 is the longest chapter and dwells on the matter of marriage—the source of so much political and legal conflagration in recent years. Are men opting out—going their own way—because marriage appears to them a worse deal than ever? (The answer, surprisingly to many, is no.) Instead, cheap sex seems to be contributing—if only indirectly—to the decline in men's marriageability, a perennial key variable for women in discerning with whom and when to tie the knot. What is occurring, then, is a massive slowdown in marriage, the result of uncertainty in the terms of exchange that has diminished its economic (but not personal) appeal among women. The institution of marriage is in recession, and cracks are appearing in the tight historical connection between monogamy and marriage. Although polyamory is a minority behavior and practiced by men and women alike, I detail why it too—like so much else in contemporary sexual patterns—reflects men's power in the mating market. In turn, women find the mating market increasingly frustrating and the process of meeting and falling in love more convoluted, despite the supposed speed and ease promised by online dating's efficiency. Organized religion appears to be marriage's key, and increasingly solitary, institutional supporter, but it too is hamstrung by the development of the pure relationship and its own decentralized and diminishing authority in America.

The book ends with Chapter 6, entitled "The Genital Life" because the data, the interviews, and Giddens's prescient perspective all point to the increasing centrality of sex and its satisfactions in contemporary life. No longer playing a supporting role in enduring relationships, sex has emerged on center stage, worthy of its own attention. It is "like a big, big, big, big part of everything now," claimed one interviewee who reported both gratification and consternation at that prospect. The book ends with eight projections about our collective relationship future. Giddens's *The Transformation of Intimacy* is now 25 years old, but a quarter-century seems like forever in a dynamic domain like sex, so I speculate about what we can expect by the year 2030. I predict what's next for sex, gender, relationships, marriage, living arrangements, and the future of monogamy. No, the sky is not falling, and I am

not interested in overreaching and sensationalism. In the end, relationships between the sexes are not at risk; only the norms and structures
around them are. For some, such changes are welcome. For others,
these are matters of grave concern. After reading this book, I hope you
will have a clearer sense of how you perceive such significant changes.
Even if you and I do not share the same conclusions, I hope you learn
much herein.

There are a variety of sex-related matters that I do not cover in-depth,
including pregnancy experiences, sexually transmitted infections (STIs),
and personal sexual assault (beyond simple reporting rates). Why not? In
part because the book's focus is on the consensual exchange relationship,
not its violations nor its desired or unwanted fruits. While intended to be
general and provide an overview of new population-based data on sex, it
cannot be all things to all readers. Any time a theme (like STIs) found no
obvious place in a discussion of sexual economics, out it went for consideration by other competent observers.

Politics, Scientism, and Realism
in the Study of Sex

It is nevertheless difficult to write a book like this one, for the following
reasons:

1. Things are changing rapidly in this oldest of subjects. It is challenging
   to keep current.
2. The topic matter is a sensitive one, subject to political and ideological
   concerns.
3. High-quality information in the domains of sex and sexuality didn't
   exist before the mid-1970s, and then only sparingly until the 1990s.
4. There has been an explosion of interest in and data collection on sex-
   related matters recently, but it has yielded both quality and dubious scientific inquiries.
5. Public—as well as researcher—expectations of what can be known with
   confidence about what happens largely in private are unreasonably high.
6. There remains popular skepticism about the reality of social structures
   and their influence.

Together these concerns can be summarized as about politics, scientism,
and realism.

First, there is the politics. Even as secularization proceeds apace, the domains of sex and sexuality remain saturated with moral idealism—what is good to do or to be, what criteria are legitimate or illegitimate, what is important to support, affirm, or denigrate. Young adults do lots of virtue signaling here. And while Americans seem to be increasingly at ease in answering questions about their sexual behavior, the process of interpreting and drawing (public) conclusions has become more difficult. Whereas not long ago conservatives policed discourse concerning human sexuality, today liberal voices have replaced them. The only thing that has remained constant is the presence of policing. It is not that quality data and arguments cannot get a fair hearing. They can. But there is struggle over who gets to be heard, what can and cannot be spoken, and what must be said or left unsaid.[16] Many "truths" in the domain of sex and sexuality seem more politically sculpted than empirically accurate.[17] There are tacit ideologies that saturate sociology, and if you trespass them you can be informally (and occasionally formally) punished.[18] The problem lies not with the scientific method, but with a politicized academic culture made worse by the pull of the media news cycle. There is wisdom to the slower pace of science.[19] And yet it is difficult to operate here with what could be considered a "neutral" perspective. I recognize that I do not. (I don't think it's genuinely possible.)

We would do well, in such a challenging context, to heed popular social networks scholar Duncan Watts's warning about how we tend to approach knowledge we dislike. Watts asserts that we tend to think of ourselves as rational actors—reasonable people—and so when we meet information which challenges us, our first impulse is to dismiss it: "People subject disconfirming information to greater scrutiny and skepticism than confirming information."[20] Watts hits upon the very human impulse toward confirmation bias, or the tendency to look for, favor, or remember information that confirms your own beliefs or hypotheses. (I am surely not exempt, either.) While we are all prone to it, the tendency toward it is even stronger when it concerns emotionally charged issues. The domain of sex and relationships is certainly that.

A second warning before leaping into the rest of the book is to beware of scientism, especially in the domain of sex and sexuality. Scientism is a perspective that suggests that empirical data collection and analysis is the only viable approach to learning what can be known about social reality. It is skeptical about meanings, values, and certainly about spirituality. (Sex and sexuality, on the other hand, seem to traffic in each of these.) It claims science can be truly neutral—again, better in theory than in the hands of

real scientists—and prefers reductionist analysis that breaks down realities into their constituent, materialist parts.[21]

This book, meanwhile, bridges macro- and microsociology, asserting in
one section claims about how survey respondents make sense of their own
personal sexual satisfaction and how interviewees discern their relationship decision-making, while offering in another section larger arguments
about macro concepts like mating markets, contraceptive "uptake," confluent love, sex as transcendence, and monogamous systems—structured,
influential realities that the people we survey and interview tend neither
to refer to nor even perceive. I caution readers from leaping to a scientism
that holds that if we cannot measure it in a survey or tap it discursively in
interviews, then claims about it cannot reasonably be offered and certainly
not believed. This book instead takes the reality of social structures very
seriously, but nevertheless holds that they are not easily amenable to inser-
tion in cross-tabs or regression models. I cannot document the influence
of "wide contraceptive uptake" simply by controlling for respondent's use
of birth control in the past month. The former is a structured reality whose
affect is difficult to avoid regardless of one's own personal decisions. The
same can be said of confluent love and the pure relationship system. They
are just not the kind of idea that is easily measured on surveys, though
some have tried.[22]

Finally, I try to be a blunt realist about empirical matters concerning
sex, sexuality, marriage, and family, because I really want to know what is
going on in social reality, even if I dislike what I see. I lean conservative
in my own life and personal perspective, but I want to know the facts,
the theories, and the best guesses of experts—whether I agree with their
interpretations of the data or not. I am not naïve about realism, though.
Even it is perspectival. Although most sociologists are quick to assert a
strong distinction between facts and values, documentation contributes
to social valuing. Hence social science contributes profoundly to values
by way of our facts. We are not simply writing down what is, because to
observe is to reinforce. Giddens wrote about that, too—he called it the
double hermeneutic.[23] Our very preferences—what we are convinced we
want and believe we have a right to—are now boxed in by what Eva Illouz
calls the "architecture of choice" framed by new "languages of the self."[24]
It is nevertheless paramount to appreciate the limits of social science, so
that we do not make the error of solely relying on science to settle questions or to resolve issues that rest well beyond the competence of the
scientific method.

I write, too, as a man, yet one who has concerns that are in histori-cal alignment with women's (and many men's) long-standing relational interests—things like commitment, stability, monogamy, tranquility, and a family. I want to help people accomplish these goals, but I won't alter my published perceptions of reality in order to do that. If the mating market is a gritty place, I do readers no favors by sugar-coating it. This book is not a clarion call to return somehow—by hook, crook, or political will—to an earlier era. That is not going to happen. This book is, instead, a documen-tary, an assessment of where things stand and an argument about how we got here, with some space at the end donated to educated guesses about what happens next. My goal in this book is to explain. There are, of course, occasional expressions of concern herein, because I think some important things have been lost, or are receding. You may or may not share those with me. But it is my hope and goal that we can all agree about what is going on in human social and sexual life. What you do with what I say here is your own business. (I do not pose many solutions, to the relief of some and the chagrin of others.) For those of you who are fans of our new relational realities—don't worry, they are not going anywhere. And to those who oppose these, I am sorry I don't have better news for you. There is, however, power and wisdom in seeing and assessing the social world realistically.

2

Cheap Sex and the Modern Mating Market

SEX IS, AMONG other things, a social transaction.[1] It is not the only way to understand the matter, and sex is, of course, not reducible to transaction. But whether we wish to admit it or not, there is a basic exchange that typically constitutes the social setting in which sexual relationships begin, end, or continue—even one-night stands. In their 2004 *Personality and Social Psychology Review* article entitled "Sexual Economics," social psychologists Roy Baumeister and Kathleen Vohs explicate the economic and market principles that characterize and shape the genesis of heterosexual relationships between unmarried adults.[2] Each person gives the other person something of themselves. Although it might appear at face value to be the same something—intimate access to each other's body—there is typically more going on than meets the eye. Men, on average, are more often principally drawn to the powerful physical pleasures of sex than women are. This does not mean that women are uninterested in pleasure, just seldom in quite the same way—or with the same single-mindedness—as men. More often than men, women's interests also include the affirmation of desirability, expressing and receiving love, the validation of worth, and fostering or reinforcing relationship commitment. Men can appreciate each of those too, and plenty do, but they will tend to be secondary or tertiary reasons for sex. Think this is a tired, unmerited, insensitive stereotype? Have an anecdote to the contrary? Too much data collected for too long suggests this claim about gender and sex may be unpopular, but it is not inaccurate.[3] Across multiple studies, women were found more likely to have regretted casual sexual interactions, while men's regrets were more often about missed sexual opportunities.[4] When we asked Kevin, a 24-year-old recent college graduate from Denver, what he wished he had known earlier about sex, he was frank:

> I wish I would have known everything I do now about … [how] girls work, how girls function, how girls think so that I when I was younger I could have taken more advantage of that …

To be sure, men can and do express regrets. But you won't hear women assert anything like Kevin just did.

I know that women can and do like sex. Rest assured, though, that men—historically, and on average—tend to want sex more and pursue it with greater abandon and single-mindedness. Sociologist Catherine Hakim documents this phenomenon over decades and dozens of data sets.[5] The vast majority of women simply do not operate like the average man—walking down the street ogling the average woman with his eyes, wondering what sex with her would be like. Men initiate sexual activity more often than women do. They fantasize about sex more often, and masturbate more. (I'll reinforce that claim later, in Chapter 4.) Masturbation, Baumeister claims, is the best measure of "excess" sexual drive, since it requires nobody else to help accomplish it. Men are more sexually permissive—in reality and not just in theory—than women. Men will take remarkable risks for sex. They need little convincing to sleep with someone they just met.[6] Many men stand ready to jeopardize their careers and marriages and risk paying a profound cost—both financial and to their reputation and family—over sex. They connect romance to sex less often. (Sarah can attest to that.) And men tend to navigate rejection with far less introspection, self-blame, and second-guessing than women.[7] Whether they actually stray from their primary partnership or not, men direct far more mental time, attention, and effort toward other potential sexual partners than do women. This is a global reality:

> Nationally representative sex surveys carried out around the world confirm that the "myth" of men having greater sexual motivation/ drive/interest than women is fact, not fantasy.[8]

Remember—all men do not have to exhibit more of such traits and behaviors than all women for a sex difference between them to be "real" and wield social consequences.[9]

Women, on the other hand, tend to be more malleable sexually, as I discuss at length later in this chapter. They are more likely to change their mind about sexual matters—either to engage or to refrain—and tend to go without any sexual activity for longer periods than men. Women take far fewer risks for sex and are more apt to regret one-night stands. Women's level of interest in casual sex with a stranger is far lower than men's. Women politicians seldom find themselves embroiled in sex scandals of their own making. (None come readily to mind.) Men's motivations are certainly more complex than simply maximizing pleasure, but they do seem more subject than women to sex-drive impulses. In the world of sex, men and women often display differences, and it has significant and far-reaching consequences.

You may think that this is all a simple matter of socialization, and that a different approach to raising boys and girls will change things. If only it were that easy. (And be careful what you wish for.) Sociologist J. Richard Udry, who helped pioneer the National Longitudinal Study of Adolescent Health, documented how boys are typically "highly immunized against feminine socialization experiences," and concluded that "hypothetical changes in the social regimen of gender," that is, efforts to make boys less masculine and girls more so, "would change [boys] little, while females would change to exhibit more masculine or less feminine behaviors."[10] In other words, you can help girls act like boys more readily than vice versa. Our interviews with 100 men and women reinforced this observation thoroughly.

So men want more sex than women do, on average. Economically speaking—at least in the heterosexual world—women have what men want. Thus, they possess something of considerable value to men, something that conceivably "costs" men to access. Historically, men have had to give something in exchange, most typically significant (economic and relational) commitments or promises, to gain access to her body.[11] Yes, men appreciate women for other reasons—and I will get to that—but that fact doesn't make this claim less true. The very same thing, sex, is not typically of value to women in quite the same way. As Baumeister and Vohs observe, women never pay men for sex.[12] Across multiple data sets over many years, I have still not witnessed a female respondent who claims to have paid for sex.[13] That is not how they operate. (And that is, on balance, a good thing.) Economically speaking, women would never need to pay for sex. She need only signal, since men are willing to provide it for free. So in the heterosexual mating market broadly understood, there is demand—interested men—and supply: women. But what if a man is attracted to another man? Then obviously that other man has something that he wants (in the way that a woman has something that a heterosexual man wants). So does men's sex objectively still have no value or only no value in the heterosexual exchange? The latter: men's sex does have value in same-sex exchange in a way that it does not in a heterosexual exchange, for men are the only ones who will pay men for sex. As you will see throughout this book, a sexual-economics approach can illuminate the relationship behavior of gay and straight by highlighting the priority and significance of long-standing male and female preferences, regardless of the objects of their affections.

Don't confuse my use of the term "market" with "marketplace." A mating market is an invisible social structure in which the search for a partner occurs, while a sexual marketplace—a theme I do not concern myself with in this book—is a visible, particular place where one searches for a partner (like a bar, a church, a gym, or a workplace). I sometimes use "mating pool" and "mating market" interchangeably, though in reality the pool is all-encompassing but within it there are distinctive markets (such as the market in short-term and long-term relationships, the marriage market, and even the market in sex for sale). Treating markets as social structures is a smart thing because it integrates perspectives from economics as well as demography, social networks, and the study of cultural diffusion.[14] Market talk sounds utilitarian, unromantic, and objectifying, but it need not be. It simply recognizes that people do not meet other people randomly. Nor do they meet whomever they wish and do whatever they want. There are constraints. And despite the sound of it, constraints actually enable and organize behavior. But there are far fewer constraints in the modern mating market than in the past.

So when does sex actually commence in a (heterosexual) romantic relationship in which sex is consensual and men desire it more than women? The theory, as articulated by Baumeister and Vohs, provides a clear answer: sex begins in consensual relationships when women decide that it should. From both qualitative and quantitative assessments, this claim garners support. Elizabeth, a 26-year-old interviewee from Denver, summarizes how it works when asked who (in her relationship with her boyfriend) decides when and how they will have sex: "Ummm ... ultimately me (laughs)." She's right. Her use of the qualifier "ultimately" aptly characterizes the typical deliberations and negotiations—spoken or implicit—that precede consensual sex. But in the end, it hinges on her permission. This is why the correlation between sexual intention and actual sexual behavior is much higher among women than among men, meaning that women are far more likely to see their sexual intentions fulfilled than men are.[15]

The gender imbalance in sex drive also means there are sexual "haves" and "have nots," by which I mean those persons who have access to sex—a willing partner—and those that do not. For women, however, being a "have not" is almost always by choice, whereas for men it is often involuntary. A woman spurned by her lover and seeking sex can find it quickly. A dumped boyfriend can only try.

The bottom line is this: women are the sexual gatekeepers within their relationships.[16] Men infrequently function as the "gatekeepers" of sex in their relationships. (If they are, they are comparatively easier to convince.) And it doesn't much matter whether we are talking about gay or straight relationships. Gay men's relationships are less likely to be sexually monogamous when compared with lesbian or heterosexual relationships, as Chapters 3 and 5 reinforce.[17] Why? It is due to stable sex/gender differences in sex drive, relationship preferences, and permissiveness. Men in gay relationships cut more deals with each other concerning outside partners, and those deals are easier both to make and to realize because men are not typically sexual gatekeepers. Men can play the role, and some do, but they are far less adept at it. It is about the difference between XX and XY, not sexual orientation.[18]

The times have changed, however. Women have plenty of agency, opportunity, and success—more than ever before—and that across multiple domains, including education and the labor market. Women can more openly pursue sex for its own sake in a manner utterly foreign to their great-grandmothers. They can try the demand side of the equation. Of course, they will succeed in their efforts. Indeed, Sarah never once recounted an unwilling first date. In her grim title *The End of Men*, author Hanna Rosin writes, "Young women are more in control of their sexual destinies now than probably ever before."[19] There is no need for qualifying it with a "probably." Rosin is right. It is not as if women receive nothing in return for sex, but they are asking for less in return—sexual pleasure, attention, affirmation, or simply an evening's worth of drinks and dinner.

What women are less in control of—in exchange—is their relational (and emotional) destinies. Today's mating market is no less dominated by men's interests, and arguably far more so than in previous generations.[20] I am not suggesting that all men direct the course and outcomes of their relationships—absolutely not. Sarah left David, but only after it became obvious that he was not going to become someone in whom she could have confidence, and with whom she would have children. Rather, it is increasingly clear that the relationships and the norms and rules about them favor men's interests, even while what men typically offer to women in return for sexual access has profoundly diminished. Kevin, the 24-year-old from Denver, was uber-confident about this, and only regrets not figuring it out sooner:

> Girls are more emotional than guys, simple as that. Girls get attached more. Girls are easier to mislead than guys just by lying or just not really caring. If you know what girls want, then you know you should not give that to them … until you see the proper time and if you do that strategically then you can really have anything you want in any way you want it, any form you want it, whether it's a relationship, sex or whatever. You have the control.

Kevin sounds like a jerk. But it's hard to tell him that his strategy will not work because it has (for him and countless others). The novelty of sexual experience appeals to him, and he has over 35 previous partners to show for it. He's hardly alone. Anthony, an attractive 26-year-old from Austin, is anything but a jerk. He, too, knew something about sexual access. Reflecting on his single days, before he met his current girlfriend:

> I felt like I could have sex anytime I wanted, you know. [*What would it usually take to have sex with someone?*] A phone call. Um, go to the bar and, I don't know. Have a few drinks and smile and laugh and I don't know. … [W]hen I got out of college I felt like it got even easier than it ever was in high school and I don't, I couldn't tell you the reasons why on that. I mean high school I think I can tell you the reasons, like I was, you know, captain of this team, that team, whatever people thought was important back then. And then now in my professional life I felt like when I was single it got much easier even than it was in high school. I don't know why that is. I think, I don't know why. Everybody's looking for a relationship I guess, I don't know.

While I hold that the modern mating market plays more to men's advantage than to women's—that is, he gets what he wants more readily and consistently than she does—that does not mean women are uniquely prone to experience the mating market's negative externalities. Men, too, get dumped, hurt, infected, and depressed. They feel guilt. And they complain. But what men seldom complain about is the price of sexual access, as Giddens discerns: "Men mostly welcome the fact that women have become more sexually available."[21] Put differently, men gravitate toward cheap sex:

> We have found no evidence to contradict the basic general principle that men will do whatever is required in order to obtain sex, and perhaps not a great deal more. ... If in order to obtain sex men must become pillars of the community, or lie, or amass riches by fair means or foul, or be romantic or funny, then many men will do precisely that.[22]

It was, Baumeister and Vohs assert, a giant trade, in which both men and women offered something of lesser importance to them in order to get something they wanted more. That's a too-active account of what was certainly a more passive process—the development of world-altering reproductive technology that boosted women's labor force fortunes. But you get the point.

Men provide the social support for cheap sex, while women provide—on average, but far less today than in previous generations—the social control against it. The double standard around sex has weakened but not disappeared. That is in part because women do not gravitate toward cheap sex but can learn to accommodate it. A minority even appreciates it, at least for a time. What neither men nor women tend to apprehend are the unintended consequences of cheap sex.

What is Cheap Sex?

Cheap sex is not a subjective thing. Narratives of regret may signal the presence of cheap sex, but they do not define it. Cheap sex is both an objective fact and a social fact, characterized by personal ease of sexual access and social perceptions of the same. Sex is cheap if women expect little in return for it and if men do not have to supply much time, attention, resources, recognition, or fidelity in order to experience it.

Cognitively, we associate cheap sex with diminished risk (of pregnancy, for example). But it is not a simple inverse function of risk. Risk tends to curb sexual access. Risk of getting (or making someone) pregnant, risk of transmitting or acquiring a significant or chronic infection (such as HIV or herpes), or risk of feeling pronounced emotional pain or regret often curbs access to sex or restricts sex to a trusted person who has promised or signaled their trustworthiness by their actions. In other words, they are a familiar partner, a faithful partner, or a partner who uses prophylactic measures.

However, it doesn't always work like this. Risk can in fact ease sexual access, typically by way of emotional pain or depressive symptoms that echo in the pursuit of sex or reduced barriers to it. For example, a woman who feels "used" or hurt after being dumped by her boyfriend may in her emotional distress pursue sex with other men either as "payback" or in an effort to make herself feel desired. Or a man diagnosed with HIV may respond to the news with hopeless resignation issuing in a reckless pursuit of sex. So cheap sex can be risky sex. It can be safe sex. It can be measured by the speed with which new partners can be found, or in the frequency with which one has sex. The key lies in the ease of access. Cheap sex charges little and costs little.

Sexual risk is old and familiar. But its risks can and often are eradicated, managed, or normalized. "Safe" sex facilitates cheap sex if the primary barrier to having sex with someone is concern about avoiding pregnancy. When a 30-year-old woman forgets to take the Pill for a couple days, or overlooks a condom on a visit to her boyfriend's place, these are instances and examples of more risky sex. But it remains cheap sex if it is subsequently still easy for her boyfriend to access it. Masturbating alone while watching porn is cheap sex—the cheapest, really—nobody will get infected or pregnant on their way to sexual pleasure or satiation, and it is easy to accomplish (that is, access).

I am not making a moral assessment of cheap sex at this point, just an observation of what it is. My central claim in this book is that cheap sex is plentiful—it's flooding the market in sex and relationships—and that this has had profound influence on how American men and women relate to each other, which in turn has spilled over into other domains. Cheap sex has made some things more accessible—including but not limited to diverse sexual experiences—and some things more difficult, like sexual fidelity and getting and staying married (long a predictable pathway to greater economic, social, and emotional flourishing).

As noted at the beginning of this section, cheap sex is more than an objective personal act. It is not just an odd way to categorize your own or

others' easy-to-accomplish sexual events like a one-night stand or an evening spent watching pornography. More significantly, ease of sexual access
has become a social fact. It has become part of Western social "doxa," to
draw upon a term popularized by the French sociologist Pierre Bourdieu.[23]
The presumption of sexual access lacking significant cost is becoming a
taken-for-granted, self-evident social value and expectation. It has rapidly
established a dominant, favorable position pivotal to the organization of
the modern sexual "field," to use another of Bourdieu's terms. Cheap sex
is "doxic," then. It's a presumption, widely perceived as natural and com-
monsensical, and hence connected by persons to expectations about their
own and others' future sexual experiences (as similarly low-cost). It has
become normative, taken for granted. And that is a remarkable—indeed,
huge—social accomplishment.

That plenty of American couples use contraception unevenly, or discover that it has failed, actually does little to jeopardize this doxic, normative status of cheap sex. This is in part because contraception's failures
are not random, but track with socioeconomic status (i.e., poorer women
are less careful to use contraception correctly). Meanwhile, the production
of public norms about cheap sex—evident in film, journalism, and other
media sources (e.g., HBO's *Girls*)—is far more the reverse, the result of
efforts by higher-SES Americans among whom complete contraceptive
failure is uncommon. In this a comparison can be drawn from the work
on marriage by sociologists like Andrew Cherlin and Kathryn Edin.[24] Both
hold that poor and working-class Americans have adopted the same mentality about marriage—its symbolic status of love, privilege, and social
arrival—even though they are in a far less optimal position to "afford" this
mentality. (As a result, fewer and fewer of them marry.) In a similar way,
poor and working-class adults perceive sex as cheap, even though their
comparatively uneven use of contraception renders sex far more costly
in terms of pregnancy. This is ironic—that the once-obvious mental link
between sex and pregnancy has weakened considerably.[25] In other words,
the idea that "sex is fun, and pregnancy is unlikely" is infectious. When
many men and women (like Sarah) never experience a pregnancy scare
despite having plenty of sex—or quietly secure an abortion—the link
between sex and pregnancy is both weakened and socialized.

The bottom line is that people think sex is for fun, and if fun can be
generated more cheaply and efficiently, why not? Women are more apt
than men to have reservations about cheaper sex, but they do so incon-
sistently, intermittently, or only in their own relationships. Hence, sex is

socially meant to be cheap. In turn, men and women alike tend to exhibit cheap sex, regardless of what they personally think about it.

Cheap sex becomes cognitively structured in the mind, affecting how men and women perceive subsequent encounters and even the purpose of sex. It becomes a mentality, not just an act. It shapes how Sarah approaches an evening out with a new man. And if her date has spent time with other women like Sarah (and he very likely has), then it affects him too, shaping his expectations for the evening or for subsequent dates. That seminal fluid is essentially sperm cells seeking an egg with which to reproduce is cognitively "forgotten" (or seldom considered) in a way that it could not readily be dismissed in an era prior to effective barrier-free contraception. When cheap sex is doxic, seminal fluid becomes cum. Its inseminating property is (largely) overlooked or, in the case of gay sex, irrelevant.

Speaking of sex in this blunt manner—as cheap—engenders many critics. And more of them tend to be women than men. Most suppose I am seeking to turn back the clock, to criticize emergent sexual norms, or to "slut shame" women. Such objections have less to do with empirical evidence than with ideology or idealism. I am, instead, excavating modern sexual activity patterns and seeking explanations for how we got here. Critics tend to only speak of the sexual exchange model by disparaging it and asserting that it is archaic—on the "wrong side of history," patriarchal, and ignores love in its many modern expressions. I understand. But this archaic idea of sexual exchange will not disappear, not because it is backed by powerful ideologies or institutions that support it—it is not—but because powerful realities do not operate well without it.

The Evolution of Cheap Sex?

Some critics suggest that cheap sex is actually very old, and it is only recently—due to greater attention paid to human evolution—that we are able to come to grips with our own deep-rooted non-monogamous natures. The authors of the immensely popular 2010 book *Sex at Dawn* do this, claiming that on all matters sexual humans have never really evolved. Christopher Ryan and Cacilda Jethá wonder aloud over the course of nearly 400 pages about why people seem to be such catastrophic failures when it comes to living up to their stated sexual moralities. Although genetically *Homo sapiens* is similar to the chimpanzee, who fights and feuds over sex, we would do well—the authors reason—to mimic the Bonobo, that likable cousin of the chimp who appears both gracious and generous in its sexual expressions. Bonobos apparently resolve their power issues with sex. And their anxiety issues. And pretty much any issue. "In terms of sexuality," the authors conclude, "history appears to be flowing back toward a hunter-gatherer casualness."[26]

They are onto something. Data from the *Relationships in America* survey—about which I will have plenty to say over the course of this book—suggest that 41 percent of adult Americans (up through age 60) say they first had sex with their current partner no later than two weeks after they began to consider themselves as being in the relationship (and often well before that), and 30 percent admit to overlapping sexual partners at some point in their life. And even though most young adults still pay deferential lip service to marriage, they are clearly voting with their feet, as I elaborate in Chapter 5. The marriage rate among 25- to 34-year-olds in the United States has declined 13 percentage points in 13 years, with no sign of slowing. Something is going on.

That something, the authors of *Sex at Dawn* proclaim, is a gradual return to our non-monogamous past, the one they declare our bodies were made for. Monogamy, they claim, is not natural. The two spend much of the book amassing evidence for their case against monogamy past and present. Much of it comes from looking at our bodies and practices today, deducing why such things exist in the shapes and lengths that they do, and what that all must have meant about human social and sexual behavior many, many millennia ago. They call it the "hieroglyphics" of the human body, and claim that such facts as the comparatively large human penis and testicles or the more vocal female orgasm testify to a non-monogamous past. They also point to the simple observation that even chaste moderns spend time resisting their sexual drives. Is monogamy natural? I have no idea. It remains, however, the aspiration—if not always the actuality—of the vast majority of Americans. Most of them—especially women—are still invested in monogamy and marriage. Only 10 percent of men and 5 percent of women in the *Relationships in America* data agree that "it is sometimes permissible for a married person to have sex with someone other than his/her spouse." Recent trend analyses of the General Social Survey reinforce this.[27] Even the book's authors admit gender distinctions in preferences for non-monogamy: "There are zones where it's always going to be difficult for men and women to understand one another, and sexual desire is one of them."[28]

I do not know enough about anthropological methods, physiological legacies, or the distant past to know whether the authors are onto something or not. They have their fans and their critics.[29] The sociologist in me, however, prefers answers to the question about modern sexual behavior that are sensibly rooted in far more recent developments.

The Modern Mating Pool

Not long ago I was watching the last episode of HBO's series *The Pacific*, in which the surviving characters return home after battling the Japanese on the island of Okinawa in 1945. One veteran in particular returns to Alabama, another to New Jersey. In the case of each, it becomes obvious to viewers that regardless of the young men's sexual wishes, marriage was considered the only intelligible way not simply to access sex but to live your adult life. Culturally, marriage was in the cards, and the men—who had sacrificed so much on the field of battle—were going to have to sacrifice some more in order to be considered marriageable by the women in their community (who protected and policed each other in the domain of relationships). Marriage was the only way that anyone could access stable, "legitimate" sex.

Then everything began to change. The advent of artificial hormonal contraception in the early 1960s brought what economists call a technological "shock" to the social system, and the mating market in particular.[30] Though no economist, Anthony Giddens agrees that contraception altered the playing field.[31] (I know of no serious scholar who denies it, but few discuss it.) Without it, the emergence of the "pure relationship" Giddens speaks of would simply not have been possible. Nor would *Sex at Dawn*'s talk of a "return" to our ancient non-monogamous roots have arisen without this very modern technology. And claims like those made by actor Ethan Hawke—that society holds a perspective on monogamy that is childish—would not have been made.[32] Our new interest in "primal" sexuality was made possible not by more rigorous historical or anthropological study but by a mid-twentieth-century invention—synthetic hormonal contraception.[33] To be sure, things did not change overnight following its debut in 1960. No social shift of significance ever does. Fertility rates did not suddenly plunge, although hormonal contraception began doing its job of regulating users' periods and preventing many pregnancies from occurring. (Legal barriers to access continued for years in some states.[34]) But change things it did.[35] The vagaries of less-reliable contraceptive devices or condoms, which men have never much appreciated, could now be avoided. Marriage plans could be stalled. Careers could be developed without fear of interruption. Women could have two children instead of five or six. This novel technology, economist Claudia Goldin correctly observes, "affected all women," including "women who were never 'on the pill.'"[36] It also, she briefly notes, affected men.

Over time the wide uptake of effective contraception split what once was a relatively unified mating pool into two overlapping (but distinctive) components or markets—one for sex and one for marriage, with a rather large territory in between comprised of significant relationships of varying commitment and duration (e.g., cohabitation).[37] Figure 2.1 displays this. The mating market—that large pool of single men and women out there looking for company of some sort—no longer functions in quite the same way it once did.[38] By "relatively unified" I mean that the majority of sex among singles used to occur in and during the search for a mate—someone to marry. My grandfathers may or may not have married the first women they slept with—I do not know—but it is safe to say that they did not approach their twenties in quite the same way that many American men do today. To them, sex implied commitments because it risked pregnancy.

Relationship security was often a value and a precursor to sex. In a survey of Americans conducted in 1970—which interviewed over 3,000 adults, some of whom were born before 1900—54 percent of the oldest men but only 7 percent of the oldest women reported having had premarital intercourse. With each successive cohort, those numbers rose, until 89 percent of men and 63 percent of women in the youngest cohort (born in 1940–49) reported premarital sex.[39] This does not mean that your great-grandparents never messed around (whatever that meant to them). But, in general, the average woman could and did count on seeing evidence of commitment before sex. If she did not—and got pregnant—her family

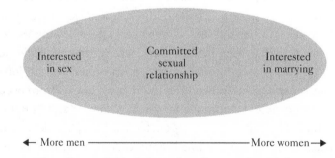

FIGURE 2.1 The split, gender-imbalanced modern mating pool

might step into the role of guarantor. Thus was born the "shotgun wedding," a once-popular phenomenon in which my maternal grandparents participated.

The mating market in this "state of nature" was populated by roughly equal numbers of men and women, whose bargaining positions—averaged together—were roughly comparable and predictable, with men valuing attractiveness more than women, and women valuing productivity and economic promise more than men.

But since pregnancy can be easily prevented now—a reality we take for granted today, but one that was unimaginable not so long ago—having sex and thinking about or committing to marry are two very different things today. Now we have a split mating market, one corner of which is for people primarily looking and hoping for sex with no strings attached (NSA) and the other corner of which are people interested in making the strongest of commitments (marriage), with a rather large territory in between comprised of significant relationships of varying commitment and duration.[40] Marriage is still widely considered to be expensive, by which I mean that it is a big deal, not entered into lightly, and is costly in terms of fidelity, time, finances, and personal investment. Sex, meanwhile, has become comparatively cheap. Not that hard to get.

If baseline interest—or change in interest—in NSA sex as well as in marriage were randomly distributed, this story would not be all that illuminating. But this bifurcated mating pool is gender imbalanced, as Figure 2.1 depicts. The sex ratio of it is uneven, and this makes all the difference. There are more men in the sex corner of the pool than women, and more women than men over in the marriage corner of the pool. You can witness the reality of all this in how men and women communicate their relational interests in online dating profiles. Some people are genuinely looking to mate for life, while some are just looking to score. Some write that they are "looking for fun," signaling that they are not really interested in a committed relationship at the moment. More of these are men than women. When women signal interest in sex, men pounce. One woman's recent anonymous account of time spent on the extramarital affairs site AshleyMadison.com noted that her posting received 200 local inquiries in the first 24 hours.[41] Author Lisa Taddeo did the same, posing as a married woman.[42] Overnight she received 164 inquiries. While a pair of anecdotes is hardly scientific, it strains the imagination to suggest that a man could garner such interest from 200, or even 164 (or 80, 40, 10, or even 5) women quite so quickly. Instead, it reinforces the assertion that women are sexual gatekeepers in their relationships—that is, they can have sex when they wish to—and that the mating market is indeed now divided.

Meanwhile, people in the marriage pool tend to signal very different things online, using phrases like "only serious inquiries, please" or "looking for an emotional connection." This approach is far more common among women than men. An advertisement for a dating service that recurs in my email markets itself in this way: "No games. Just real women looking for a faithful guy." The service is attempting to capitalize on the popular (and accurate) assumption that women are more interested in securing commitment than men. Hence, when a woman signals that she is more interested in sex than stability, men gather, but she can be as picky as she wishes. As people age, they tend to drift toward the marriage market—meaning they more intentionally wish to pursue marriage and intend for their sexual behavior to serve that goal. But given their distinctive biological clocks and sexual preferences, men and women tend to drift over at different paces and ages, on average.

It is a basic economic idea that relative scarcity or abundance affects human behavior in lots of important ways. So why in the world would anyone think that newfound abundance and scarcity in the modern mating market does not affect our relationship decision-making? Probably because the dominant liberal and conservative interpreters in this domain have been more concerned with (feminist and romantic) idealism—how they think our relationships ought to form, proceed, and conclude—than with realism about how they actually do come to be, what they look and transpire like, and when and why they end as they do.

I am not suggesting analysts or readers drop their ideals, but I do recommend they not allow their ideals to trump their ability to see what is going on in social reality. Some will try, though. University of Texas psychologist David Buss relays this anecdote: "After a lecture of mine on the subject of sex differences in mate preferences, one woman suggested that I should suppress my findings because of the distress they would cause women."[43] If sociologists cannot first describe accurately what is going on, our project is lost and our discipline has wandered away from privileging the empirical in favor of the imperative.

The Sex-Ratio Hypothesis

The sex-ratio hypothesis holds that an oversupply of unmarried women in a community or group gives men therein considerably more power in romantic and sexual relationships, which translates into lower levels of relationship commitment, less favorable treatment of women by men, and a more sexually permissive climate wherein women receive less in exchange for sex.[44] Keep in mind this occurs not because women are more permissive but because men are. How does this process work?

It's about power. The split mating market, the gender imbalance in it, and the age-graded drift patterns—all of it affects expressions of power in relationships. Social psychologist Karen Cook spells out the basics of how this happens:

> Differences in the nature of the valued resources among actors result in interdependence and thus the need for exchange. They also serve as the basis for emerging inequalities in exchange outcomes as well as power differentials between actors linked by exchange.[45]

In this case, men and women seek to be in relationship with each other, but tend to value different things—hence the need for an exchange relationship. Nevertheless, you should expect inequalities and power plays to develop. And they do. Power is relational; it's a function of the dependence of one actor upon another. While Cook continues, imagine A and B here as a young man and woman, respectively, who tend to want different things in the mating market. In the (sexual) exchange relationship, y is sexual access while x represents desirable resources of various types:

> In an exchange relation between two actors, A and B, the power of actor A over B in the Ax:By exchange relation (where x and y represent resources of value) increases as a function of the value of y to A and decreases proportional to the degree of availability of y to A from alternative sources (other than B). These two factors—resource value and resource availability—determine the level of B's dependence on A and thus A's power over B. The more dependent B is upon A, the more power A has over B.[46]

Power within relationships is determined not simply by such things as inequalities in the social status or physical attractiveness of the partners but also by surrounding market realities, like the availability of sex from other sources.[47] The key is the level of a partner's dependency. All else being equal, the availability of attractive alternatives outside of the relationship yet inside the local market tends to reduce an individual's dependency and result in lower levels of commitment to and investment in a relationship. Alternatives are more available in markets where there is an oversupply of the opposite sex.

Some demographers hold that since women are apt to consider a wider (age) range of men, then the actual marriage market contains more men than women, which ought to afford the latter "greater marital bargaining power" over the former.[48] But this matters little because the marriage market is sensitive to far more than just sex and age distributions. For example, women have long preferred marrying men with at least as much education as they have—a reality that is beginning to decline due to its increasing impossibility (as Chapter 1 indicated). But more important than any of this, however, is the game-changing reality that the mating market itself is now split—as Figure 2.1 displayed—with rather prominent sex-ratio disparities in what men and women are looking for. If the sex corner of the mating market has more men than women in it, then women there have greater bargaining ability and can be more selective, as the Ashley Madison enrollee's testimony confirms. It is hardly surprising, then, that young women tend to feel empowered by sex appeal. It is very empowering in the market for short-term (exchange) relationships. But sex appeal that generates "interest from men" is hardly the same as "potential for marriage"—not in the post-Pill mating market. And the very reason there are fewer women than men shopping for sex is because most women tend to prefer sex in stable, committed, romantic relationships. This is not new. Most evolutionary psychologists, save perhaps for the *Sex at Dawn* authors, would agree.

Meanwhile, we see more women than men in the marriage corner of the mating market. The gender disparity there may not seem like a massive one, at face value. Among unmarried respondents under age 40 in the *Relationships in America* survey, the sex ratio of those who said they would prefer to be married is 0.82, which can be translated that for every 82 men who wished to be married, 100 women said the same. But the ratio need not be profoundly divergent for the effect on power dynamics to be keenly felt. This allows men to be more selective, fickle, cautious, and insist on extensive sexual experience before committing. Pickiness is not a personality trait. It's a result of the new ecology of choice.[49] Sociologist Eva Illouz explains:

> [M]en are more likely to view the marriage market as a sexual market and tend to stay longer in such a sexual market, whereas women tend to view the sexual market as a marriage market and would tend to stay in it for less time.[50]

Jessica, a 29-year-old from Austin, learned this lesson the hard way. While engaged now to a man she adores, she had spent four years in a dead-end relationship not long after completing college. It began as a "friends with benefits" arrangement, but she always hoped it would turn into something more:

> I really thought that it was sexual but would lead to romantic, ... and apparently for him it was just sexual. And I just did not, I mean, I had to be hit over the head with it to see that "You know, that's right, it really wasn't what I thought it was." ... [*And so did you eventually confront him and he told you, or what, how did you* ...] No, I just, I started taking a good look at the things that had happened in the past. He would only call me when, we would have, you know, these big heartfelt conversations, but ... I began to realize it was only like, at two in the morning, when he was drunk and couldn't get a hold of anybody else. And I just never really thought of that before. So I just needed somebody to help me put it into perspective.

To plenty of women, it appears that men have a fear of commitment. But men, on average, are not afraid of commitment. The story is that men are in the driver's seat in the marriage market and are optimally positioned to navigate it in a way that privileges their (sexual) interests and preferences. It need not even be conscious behavior on their part. And their ability to do so seems to improve with age, up to an unclear tipping point (but likely before age 40). The sex-ratio difference prompts an oversupply of women searching for a marriage partner, compelling them to compete for marriageable men in a far more evident fashion than among prior generations. This competition prompts some women, economist Tim Reichert claims, to cut poorer deals.[51] That is, to marry and then regret it.

Any talk of the emerging power of "cougars," that is, sexually experienced older women pursuing younger men, is limited to the market in sex, a domain in which they can compete with younger women by appealing to their own experience and skills (and find ready interest, given high demand). Age, divorce, diminished fecundity, and the presence of other men's children curb the abilities of cougars to compete effectively in the marriage portion of the mating market. It is not that they cannot remarry; they can, and plenty do. The competition to do so, however, is taller, men's selectivity greater, and the pathway to successful remarriage no less daunting than that facing women in the (first) marriage market.

The mating market "split" is not absolute, of course. The divide is real, but invisible. Men and women can and do participate in both corners of the mating market at the same time—drifting over from marriage-mindedness to pursue a one-night stand, and then back again.[52] That was the case with Abby, a 30-year-old Austin woman who told us she was definitely searching for a long-term partner, but had a one-night stand recently after meeting a man at a Longhorn football tailgate party. She said she knew nothing would come of it and expressed no interest in a relationship with the man she slept with. Indeed, most Americans do not perceive the market as bifurcated at all, and many women (and some men) engage in sexual intercourse with varying degrees of hope or expectation that they will eventually marry their partner.

It is not true, of course, that starry-eyed women are now simply being more efficiently duped or hoodwinked by skirt-chasing, commitment-phobic men. Not at all: many, many women don't mind the new mating market and its dynamics, at least for a while. Plenty of them like to spend some time in less-serious relationships before hoping for a more significant commitment, and more than ever are eschewing marriage entirely (though not always voluntarily). But ignoring the economics of this doesn't mean you can escape it. There is an exchange whether either party recognizes it or not. And the "price" of sex is conveyed—that is, socialized. The irreligious author of *Chastened* experimented with a high price for sex, electing to go for a year without it.[53] At the conclusion of her year of chastity, she opted back in to a life including sex but noted her time spent away from it "has really changed everything. And it [sex] seems to proceed at a much slower pace [now]." When asked what she would do differently if she could relive her twenties, she responded with new terms of exchange:

> I'd be more assertive about my right to be romanced. And I think
> that would have probably sent some of the cads running, and then
> I might have then noticed some more interesting fellows.[54]

The Emergence of Love in an Era of Cheap Sex

Sex ratio imbalances. Deceit. Conflict. Power plays. It's starting to seem like a wonder that any couple ever actually elects to commit in a world awash in cheap sex. But people do fall in love, and many still marry. Observation and experience, together with evidence from the psychology of interpersonal relationships, reveals that a common shift occurs wherein love—and trust, confidence, and self-sacrifice—emerges in relationships.[55] It is quicker to develop in women, on average, though that is hardly always the case. But the exchange model would seem to suggest that men willingly, eventually, pay a much higher price for sexual access than they need to, confirming that the pricing of sex is hardly a straightforward supply-and-demand function. Why?

Because they want to. Men are more than just consumers of sex, objectifying women and feigning commitment as a ruse to gain sexual access. (We're not that simple.) But there tends to be a more significant and difficult transition away from a consumptive mentality about relationships in men than in women. Psychologist and cohabitation expert Scott Stanley perceives it, too, noting that a man's developing commitment—typically visible in daily sacrifices—uniquely signals a transition from a winner/loser, zero-sum scenario to that of trust and expectation of a future together.[56] Such signaling, in turn, reinforces additional sacrifices, fostering "an exchange market (between partners) that is noncompetitive, where the goal is to maximize joint outcomes."[57] The key word here is noncompetitive, that is, external options become decreasingly attractive and the couple invests in the good of each other. In other words, love.

Love—and here one cannot but break from straightforward exchange language—emerges. That is, an intrinsic relationship like love is not something one could readily model statistically as the product of units of joint attraction, educational match, sexual interest and compatibility, personality fit, rational evaluation, and happenstance. Nor is love a "threshold" of sorts, below which is "not love." No, love "emerges," occupying a reality heretofore nonexistent and yet one that tends to act back on the two individuals (as well as outward onto others).[58] The emergence of love, however, is a mysterious process. It hinges on the exchange relationship, but that is far from sufficient to generate it. It involves attraction, of course, but falling in love defies simple hormonal or economic or psychological descriptions and requires—when asked about it—lengthy personal narratives to do it justice, since these are more holistic and rooted in a lived experience. You can learn more about love in a novel than in a textbook. Indeed, "falling in" love is an unfortunate way of speaking about it. Love emerges, sometimes promptly, oftentimes more slowly. Cheap sex, however, is poorly adept at generating love, if the interviewees are to be believed. It can, however, harm or unravel love, as countless breakups and divorce proceedings attest.

Historically, signaling love by sacrificial acts has been particularly important for men, given the nature of the exchange relationship and the lopsided cost to women of pregnancy and childbirth.[59] Without such acts, a more committed partner becomes aware of their more vulnerable position (in terms of power) in the relationship, senses little or no recognition, and is more apt to feel devalued and taken advantage of.[60] In his 1964 classic *Exchange and Power in Social Life*, sociologist Peter Blau observed that "if one lover is considerably more involved than the other, his greater commitment invites exploitation or provokes feelings of entrapment, both of which obliterate love."[61] This scenario is remarkably common, and becoming even more so, not just because young adults are spending more time on the mating market than previously, or because fewer of them are marrying, but because Stanley and his colleagues perceive a thinner association between romance and commitment today. It means they detect cheap sex:

> The linkage between romantic attachment and dedication has weakened over the past few decades as romantic and sexual connections fueled emotional attachments without necessarily leading to the development and clarification of commitment.

Instead, premature "entanglements" are apt to lead to ambiguity, frustration, anxiety, and power plays—not exactly fertile soil for commitment to emerge.[62] It's prompted Stanley to distinguish "sliding" into cohabitation from "deciding" to do so.[63] Sliding adds constraints (e.g., shared rent, pets, debts) on a relationship before commitment has been amply signaled and trust matures. The future for such unions—about which we heard plenty in the interviews—is often a short one.

All of this suggests that men are considered safer marital bets as they age. Some men are prepared for the costs and responsibilities of marriage at age 20, but not very many. Even Kevin wants to get married someday, and "is almost 100 percent positive I will," but not yet, "because I am not done being stupid yet. I still want to go out and have sex with a million girls. I still want to do stupid stuff. I still want to make mistakes." Kevin anticipates willingly committing to one woman someday. Just not yet. Many men anticipate their own greater willingness to eventually pay the elevated price (of marriage), in no small part because sex does not remain a solitary pursuit; other motivations encroach. They want to fall in love. They want children. Their autonomy becomes less valuable to them. They may perceive their own attractiveness begin to decline. And even though they may feel like they're in the driver's seat in the marriage market, ideal spouses grow less numerous with time. (The market, it seems, has a sense of karma.)

But at 24, Kevin is not yet interested in those things. Commitment—a pledge of monogamy, acts of self-sacrifice, and investment in growing a relationship with one woman—seems unattractive to him, and unnecessary. Long-term monogamous commitment—less sexual variety, a shorter search, and a more circumscribed social life—is a much taller order for gay and straight men alike at age 24 than the very same thing at age 34. The rising median age at first marriage reinforces this claim. In sum, then, commitment and its boundaries (and benefits) become more attractive to men over time.

So why care about sex and marriage markets, ratios, prices, early entanglements, and exchanges, since people should be free to do whatever they want, right? Choice and options are sacred, the "defining cultural hallmark of modernity," after all.[64] So long as love isn't forced and consent is our byword, let people do what they want, no? But truly free choice does not exist here. It never has. We have exchanged an older set of challenges for a newer set now that the general mating market has morphed into two distinctive components and given rise to vastly different power dynamics within each. Talk to most any thirty-something woman who wishes to marry and you are apt to get an earful, a window into the vagaries and frustrations of finding a mate today.

It is a very different world than before. The physical risks of sex have been dramatically lowered and the independent, economic trajectories of women have soared, both a product—directly and indirectly—of significant advancement in fertility control. Thus this new era has been remarkable for women in terms of career options and labor force successes, but more challenging on them relationally. This is not the account of every young woman, for sure, but the route to marriage—something the vast majority still holds as a goal— is more fraught with years and failed relationships than in the past. Once-familiar structures, narratives, and rituals about romance and marriage—how to date, falling in love, whom to marry, why, and when—have largely collapsed, sustained only in subgroups, and that with increasing difficulty.

After the Gender Revolution, Does the Exchange Model Still Work?

Some critics argue that fertility control and women's flourishing careers are clear signs that the exchange model of sex-for-resources is breaking down, since women no longer need men's resources. Certainly the latter observation is accurate. In reality, both sides of the exchange model have taken a hit, since men's options for accessible and satisfying sexual experiences have likewise increased. Do these mean the underlying model is faulty? Am I leaning on a house of cards?

No, the underlying model is not faulty because the exchange model is rooted in stable realities about male–female differences that are not socially constructed and will not disappear. In a July 2015 *New York Times* article about the slow normative uptake of state-mandated campus sexual consent laws, Kinsey Institute graduate and health education professor Kristen Jozkowski critiqued "traditional sexual scripts," that package of behavioral norms "whereby men are the pursuers and women the gate-keepers of sex, trained by society to be reluctant." Her aggravation is predictable, and yet she nevertheless admits, "Studies have found these stereotypes, even in the age of hookup sites like Tinder, to be generally true." Yes—empirical data still reinforce the fundamentals of the basic sexual exchange model, even if you wish it was not so.

Why Don't Women Ask Men to Marry Them?

A very liberal acquaintance of mine recently became engaged, not long before turning 35. She told me she never intended to avoid marriage, but was never entirely attracted to it either. She became engaged, however, by proposing to her boyfriend—baking a cake with the words "Want to Get Hitched?" spelled out on it. He said "yes." The unique experience prompted me to reflect on the gendered way in which (heterosexual) marriage decisions happen. One of the most enduring distinctions around relationships is the practice whereby men ask women to marry them. Marriage may be in decline as an institution. (It is.) The age at first marriage may be rising. (It is.) The share of Americans who are married may be shrinking. (It is.) And some women may hint and wonder aloud about marriage and all but outright ask men to marry them. (Plenty do.) So how come so few women actually explicitly ask men, "Will you marry me?" Why does a marriage proposal from a woman to a man feel or sound so egalitarian and appropriate to this era in the United States, and yet so illegitimate? It's because it seeks to overturn or reverse the exchange model of relationships, if only symbolically and momentarily. And that's a difficult thing to do. Indeed, that so many modern, egalitarian relationships still await a man's proposal of marriage is ironic.

Same-sex marriage proposals by definition witness something different here. In that case, a man will, of course, propose to another man, or
a woman to another woman. In plenty of accounts the proposal is not
quite formal, but more of a conversation (which, of course, someone must
broach). In reality, that is what my friend did with her fiancé, avoiding
the classic will-you-marry-me question in favor of something more subtle,
couple-focused, and egalitarian-sounding—a "what do you think of this
idea" method.

It is nevertheless testimony to the historic robustness of the exchange
model, even in the absence of an obvious exchange, that a man is still
expected to ask a woman to marry him rather than vice versa. But given
the progress of confluent love, might we witness a shift here too, such that
far more women than in the past will propose marriage to men? I don't
see it. Men have the advantage in the contemporary marriage market and
"conceding" to marriage proposed by a woman is just not how they roll.
Evidence of a shift here remains anecdotal and rare. Clare, a 30-year-old
African American living in Austin, tried it—asking her boyfriend to marry
her after a year together. He said no. They lasted awhile longer, and then
it was over.

More significantly, what do women offer in a marriage proposal that
they are not already commonly providing? A man's proposal to a woman,
on the other hand, typically signals a significant shift in intentions, readi-
ness, commitment, and willingness to sacrifice for one woman whom he
has grown to love and trust (whether she needs the provisions or not). My
best guess is that we will not see any turnaround in marriage rates due to
women pursuing it more doggedly than men. The exchange model can
neither be reversed nor declared dead.

The Exchange Model May Bend But It Won't Break

The model may be old-fashioned, but it is not faulty. For the exchange
model to fail, men and women would have to alter their (collective, not
just personal) preferences and long-standing sources of status. That is,
men would no longer be known (and socially rewarded) for seeking sex,
while women would begin to seem more commitment phobic. More men
would be longing for emotional satisfaction and validation, while more
women would pursue bedding complete strangers. Men would pine to
stay at home longer with their infants. Women would play fantasy football. All unlikely scenarios. Rather, what has happened is that each side of

the model—the supply of sex and the supply of resources—is increasingly being met outside of a relationship between persons in a manner that is perceived to be less costly or risky to each, rendering their sexual unions less consequential and less stable.

And yet men and women themselves continue to make use of economic signaling that highlights the exchange model. That has not disappeared with the shrinking earnings gap between men and women. As historian Yuval Harari accurately points out in his tour-de-force book *Sapiens*:

> Previously bride and groom met in the family living room, and money passed from the hands of one father to another. Today courting is done at bars and cafés, and money passes from the hands of lovers to waitresses. Even more money is transferred to the bank accounts of fashion designers, gym managers, (and) dietitians.[65]

Harari is right: relationships are still being brokered, and resources are still being expended. While American fathers and mothers often have little to do with whom their children marry today, and have not for quite some time, online dating is a very blunt market tool wherein people assess the gain-in-trade they would make for simply going out with another person. If anything, the modern mating market feels more nakedly economic, and far less social, than the pre-Pill one. There is little shelter offered anyone, and every man and woman is now on their own to discern their feelings and to make "authentic" decisions to live in step with them. Eva Illouz gets it:

> What we call the "triumph" of romantic love in relations between the sexes consisted first and foremost in the disembedding of individual romantic choices from the moral and social fabric of the group and in the emergence of a self-regulated market of encounters.[66]

Interdependence has faded, leaving only independence. It is freer but also far more vulnerable than many wish to acknowledge. Moreover, the cultural suppression of female sexuality that many presume the exchange model depends on was never the concerted accomplishment of men—the patriarchy—but rather of women.[67] In fact, men's actions were far more scrutinized than women's.[68] Only sexual economics could have guessed that. That era is gone, deconstructed by the uptake of contraception. Baumeister and Vohs even call it a "market correction":

Men's access to sex has turned out to be maximized not by keeping women in an economically disadvantaged and dependent condition, but instead by letting them have abundant access and opportunity. In an important sense, the sexual revolution of the 1970s was itself a market correction. Once women had been granted wide opportunities for education and wealth, they no longer had to hold sex hostage.[69]

The idiom and language they use implies an active process, but in reality the developments were passive ones. And suggesting that the exchange model depends on sexual suppression or repression or "holding sex hostage" is an overstatement.

Romantic and sexual choices have not been altogether deregulated. Rather, the guiding morality of one's group and community has been replaced by that of the corporation and consumer culture, the sources of modern centralized ethics and the commodification of sex and sexuality.

Fifty Shades of Exchange

Love it or hate it, the wild popularity and success of the *Fifty Shades of Grey* film and book series reminds us of the dominance of men, as well as the corporation, in the mating market. One could simply perceive in it the triumph of a sadomasochistic sexuality—there is that—but I think it would be shortsighted to see no more than that. What its publishing and box office success (among women, largely) suggests to me is threefold: (1) that the exchange relationship between men and women is alive and well, (2) that men and women tend to appreciate that, but that (3) men have the distinctive upper hand in this mating market. In order to be with a desirable man, it is the woman who makes the sacrifices. The "contract" that wealthy and handsome Christian Grey offers to Anastasia Steele stipulates that she agree to "any sexual activity deemed fit and pleasurable by" Grey, after procuring "oral contraceptives from the physician of [Grey's] choosing." The list continues and includes monogamy on Anastasia's part, as well as good diet, dress, and exercise.[70] And what does she get? Him.

- Anastasia: So you'll get your kicks by exerting your will over me.
- Christian: It's about gaining your trust and your respect, so you'll let me exert my will over you. I will gain a great deal of pleasure, joy even, in your submission. The more you submit, the greater my joy—it's a very simple equation.

- Anastasia: Okay, and what do I get out of this?
- Christian (shrugs and looks almost apologetic): Me.

What about dinner and a movie? "That's not really my thing," Christian levels. I recognize that *Fifty Shades* is fiction. It's made up. But when you sell 100 million copies in two years, your narrative is resonating. There's something to it.

Its success dismayed not only religious conservatives—a predictable response—it also irritated many feminists, who perceived in it a significant step backward by admitting, and even glamorizing, uneven power relations between the sexes. *Fifty Shades* is not very egalitarian, to be sure. But perhaps sexual relationships don't thrive on egalitarianism. Sociologists analyzing data from the National Survey of Families and Households recently examined how husbands' participation in what they called "core" and "non-core" (or traditionally female and male, respectively) household tasks corresponded with their sexual behavior self-reports.[71] The authors wondered whether tweaking the exchange model to accommodate egalitarian norms might work here. Perhaps wives, they surmised, would use sexual access to convince men to do more domestic tasks—the "sex begins in the kitchen" hypothesis. (There is no shortage of "academic work predicated on the demise" of forms of non-egalitarianism.)[72]

So do egalitarian men find a fairer division of labor rewarded in the bedroom? No. Regardless of who reported on sexual frequency—husband or wife—it was apparent that the more that men did traditionally women's housework, or women did men's tasks, the less marital sex they reported, controlling for lots of alternative variables and pathways. (The converse is also true.) Moreover, the bedroom penalty was the most severe when men did traditionally women's work rather than vice versa. Household egalitarianism talks a good game about sex-positivity. That it fails to live up to it should surprise no one.

A gendered exchange model is clearly evident whether we observe men and women in a buttoned-down society or in a libertine *Fifty Shades* one. It rests, rather, on the stable observation that men and women tend to seek different goals in their sexual relationships and tend to display or value different aspects of sexual connection, and reward distinctively sex-typed behaviors.

The "Paradox"

But some still remain unconvinced. What about independent women with a high sex drive? Female versions of Christian Grey, that is. They seem at face value to need none of men's available resources, and they mimic more masculine values. Don't they alter the exchange model by utterly ignoring it? Not really. The fact that some women actively pursue sex signals little power. It just means they will have predictable success in accomplishing that goal, which is not really an accomplishment once you understand men. But they tend to have greater difficulty in navigating successful, long-term relationships of the type many claim to want.

Alyssa, a 27-year-old from Milwaukee, told us she had a higher libido than her live-in boyfriend. While nearly everything about her past shouts "cheap sex" and the problems that often accompany it, she cannot shake the idea that the exchange relationship between men and women is in the order and design of things. (I'm not talking about religion, either, since she professes none.) When we asked her whether she thought sex is something men should "work" to get, the words spilled out:

> This is a tough question. I know in my mind, and from my feminist perspective, that sex is something that people come together for, that women and men should enjoy equally, and that there shouldn't be any work on either part, there's no trade-offs, there's none of that. But culturally, there's definitely ingrained in me something that says that it's a gift that a woman is giving a man, and that he needs to deserve it. And so, yes, he should work for it ... (but) it's conflicting! It's something that conflicts like on a daily basis, it's hard for me to deal with! Um, but yeah, the idea of like, if I, like what I said to my boyfriend yesterday, "Are we splitting this or are you paying for it?" When we first started dating, he paid for everything, and I assumed that he would pay for everything, and that's apparently why he paid for everything. He didn't like it—he never liked it. He never thought that that was a good idea. He thought it should be equal. But I was like, "I thought we were dating. Are you not courting me? Are we not trying to establish a boyfriend-girlfriend pattern? Isn't this what you do?" That's how I thought. I feel entitled to be taken out on dates. And like I said, that conflicts with a part of me inside where I'm like, "No you don't! What are you talking about, like, you make the same amount of money, there is no reason for this, cough it up (chuckles), and stop feeling so deserving, like why are you so special? You're getting just as much out of this as he is." So, it's a conflict. [*So you have this tension?*] Yes. So um, what we came to decide in our relationship, is that there

was a courting period in the beginning, and now it's over, and he can't afford to do that forever, and so we split everything evenly, we are, have been in the process of the last few weeks of looking for a joint bank account, so, to make it easier to split things evenly. And um, in that way, he is no longer working for it. But, at the same time, last night, when he said "Is this a date or are we splitting it?" (I realized) that has a direct relationship to how interested I would be in having sex that night. [*And in what way? Describe that relationship.*] Um, when I feel like I have been taken out, I feel a lot more romantically inclined because it just feels more romantic, it's less like utilitarian, like um, I'm willing to do it, but it doesn't feel good. It feels much better, romantically, and it's more arousing to be taken out and treated well, to have gifts, to have all of that stuff, and like it. [*And have you known this for a while, or is this a new revelation for you?*] It was kind of a new revelation (chuckles) because I've been fighting it for so long, 'cause I thought that it was wrong, and I still do, kind of. Like I said, it upsets me that I feel that way, but I acknowledge that I feel that way and I try to work with it and make it reasonable.

Lots of women we interviewed, many of whom had extensive sexual experience, would say that Alyssa is right on. And yet at the same time most would acknowledge that they too, like her, have often strayed from the model's assumptions—that is, the provision of sex with few resources in return. They feel tension: freedom to do what they wish, craving for the recognition and status that relationships can (but don't necessarily) provide, raw desire, and yet the suspicion that offering sex and signaling commitment with little in return is giving away too much.

A key source of this tension rests in another of the model's assumptions—the availability of y (sex) to A (him) from alternative sources besides B (her). It means women have a *social* problem (not just a personal one) getting the x (treatment or resources) they want. Kendalia, a 32-year-old African American woman from Milwaukee cohabiting with an unemployed man who spends most of his days playing video games and watching pornography, knows this only too well. When asked if she's ever felt guilty about sexual activity, she doesn't have to think very hard, or very far back in time: "I just don't feel like he deserves it at times. Like sex should be deserved sometimes. [*So you feel guilty for . . . ?*] Giving in, just letting him have it."

Leslie Bell, a combination of sociologist and psychotherapist, perceives such women's lives as profoundly enigmatic. (Alyssa would agree.) Why? Because, she laments, their "unprecedented sexual, educational, and professional freedoms" have spawned "contradictory and paradoxical consequences" in the realm of sex and relationships.[73] The skills they developed "in getting ahead educationally and professionally have not translated well into getting what they want and need in sex and relationships."[74]

Nonsense. The only contradictory and paradoxical thing here is the unrealistic expectation of so many that the securing of ample resources independently of men should have no consequences, or only positive effects, on the success of their intimate relationships. It's not surprising that women would expect it. The emotional energy bred by success would seem to be transferable. Instead, what Bell uncovers—and labels as enigmatic—is the straightforward economic reality that sex and even marriage are, at bottom, exchanges. If women no longer need men's resources—that which men can and will always be willing to exchange, if necessary—and can minimize sexual risk, then sex simply becomes less consequential, easier to get or give away, and relationships far more difficult to navigate because strong commitments and emotional validation are just plain less necessary (and thus slower to emerge) from men. Women still want them—they want love, which is a noble pursuit—but the old terms that prompted men's provisions are on the rocks. There is no paradox here. Rather, it is what you should expect.

Given this turn of events, the recent rise in popular defense of the short-term relationship is not surprising ("When life gives you lemons . . ."). But participating in a "mate circulation" system of sexual partners is far less of a social accomplishment—and typically less satisfying—than is partnering long-term and exiting the market through marriage. While Giddens was on target to hold that "sexual freedom follows power and is an expression of it," it simply does not spell the power to make relationships flourish and last.[75] To be sure, many men fall head-over-heels in love, seek to accelerate a relationship faster than she prefers, and even propose marriage. But most such men are not so speedy. New partners remain available without great difficulty, and the historic signposts and transitions from sexual partnering to cohabitation to marriage seem far less distinctive anymore. The marriage process slows down, but the sex speeds up.

When Gender Egalitarianism and Men's
Mating Market Power Collide

Gender egalitarianism, or the commitment to equal treatment and opportunity for women (and men), is a sacred commitment among sociologists. It's challenging to realize, however, in the domain of committed relationships. That is because women's remarkable advances—their unprecedented educational, professional, and sexual freedoms—did not simply collide with, but rather helped create, the newfound power that men hold in the marriage corner of the modern mating market. The only paradox here is that it caught people off guard and continues to confuse them. It does so because so many earnestly wish that the sex act would no longer have anything to do with exchange relationships and that men and women would perceive and pursue sex in comparable ways, displaying equality. That power asymmetries could have been worsened by egalitarianism is almost unthinkable. Eva Illouz describes the contest:

> Feminism and scientific language have in common the aim of controlling relationships, of making them the object of procedures and rules, of subsuming them under abstract principles and procedures that derive from the legal and economic spheres.[76]

Eros cannot but suffer under these circumstances. Alyssa's compelling internal dispute characterizes both how exchange relationship dynamics have shifted in light of growing equality among the sexes, and yet how some things may never change. There is no paradox here, but there is certainly tension.

Such tension is being keenly felt on America's university campuses as administrators (finally) seek to curb sexual assault. Even former President Obama weighed in on the matter, suggesting that 20 percent of women are sexually assaulted at some point in their collegiate careers.[77] And he is right, or very nearly so. In the *Relationships in America* data, among women no older than age 25 who have already earned a college degree, 19 percent of them report having been physically forced to have sex against their will at some point in their life.[78] I am unable to say anything about the when, where, or by whom of such assaults, but the reality of significant sexual violence is a fact. There is a social problem here. The problem, of course, extends well beyond college campuses.

Where facts turn to fiction, however, is when the discourse about sexual violence formally ignores (yet implicitly admits) the robust reality of sexual exchange. This is evident in how scholars, administrators, journalists, and activists talk about such violence and the key way in which campuses are seeking to reduce it—by pressing for more explicit consent laws.[79] On the one hand, it is heartwarming to see universities wonder aloud about how to ensure the sexual behavior of their students could be more wanted and mutual. On the other hand, presuming the sex act is malleable by fiat and subject to bureaucratic oversight is hubris.[80] And sexual consent, while no doubt a key value, is more of a spectrum than a dichotomous variable.[81] There is no way to create sexual encounters free of nuance, judgment calls, and the possibility of regret.

What does this recent turn have to do with sexual economics and the exchange relationship? Plenty. The concept of consent implies the giving and receiving of something valued. Normative and legal forms of consent—whether "yes means yes" or "no means no"—presuppose distinctive roles, with men as primary pursuers and women as the recipients of sexual pursuits.[82] The nature of heterosexual exchange is deeply imprinted on our collective psyche. It's more than a mere cultural script, as some sociologists suppose.[83] "[E]quality," Illouz observes, "demands a redefinition of eroticism and romantic desire that has yet to be accomplished."[84]

To imagine pressure-free, sex-positive, egalitarian utopias is to ignore the real world of men and women who, for all their fine qualities, nevertheless experience and demonstrate no shortage of brokenness, lying, cheating, deception, and aggression. Collectively, we remain unwilling to wrestle with the dark side of human personhood, concluding instead that enforcing speech laws will reform people's motivations and actions.[85] We want men to act better, but are unwilling to admit that men are more apt to do the right thing when they are socially constrained, not just individually challenged. Since women's freedom to choose—that is, the freedom to have sexual encounters—will not be questioned, we seek instead to alter how their encounters must transpire. It is a fool's bargain. The sooner we recognize that campus "rape culture" and "hookup culture" are both children of the same parent—the split, gender-imbalanced mating market depicted in Figure 2.1—the quicker we will see the wisdom of privileging some sensible social control (of sexual behavior), not just self-control. Thoughtful restrictions on Greek social functions (i.e., parties), as well as sex-segregated residence halls with sensible visiting hours, make sense in this light. These do not prevent lovers from being together. Rather, they undermine social situations that promote cheap, as well as unwanted, sex.

Everyone wins. Because men, argued Alfred Kinsey, will pursue diverse sex partners their entire lives were it not for social restrictions.

Does Sexual Economics Only Apply to Heterosexuality?

It is increasingly impossible to talk intelligently about heterosexual behavior without making reference to nonheterosexuality and its forms and expressions. While I pay more attention to heterosexual relationships than to gay and lesbian ones in this book, it is certainly the case that the two do not orbit different planets. Scholars increasingly recognize this. Moreover, a sexual economics approach concerns the distinctive relational interests of men and women, whether they are gay or straight. In fact, it proves an optimal test of aspects of the exchange model. Has the advent and uptake of cheap sex, something valued from Chelsea to Chattanooga, affected nonheterosexuality? Certainly. One of the key observations Giddens made in *The Transformation of Intimacy* concerned the malleability of human sexuality, which he linked to our dramatic advancement in fertility control:

> The creation of *plastic sexuality*, severed from its age-old integration with reproduction, kinship and the generations, was the precondition of the sexual revolution of the past several decades.

And of that sexual revolution, in turn, he had more to say. It was not "gender-neutral." Instead, it was "a revolution in female sexual autonomy," one that nevertheless held "profound consequences" for male sexuality. Finally, it prompted "the flourishing of homosexuality, male and female."[86] Giddens draws an arrow from the advent and uptake of contraception— and with it the dramatic decline in the cost of sex—to the plasticity made possible by the sexual revolution, and then from there to sexual experimentation and the flourishing of non-heterosexual expressions.

We now think and act quite differently in regard to sexual orientation, and not primarily because of a recession in religious authority or emergence of political progressivism (though those have certainly mattered). Social psychologist Jean Twenge detects an upswing in same-sex sexual behavior among women that cannot be accounted for by controlling for greater acceptance of such relationships, suggesting it's not just about shifting attitudes.[87] It is the new attention people are able (and perhaps encouraged) to pay to sexuality when it is no longer "held hostage" to reproduction. If sex is less risky and life-altering, as well as more accessible, then it is far more conducive to exploration, personal discovery, and cultivation. Sexuality became "something each of us has ... no longer a natural condition which an individual accepts as a preordained state of affairs" but, rather, is malleable, "a prime connecting point between body, self-identity and social norms."[88]

Giddens held that gay and lesbian relationships were thus in the vanguard of the pure relationship form, the pioneers of the confluent love model. But they would not remain alone, eventually joined by non-marital—and then marital—heterosexual relationships. It seemed simply a matter of time back in 1992. Today, scholars are increasingly recognizing that sexuality and desire can be cultivated. Immutability, a foundation for legal shifts in LGBT rights as recently as 2015, seems on the way out. It does not adequately capture the complexity of sexuality or give credit to the social directedness of desire—especially among women. Jane Ward, a sociologist of sex, gender, and queer politics at UC-Riverside, thoughtfully captures the dilemma that survey self-report data pose to the idea of immutability:

> If we all really believed that sexual orientation was congenital—or present at birth—then no one would ever worry that social influences could have an effect on our sexual orientation. But I think that in reality, we all know that sexual desire is deeply subject to social, cultural, and historical forces.[89]

Self-identified sexual orientation appears both more discernible and more stable for men than for women.[90] Psychologist J. Michael Bailey agrees with Ward that women's sexual orientation is more sensitive to social influence and more subject to personal decision-making:

> Even if they had the potential to enjoy sex with men and women, most women might choose men due to overwhelming socialization pressures. From early childhood most people are exposed to a largely heterosexual world, are encouraged in various ways to behave heterosexually, and discouraged from behaving homosexually. ... Current social forces in most of the world work to mold heterosexual lives.[91]

Kara, a 31-year-old from Washington, DC, exemplifies this. She had explored oral sexual experiences with women both when she was in college and then again a few years later, but suspected it would not be an enduring phenomenon with her. She is confident that she's not a lesbian, but self-identified to us as bisexual. Nevertheless, that too wouldn't likely last, she believed: "I prioritize males ... I guess you could say (I'm) bisexual, but I know when I get married I probably won't be doing all that [i.e., having girlfriends]." Not so for Uneek, a 24-year-old from Maryland. After finishing college, she began work as a health outreach coordinator, a placeholder position until she goes back to school to become a physician's assistant. Uneek identified as "gay," but has had sex with men, including recently. Moreover, "most of the girls I have sex with are straight," she claims. She's religious, too—she attends an AME Church every Sunday. Her name character-izes her, because stereotypical she is not. It all makes for a socially awkward existence, but Uneek seems to handle it with aplomb. Her parents back home in Missouri are not thrilled, but that did not sur-prise her. Nor did the malleability of the women she has slept with, because she knows all about that. When we inquired of whom she confides in about relationships, Uneek expanded upon the impulse she observes in others to "cultivate" sexuality. It becomes challenging for her to navigate:

> I just don't think you should discuss sex with friends because, one, I have learned that I don't talk to straight people about gay sex, because they want to do it and that's half the issues I have in my life. And then—yeah, they want to do it, and so I don't even like to tell people I am gay, but they find out that I am so gay, so. (Laughs) I just don't do it because they are going to want to know. They are going to want to try it and I have ruined (my relationship with them) and that's why I don't have any friends. [*So do you have any gay friends that you can talk to about it ... ?*] I mean I have, like, one or two but they are not like me. They are not the same. [*How do you mean?*] They are not like me, like they are studs. They are like girls that just try guys.

The same fluidity at work in Bailey's description is evident in Leslie Bell's qualitative study of northern California women.[92] Half of the les-bian, bisexual, and queer women Bell interviewed experienced no clear sexual identity transformation in moving between male and female partners. Kara and Uneek highlight how we cannot ignore the effects of non-heterosexual behavior in heterosexual life. They overlap, sometimes briefly, sometimes for much longer. Toward that end, Figure 2.2 displays the share of American adults ages 18–60 who self-report being completely heterosexual (or straight), graphed by age, in the 2014 *Relationships in America* survey. Whereas men's self-reported heterosexuality varies only modestly with age, women's does not, displaying instead a U-shaped curve whose trough—the lowest share self-identifying as entirely heterosexual—bottoms out in the mid-twenties. Shortly before age 50 the share of women self-reporting heterosexuality eclipses that of men for the first time.[93] A similar U-shape curve is visible in the 2011–13 NSFG estimates on sexual attraction (not shown).

Women nevertheless face a fixed fertility schedule. Thus we should not be surprised to see an age-graded shift in self-reported sexual identity around the time their peak fertility years begin to decline with the advent of their thirties.[94] The distinctive U-shaped curve visible in Figure 2.2 is evidence of that. As an aside, bisexuality follows the same curve, with the self-reported orientation peaking among women in their early twenties (at 8 percent, not shown). Ditto for the share of women who claim to be "mostly attracted to males." It peaks at 15 percent in the early twenties, and bottoms out at 7 percent in their early forties.[95]

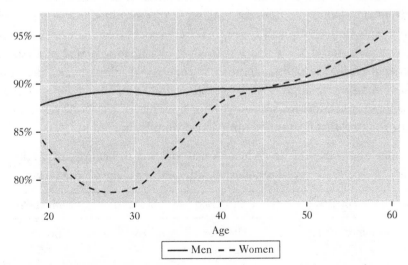

FIGURE 2.2 Percent self-identifying as "100% heterosexual," by age and sex
Source: Relationships in America.

Mating Market Dynamics and
Sexual Malleability

The malleability of female sexuality and the age-graded trends in self-reported sexual identity raise questions about a possible role of the wider mating market and its dynamics on the formation of some share of same-sex relationships among women. Sexual economics has not often been a lens through which to understand developments in same-sex relationships. While I understand why that is the case, I think it is premature to write off mating market dynamics as having nothing to do with men's and women's same-sex relationships, especially in this era of experimentation, cultivation, later marriage, and more and better data.

Let me recount a story as an example. Recently I was chatting with a friend of mine whose sister Amanda is in a same-sex relationship. I asked her to relay the account of her sister's "coming out" as a lesbian and was told that it coincided with early twenty-something difficulty navigating the relationship world of men as a tall, athletic woman. She didn't fit in and was seldom asked out. I am not at all suggesting this experience was a key reason for trending toward relationships with women. Most women in her situation do not do this. But my friend wondered aloud whether at a critical time in normative sexual relationship development—the late teens and early twenties—her sister found little relational interest from men. Indeed, a competitive hierarchy based almost entirely on sexual attractiveness has emerged from the long-standing embeddedness of men and women within group and communal frameworks that characterized earlier eras.[96] And it happened for Amanda in a historic period of political change around sexuality, a local social context (Washington, DC) that was becoming increasingly open to sexual exploration and the generation of same-sex relationships, and a city known for having the worst sex ratio in the country (that is, far more unmarried women than men).

Table 2.1　Share of "100% homosexual" and "mostly homosexual" adults reporting a sexual relationship with someone of the opposite sex

Sexual Orientation	Time Period	Men (%)	Women (%)
100% homosexual	Lifetime	30.7	69.4
	Past year	0.3	4.6
Mostly homosexual	Lifetime	77.8	69.0
	Past year	15.2	22.3

Source: *Relationships in America.*

Very few scholars—perhaps paralyzed by fear of being wrong about the matter—have wondered aloud about why exactly it is that the early twenties is the period of greatest experimentation with same-sex relationships among women, as attested in Figure 2.2. It may be in part the product of the time (and following that, mentalities) created by wide contraceptive uptake, allowing—as Giddens asserts—the social space to cultivate and explore sexuality with diminished risk. As Table 2.1 documents, 69 percent of women who self-identify as homosexual in the *Relationships in America* survey reported having had sex with a man at some point in their life. The figures on having had sex with a man in the past year are far lower, but well above (15 times) that of recent sex between self-identified gay men with women.

Amanda eventually married a woman. For others (like Kara), following the trend line, their experiences do not fit well and they shift toward relationships exclusively with men. So does a poor experience with the mating market—whether by problematic interaction with men, sexual violence, or, in Amanda's case, a lack of interaction with them—lower some women's barriers to a same-sex relationship they otherwise might never have entered? Anecdotes and indirect observational data (like that cited just above) are unfortunately about all we have to go on, but they nevertheless suggest so. If scholars like Giddens and Bailey are right— that women's sexual plasticity and autonomy have increased—then we should expect that some share of women will respond to perceived mating market constraints and struggles by experimenting with same-sex relationships in a way their grandmothers could not have imagined. This need not be the case for all or most self-identified lesbians or bisexual women. No matter. In Amanda's case, she told her sister that she very well could have settled into a relationship with a man had interest from such been expressed and received at critical times. But it did not happen.

Frustration with the mating market may not be a primary (and certainly is not a conscious) reason for the pursuit of many women's same-sex relationships. I hold, however, that it may be an indirect effect—a factor that contributes to the consideration of alternatives or options otherwise unlikely to occur if the general mating market was "clearing" more efficiently. That is, if it were more quickly enabling men and women to meet, fall in love, and "get out" of the market and into permanent (or long-term) relationships. That clearing process has slowed down dramatically, as attested to by the rising age-at-first-marriage and the diminishing share of married twenty- and thirty-somethings (more on that in Chapter 5).

The diminishing price of sex has no doubt made the market in relationships more inefficient—in lots of ways. And following Giddens's logic,
only a Pill-era mating market is even poised to witness and enable participants' experimentation with numerous types of relationships (e.g.,
long-term, short-term, same-sex, non-romantic, etc.). Prior to it, pregnancies would have sealed many sexual relationships promptly, if also prematurely and unhappily.

Markets constrain and enable, and so what alters market dynamics—in
this case, reproductive technology—matters a great deal for what is possible, including women in same-sex relationships who have previously
been in relationships with men. Reproduction, Giddens claimed, was
once far more squarely embedded in nature. But now that conception can
be avoided or artificially generated, heterosexuality is at risk of becoming
"one taste among others."[97] And if Bailey is correct—that women's sexual
behavior and relationship decision-making are more subject to social cues
than men's are—then the cultural expectations of women's behavior in
the mating market matters.[98] The bottom line is that as Americans' sexual
culture becomes less heteronormative, which appears to be the case, the
effect of it on mating market dynamics is almost certain, but is not simple
to predict. For that reason alone, we ought to pay attention.

Conclusion

Heterosexual sex exhibits an exchange relationship wherein men access
sex that women provide, typically in return for desired resources. Sexual
access today, however, has gotten easier or "cheaper." It is the cognitive
and behavioral norm today. Some say we have simply recognized our
ancient amorous natures, but the more recent invention and uptake of
synthetic hormonal contraception seems a far more plausible explanation
for the diminished price of sex. The Pill's injection into the mating market altered much about modern life and relationships, reducing women's
dependence on men's resources while dropping the price of sexual access
for men. It also split the mating market in two, laying bare men's long-
standing hopes for sex with fewer strings alongside women's stable interests in stronger signals of commitment first. This altered power dynamics
between them, since power in developing relationships is determined in
part by the ability to secure things outside the relationship. In this case,
women want men but don't need them while men want sex but have more
options now. Relationship frustrations, especially among women, mount,

but are mischaracterized as a paradox when they are instead quite predictable. It's not that love is dead, but the sexual incentives for men to sacrifice and commit have largely dissolved, spelling a more confusing and circuitous path to commitment and marriage than earlier eras. The exchange relationship isn't dead, either. Bona fide egalitarianism is punished in the bedroom—and on the big screen—to the chagrin of ideologues. An examination of sexual self-identity and behavior patterns suggests Pill-altered mating market dynamics even reach beyond heterosexuality to affect how women navigate same-sex relationships. Markets constrain and enable, and thus whatever alters their dynamics—in this case, reproductive technology—matters.

3

Cheaper, Faster, Better, More? Contemporary Sex in America

NOT A WEEK seems to go by without a new journalistic probe into the world of hookups. I certainly didn't start it, but I contributed to it back in 2011 when I wrote a piece for *Slate* entitled "Sex is Cheap." (Obviously I still believe it.) It was the ninth-most downloaded article in *Slate* that year. It struck a nerve, as discussions of this subject matter typically do. One very popular iteration of the genre appeared in the September 2015 issue of *Vanity Fair*, describing how the dating app Tinder has exacerbated the hookup culture and created what author Nancy Jo Sales dubbed the "dating Apocalypse," the catastrophic collapse of romance.[1]

In truth, I was wrong about Tinder (though nobody knew it because I never publicly wrote about it). Tinder came about as a "straight" alternative to Grindr, a popular meetup app for gay men. I surmised that women would not take to Tinder, given it features no clue about a man's resources other than that which can be discerned in a photograph. (Grindr's popularity, on the other hand, makes more sense.) But I was wrong.

"Sex is easy," penned Sales. But what neither she nor many women wish to admit is that when you say "sex is easy," what you mean is that sex is cheap. And that is something men will commonly appreciate more than women. Again, this fact does not debunk the exchange model; it just signifies that increasing numbers of women don't really need men's resources anymore, and that they outnumber men in the market for committed relationships. That is not to say that they prefer anonymous sex—few do—or are happy that little resources are expended for their company. They are not. Sales quotes frustrated women at length, women who do not recognize that they are competing for men now. But when the supply side rises to meet demand, the price of anything—including sex—will fall.[2] Tyler, a 28-year-old from Denver with whom we spoke, makes an astute observation about dating in an online era. It is, he calculated, "somewhat of a numbers game." How so? "As many potential contacts that you can make with members of the opposite sex, you know, the more likelihood is that you're gonna be able to have sex with one of them."

It may be crass, but it is not unscientific. Sales interviewed psychologist David Buss, an expert on the evolution of mating strategies. He spells out the discouraging scene:

> When there is a surplus of women, or a perceived surplus of women, the whole mating system tends to shift towards short-term dating. Marriages become unstable. Divorces increase. Men don't have to commit, so they pursue a short-term mating strategy. Men are making that shift, and women are forced to go along with it in order to mate at all.[3]

It is far from the only economic reference in her piece. In fact, the *Vanity Fair* feature is rife with exchange claims. A short sample includes:

- "Dating apps are the free-market economy come to sex."
- "The act of choosing consumer brands and sex partners has become interchangeable."
- "A few young women admitted to me that they use dating apps as a way to get free meals. 'I call it Tinder food stamps,' one said."

Sales goes on to interview Elizabeth Armstrong, a sociologist (at the University of Michigan) and co-investigator of a fascinating look into the lives and sexual decisions of Indiana University undergraduate women. Armstrong makes a common qualification—predictable among sociologists because it is in the air they breathe—when she begins by making reference to unacceptable inequalities:

> For young women the problem in navigating sexuality and relationships is still gender inequality.... Young women complain that young men still have the power to decide when something is going to be serious and when something is not—they can go, "She's girlfriend material, she's hookup material." ... There is still a pervasive double standard. We need to puzzle out why women have made more strides in the public arena than in the private arena.[4]

Like Leslie Bell, Armstrong is puzzled by the paradox. Being a sociologist myself, I understand the language of my peers. Many feminists fear the gender revolution is only partly successful, having stumbled not in the workplace but in the bedroom. But family historian Stephanie Coontz's blinders make Armstrong's seem mild by comparison when she asserts that somehow men have failed to evolve:

> Exploitative and disrespectful men have always existed. There are many evolved men, but there may be something going on in hookup culture now that is making some more resistant to evolving.[5]

Evolution—whether the real or the rhetorical kind—has nothing to do with this because men's sex drive will nearly always trump their manners in the absence of social and community pressure to the contrary. Coontz wants men to behave nicely in the domain of sex and relationships, just because. Again, the only paradoxes here are the unrealistic expectation that economic and educational equality should spell the same in determining how their relationships transpire, and the equally striking failure to recognize that in the domain of sexual expression, women's unique power to accomplish what they want is in gatekeeping. Even Sales, who writes not with amusement or approval of the hookup scene but with alarm, fails to appreciate how the exchange model works:

> Men in the age of dating apps can be very cavalier, women say. One would think that having access to these nifty machines (their phones) that can summon up an abundance of no-strings-attached sex would make them feel happy, even grateful, and so inspired to be polite. But . . . the opposite seems to be the case.[6]

There is no puzzle here. The double standard is not a mystery. It is not something to which one "subscribes" or a structure that one can reject at will with few repercussions. It is about robust, deep-seated distinctions between the sexes that may be malleable but are not simply socially constructed. And it is about women devaluing (or in the case of Tinder, altogether ignoring) men's productivity and winsomeness while still expecting to be esteemed and not objectified in relationships. That is not how men work. In her excellent and kind review of my previous book, *Premarital Sex in America*, NYU sociologist Paula England chides my co-author and me for suggesting that the double standard is not a social construction: "Instead of recognizing it as a socially constructed piece of culture that could be otherwise, they explicitly state that it cannot ever be changed. They see it as a logical deduction from the 'sexual economics' theory when combined with the assumption that men want casual sex more than women."[7] She is right that I do not recognize it as a socially constructed piece of culture (and hence in need of constant social reinforcement), but she's mistaken to believe that I deduce it from sexual economics. No, the double standard precedes sexual economics. The contemporary mating market does not cause men to, in her words, "morally disrespect women who, when they find themselves competing with more women for men, switch to offering sex with fewer requirements for commitment." Men are more apt to morally disrespect such women as possible long-term partners and spouses due to their concern about future fidelity in the exchange relationship. At the same time, they value them as possible short-term partners. This is maddening to many, I understand. But it is going nowhere fast, even as women are increasingly besting men in the labor market.

Tinder—and online dating in general—did not cause cheap sex. It simply made the acquisition of it more efficient. And it is not just a New York problem, or one confined to university campuses. Jennifer, a 24-year-old from Bristol, Tennessee, waxed eloquent on the dating scene in and around the Tri-Cities area:

> Today, and I'm speaking for myself and what I also know from my girlfriends, guys don't ask girls on dates. They, it's you know, "Do you wanna go get a drink? Do you wanna do this?" It's never a formal date where a lot of times she'd get dressed up and he would take her out and, you know, try to woo her. . . . That doesn't really exist. Not here anyway (chuckles). [*Do you have thoughts as to why that is the case?*] I feel like the guys don't do it because they don't have to. [*OK.*] I feel like the girls don't make them, they don't express that they should be doing this, you should be taking me out when you meet me and trying to win my affections. They make it almost too, I feel like, well the guys, what's the point when you're not gonna make me if I can get it easier? [*Are you referring to sex when you're talking about this?*] Sex, relationships, I mean either way, you know, what you would expect or want when you start a date with somebody, hopefully it's not just sex, you know. If you're going on a date, then hopefully they like you and you like each other. I don't feel like that even exists for people who just, you know, have a connection or are attracted. I feel like it's just too easy for guys just to say "Hey, let's you and I hang out and see what happens."

Why such modest investment by men? Jennifer knew, even as she participated in it:

> Because they don't have to. And the girls aren't saying, "You need to do this." [OK.] You know, to win my affection, you need to take me out. You know, guys aren't gonna do it, I guess, if we're not making them. [*So why do you think girls are not making them?*] I don't think they put enough value, and this is myself included, on and in themselves to think that a guy would take them out on a date. To make them, I think that they don't have, and this is, you know, maybe just me, but there's gotta be a reason and when I think about it I think they wouldn't want to on this. They wouldn't want to put forth the effort. . . . I should be asking, you know, "You need to take me out, you need to show me a good time. . . . You need to woo me. . . . But we don't, and I think that has something to say about our value on ourselves.

The dating scene in Bristol sounds as blunt as it does in the *Vanity Fair* description of New York City, a world away from eastern Tennessee both economically and culturally. It highlights the social challenge of the "collapsed cartel" among women, about which I will have more to say in Chapter 5. Jennifer identifies what amounts to a collective problem among women—a low price for sex and a concomitant failure by men to woo them. It is collective because she can identify its sources yet feels personally powerless to do anything about it. This is what cheap sex hath wrought: men perceiving women (and women in turn perceiving themselves) as having diminished "value," to use Jennifer's own term. Sociologist Eva Illouz would agree, having diagnosed modern women's assessments of their own value not as "less dependent on a man's gaze," as we might suppose in our more egalitarian era, but more.[8]

In a near-miss attempt at explaining the problem, Sales revisits Naomi Wolf's theory, articulated in her 1991 book *The Beauty Myth*, that "as women achieved more social and political power, there was more pressure on them to be 'beautiful' as a means of undermining their empowerment." Then Sales wonders aloud, "Could the ready availability of sex provided by dating apps actually be making men respect women less?" However, apps don't provide sex, people do. The apps simply make more efficient the historic male pursuit of sex. That smart people continue to misunderstand this is befuddling.

When relationships start with sex—as I will shortly document that many do—the odds that women will flourish and enjoy a long-term relationship are dramatically lowered. It is not impossible, just rare. It reminds me of social network scholar Duncan Watts's assertion that people are "always convincing ourselves that this time we are going to get it right, without ever learning what it is that we are doing wrong."[9] And since men tend not to make for diligent sexual gatekeepers, it turns out the puzzle here is not of Sherlock Holmes caliber. The question to ask is not why double standards exist or why women's strides in the private arena have not matched their gains in the public arena. The question to ask is why women demand so little of men in return for offering men what they want—what they are willing to sacrifice a great deal for. And the answer is economic: it is because many do not need what men can offer. And that is not going to change.

The gender revolution is a profound one, but it stops here. It cannot make men "better behaved," save perhaps by force of law. But law here will only foster modestly better external behavior. In an increasingly sexualized world, law will not alter interior motivation and mentalities. Until the exchange model no longer works—and I do not perceive how that would happen—sex will continue to be cheap, journalists will have plenty to write about, sociologists will continue to overlook the obvious and feign consternation, and women will find themselves frustrated.

Like much of the investigative journalism about hooking up, the *Vanity Fair* piece is illuminating and highlights the reality of sexual economics at work. But like almost all such narratives, its sample is a decidedly nonrandom one, comprised of the people the author elected to speak with. For all we know, they may be acquaintances of hers, or friends of friends. Not exactly the sort of data one wants to rely upon for making claims about what is going on in the population as a whole. Perhaps young-adult New Yorkers are providing an account of what is going on in their relationship lives that is not consonant with the rest of America. Heck, even Tinder criticized her sampling strategy.[10]

Is Online Dating a Cheap Sex Delivery System?

Dan Slater is the author of a variety of manuscripts about online dating and two books on the same. His *Love in the Time of Algorithms* levels with readers about the consequences of online dating for the mating market. But first he reminds readers of what came before:

> For virtually all of human history the search for a mate has been predicated on scarcity: One met only so many people in his or her lifetime. They optimized their options within a circumscribed pool,

chose someone, settled down, and, in the best of cases, found something they called happiness.[11]

Online dating forces participants to play by its rules—a carefully
selected photo, a honed narrative about ourselves—hemmed in by
what sociologist Charles Cooley called the "looking-glass self" (way
back when a mirror was called a looking glass).[12] Cooley asserted that
people imagine how they appear to others, interpret those others'
reactions to them, develop a self-concept accordingly, and then live in
consonance with that self-concept. It seems an almost juvenile claim
when contrasted to our contemporary clichés about the self—that we
can become whoever we wish to be, achieve our biggest dreams, and so
on. But the looking-glass self characterizes us more today than when
it was coined.

Let's not get too far ahead of ourselves, though. Although common,
online dating is not yet the modal or typical way heterosexual couples connect. In a recent study of how couples meet, it was the third-most likely
way among them, after the mediation of friends, and was comparable to
meeting at bars, restaurants, and other public places.[13] But demographer
Michael Rosenfeld finds that for gays and lesbians, who endure what he
calls "thinner" markets—that is, fewer possible social ties with potential
romantic interests and less help from family or schoolmates—online
meetings are the most popular source of relationships, by a long shot, and
have been for some time now:

> The most striking difference between the way same-sex versus het-
> erosexual couples meet is the dominance of the Internet among
> same-sex couples who met after 2000, with over 60 percent of
> same-sex couples meeting online in 2008 and 2009. Meeting
> online has not only become the predominant way that same-sex
> couples meet in the United States, but meeting online is now dra-
> matically more common among same-sex couples than any way
> of meeting has ever been for heterosexual or same-sex couples in
> the past.[14]

From this distinction we know nothing of what online dating users intend,
male or female, gay or straight. Grindr's popularity suggests that gay men
often use the site for sexual couplings, but Tinder's surprisingly comparable rapid emergence among straight couples undermines any blanket

statements about what particular users of such media hope. While writers at *Slate* were content to declare that the uproar over the *Vanity Fair* article simply signaled age-old anxiety about the emerging equality of women and their own pursuit of sexual pleasure, Tinder itself took to social media to assure the concerned that plenty of men and women do not use it solely for sexual hookups.[15]

Tinder is not Match.com, and both of those are distinct from eHarmony or religiously inspired dating services like Catholic Match and Christian Mingle. But a comparable underlying template to each of them boxes in most users of such platforms, and it is one dominated by market-driven questions: What does he have to offer? How attractive is she (or he)? Is she out of my league? Is there a better fit out there? (Probably.) How good is "good enough"? While online dating sites turn qualitative traits into quantitative rankings, algorithms nevertheless figure out pretty readily that what you say you want—in your profile—and how you actually behave online can be quite different. As I stated at the outset of this book, reality—how relationships work— is always more interesting and compelling than ideology, how we wish they would work.

As online dating increases in popularity, there is growing interest in evaluating its successes and failures, and especially what sorts of people tend to be attracted to other sorts of people.[16] That is all interesting, I suppose, but it is often intuitive and utterly unsurprising. From a sexual economics perspective, on the other hand, the most relevant thing about online dating is not its ability to match preferences before you meet but rather that it enables people to sort through sexual and romantic "options" more efficiently. What it signals socially is that while persons are not commodities, sex is often considered exactly that (especially by men), and online dating is a means by which sex can be secured. It may link you to your eventual beloved spouse, but along the way online dating is a remarkably efficient cheap sex delivery system. It puts far more choices— in human beings and relationship types—in front of us than we have ever had before. It's like a platter of people.

And if social media use in general fosters relationship discontent—and a recent study using the NFSS data demonstrates it does—then it would be prudent to suspect that online dating encourages even greater discontent.[17] Have an awkward time on a second date? A petty dispute on your third date? Why bother working at it—log on and see who else is interested in you. It gets better, right?

Online dating's superior efficiency works against relationship development, and problem solving, and positively rages against the goal of efficient marriage market "clearing," that is, people exiting the market for good by having found someone who fits them. Slater agrees: "What do you think will happen to commitment when people discover how much easier it's become to find new relationships?"[18] In a conversation with Jacob, an experienced online "dater" who had just concluded a two-year-long cohabitation with a younger, attractive woman he'd met online, Slater's interviewee approaches the answer:

> "I'm about 95 percent certain," he says, "that if I'd met Rachel offline, and if I'd never done online dating, I would've married her. At that point in my life, I would've overlooked everything else and done whatever it took to make things work. Did online dating change my perception of permanence? No doubt. When I sensed the breakup coming, I was okay with it. It didn't seem like there was going to be much of a mourning period, where you stare at your wall thinking you're destined to be alone and all that. I was eager to see what else was out there."[19]

Note Jacob's choice of words. Not who else, but what else. It reminds me of Zygmunt Bauman's observation, "Once permission (and the prescription) to reject and replace an object of consumption which no longer brings full satisfaction is extended to partnership relations, the partners are cast in the status of consumer objects."[20] Online dating could simply be a more efficient way to meet potential romantic interests and democratize the marriage market, maximizing the likelihood of locating a spouse who is more desirable to you (and vice versa) than to most other people. I have seen it work that way. But more often, we are allowing ourselves to treat human beings as commodities, even while we purport to be better than that. Back to Slater:

> One industry insider admitted wondering whether "matching you up with great people is getting so efficient, and the process so enjoyable, that marriage will become obsolete." Match.com's parent company CEO was realistic: "Look, if I lived in Iowa I'd be married with four children by now. That's just how it is."[21]

When my own girlfriend (now wife) dumped me in 1991 after I was being distant, unpleasant, and uncertain about us, she promptly went to the annual Chicago Auto Show with another man, on a date. I stayed in my dorm room watching *One Flew Over the Cuckoo's Nest*, a course assignment. Questioning my own sanity, I quickly perceived my options as limited, the search costs fairly tall, and the challenges of my romantic relationship not so bad. We were back together before the weekend was out. But that era is over. Today I might have logged on and moved on.

Online dating encourages throwing a potential relationship away and starting with a new one (again). And sites like Grindr and Tinder privilege sexual attraction—a notion that is actually distinct from beauty—as the primary currency in (early) relationships.[22] It fosters overlapping sexual partners, since options can be kept open. Not exactly the pinnacle of modern enlightenment or "evolution." That is because very little about men (and women) has evolved or become enlightened. The exchange model is not only old, it's robust. Slater explicitly respects the sexual economics of online dating, noting that historically heterosexual men who wished to pursue what he calls "a short-term strategy" faced three barriers to their wishes, all of which have been dramatically lowered (in part) by online dating:[23]

1. Sexual variety was hard to get.
2. Identifying which women were "sexually accessible" was difficult.
3. Minimizing commitment and investment in a sexual relationship was a challenge.

Just like the psychological impulse to check your email frequently—so too with online dating. It has altered how we approach getting to know people. And like pornography, very many people spend lots of time circulating through hundreds of photos (i.e., profiles) on your way to finding "just the right one" that they're looking for. And given the ubiquity of online dating today—again, like porn—this psychological process is becoming difficult to avoid.

Finally, there is the basic economics of the online dating industry to remember. There is a good deal of money being made in the circulation of partners, but no profit at all in the successful cessation—via marriage or even monogamous cohabitation—of an online dating career. Like most organizations, when you peel back the layers you realize it is built to survive more than it is to help its clients. Such companies want you to keep dating. They want you to commodify persons and sex, even while they are trying to convince you that they are doing their best to help you get off the mating market for good. Social embeddedness in a community, not the efficient circulation of potential partners, is what promotes stable relationships and the formation of marriage.[24]

So yes, online dating has become an efficient cheap sex delivery system. Its very efficiency powerfully functions, if even only as an unintended consequence, to foster a short-term relationship mentality.

Oversexed? The Frequency of Intercourse among Young Adults

Are the men featured in the Vanity Fair article unique in their sexual access? Probably. On any given day—across America as a whole—19 percent of young adults between ages 24 and 35 have sex.[25] Of course, sex is not randomly distributed among them. There is an inequality to it that is directly connected to opportunity: 25 percent of cohabiting young adults have sex on any particular day, compared with 22 percent of married young adults, and only 10 percent of never-married young adults. But few have ever considered inequality in sexual frequency a problem.[26]

How much more sex are we talking about? Not that much: cohabiters reported a sexual frequency of about 2.9 times in the past two weeks, compared with 2.6 times among married respondents. The difference is a statistically significant one, though only in the full sample of 18- to 60-year-olds. It holds up in regression model results (in appendix Table A3.1) that control for age, sexual orientation, race/ethnicity, gender, church attendance, health, education, and number of children. In other words, it's robust: cohabiting adults report having more sex than married adults. When I limit the sample to young married and cohabiting adults, the difference is not a profound one.

Any suggestions that average young Americans are oversexed, then, are not borne out by the data. Psychologist Jean Twenge notes—using GSS trend analyses—that a higher share of young adults ages 20–24 are reporting complete sexlessness than in previous cohorts. It would be unwise, however, to presume from this that partnerless young Americans are simply failing in their efforts to access sex. Slightly more of them are opting out of the market, at least temporarily.[27] Hence, some have more sex than others. (Nothing new about that.) The following list reveals the types of young Americans age 35 or under (and currently in a relationship) who report having statistically more frequent sex:

- Those who have had more than one STI, compared to those who have never had one
- Those who have been sterilized compared with those who have not been
- Those who have ever had anal sex, compared with those who have not
- The happiest people (top of the scale), when compared with less-happy respondents
- Self-identified heterosexual women, compared with self-identified homosexual women
- Persons with a college degree (or less), compared with a master's or doctor's degrees

I will not argue causality here, especially since effects are often two-way. Sterilization predicts more sex, but one can also guess that frequent sex—combined with concern about pregnancy—may also predict a decision to sterilize. More sex and greater happiness is likewise a two-way street. The STI and anal sex links are most likely a selection effect; that is, persons who have had anal sex or have acquired an STI are also more apt to be the same persons who pursue more frequent sex, and with more people.

What may surprise some readers is what is not on this list: nearly everything else. Political perspectives, religion, health, race—you name it. While each of them may be factors that predict being in a relationship rather than not being in one, or having had more or fewer sexual partners, among those already in a relationship they are not remarkably influential as far as sexual frequency is concerned.

Sex Is for Singles?

After sex columnist Anthony D'Ambrosio split with his wife of three years, he penned a popular autopsy for matrimony entitled "Five Reasons Marriage Just Doesn't Work Anymore."[28] While I seldom hold out hope for genuine insight in such places, D'Ambrosio offers some thoughtful explanations, most of them rooted in technology. Social media, he claims, uproots us from physical space and materiality, invites too many people (if only virtually) into our relationships, and encourages the desire for attention rather than for genuine love. I think he's onto something. Where I think he strikes out, however, is in his claim that married people just don't have sex. Consistent sex remains a normative expectation for most married Americans.[29] A 2007 Pew Survey found that a happy sexual relationship was the second most important predictor of marital satisfaction, with 70 percent of adults saying it was "very important" for a successful marriage.[30]

D'Ambrosio's impression raises the question of just how widespread sexless marriages are in this era of increasingly confluent love and elevated sexual expectations. Baumeister argues that marriage typically witnesses the return to a "natural" (and lower) level of female sexual interest unburdened by concerns about closing the deal that is marriage, a move he holds frustrates many husbands who didn't see it coming.[31] Is it true that there are a great many sexually frustrated husbands (or wives)?

Yes and no. It is the case, at least in the *Relationships in America* data, that 61 percent of married women say they are satisfied with the amount of sex they are having, a figure higher than that of any other arrangement (including cohabiters, divorcees, and the unmarried). But it is not far higher: those other arrangements hover around 50–54 percent satisfaction. Baumeister and Bettina Arndt, an Australian clinical psychologist and sex therapist, would hold that the best test of whether the exchange model collapses in marriage—with husbands living sexless lives against their will—is by assessing the sexual wishes of husbands.[32] But among them the story is not that different than among wives: 53 percent of married men say they would like to have more sex, a figure only modestly north of the 46 percent of cohabiting men who say the same, and below that of divorced and widowed men (at 57 and 64 percent, respectively). Married men are very unlikely, however, to say they want less sex. Only one-half of 1 percent said so.

Moreover, sexual inactivity in marriage is neither new nor terribly surprising, and is sometimes rather explicable.[33] In their 1992 landmark study of human sexuality, sociologist Edward Laumann and his colleagues reported that 1.3 percent of married men and 2.6 percent of married women between the ages of 18 and 59 had not had sex within the past year. By contrast, twenty years later—in the *Relationships in America* data—4.9 percent of married men and 6.5 percent of married women in the same age range report that it has been over a year since they have had sex with their spouse.[34] Just under 12 percent of all married persons ages 18–60 reported not having had sex for at least three months prior to participating in the survey. What about younger adults? Sexless relationships characterize only 5.8 percent among married respondents aged 24–35, just slightly above the figure among cohabiting young adults (4.5 percent).[35]

Although the questions were asked in slightly different manners—and thus not directly comparable—could it be that there has been an uptick in marital sexual inactivity in the past twenty years? The General Social Survey, which has consistently employed the same question since 1989 to determine sexual frequency, confirms this trend (results not shown). Commuter marriages have, no doubt, increased in frequency.[36] But a 12 percent sexless (in three months) figure is nothing to dismiss lightly. What prompts sexual inactivity in marriage? The presence of children? Age-related sexual disinterest? Or something less relationship-oriented, such as spouses working and living in two different places?

Unfortunately, it's difficult to assess the last of these—the share of those who live apart—in a social survey that also includes sexual behavior questions. (I don't think such data exist.) But commuter marriages have most certainly grown more numerous. In fact, the number of them has increased 17 percent since 2003, according to the 2015 Current Population Survey.

For those couples whose sexual inactivity is not explained by being in a commuter marriage, sociologist Denise Donnelly of Georgia State University argues that habituation may be at fault: while sex may be exciting at first, over time one becomes accustomed to sex with a spouse, until what was exciting becomes dull and predictable.[37] Such an explanation is also increasingly on the lips of non-monogamy proponents.[38] This is hardly new news, of course, and not an uncommon experience.

Habituation—if you were to measure it by duration of marriage— may well be responsible for sexual inactivity in relationships. Analysis of *Relationships in America* data (not shown) reveals a tight association between sexual inactivity rates and the length of time a couple has been married. Those who have been married for longer are quite a bit more likely to be sexually inactive. But length of marriage and age are highly correlated, making it appear as if the length of a marriage is responsible for sexual inactivity, when in reality the age of the respondent may be the culprit. So what happens to sexual inactivity among married couples when I account for the effects of age? For starters, older couples are much more likely to be sexually inactive, as you would expect. Older people are more likely to be ill, have lower energy levels, and experience decreased testosterone and libido, all of which contribute to decreased sexual activity.[39]

For most age groups, there emerges a brief "honeymoon phase" where sexual inactivity levels are lower for those who haven't been married for long, but then increase sharply for those married a few years. However, after the first several years of marriage, sexual inactivity levels off (or trends downward), meaning that those respondents who are the same age—but who have been married longer—are actually less likely to be sexually inactive than their comparable-age peers who were married more recently. As length of marriage increases, sexual inactivity actually decreases.[40]

What else predicts being in a sexless relationship? Not much. Those who are in sexless relationships tend not to be on artificial contraception (which makes sense), and unhappy both personally and with their relationship. No surprise there. It is also slightly more characteristic of respondents who report having been sexually abused by a parent or other adult caregiver at some point while they were growing up, an experience that can (but does not always) echo into respondents' futures.

In the case of Anthony D'Ambrosio, however, there is a good chance that simple mismatch in interest was to blame. (He's hardly unique in that, however.) For a sex columnist who describes himself as "very sexual," all but a high frequency of sex will not likely suffice. It is quite possible, however, that he misses cohabiting far more than marriage. Many young adults—saturated in Hollywood narratives about the single life—worry that marriage spells the end of stable sex. As I just demonstrated, it is not true. And yet married Americans report slightly less sex, on average, than

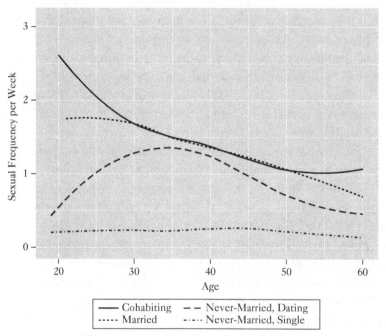

FIGURE 3.1 Sexual frequency per week, by age and relationship status
Source: Relationships in America.

cohabiting couples. And bona fide singles? When I restrict the analyses to those people who have never been married but who are currently romantically involved with someone, they report having sex 1.1 times per week, just under the married couple rate. Altogether un-partnered adults report a more modest average of 0.3 times per week.

It might seem that moving in with a significant other increases sexual frequency (by expanding opportunity) but that getting married reduces it (by familiarity). Figure 3.1 illuminates the age-and-relationship association with sexual frequency. To be sure, cohabiting couples still report more frequent sex than married couples, but the difference is brief—it is only pronounced until around age 25, by which time married and cohabiting couples display parallel patterns of similar sexual frequency. Moreover, the decline with age is not a very pronounced one. By contrast, never-married singles report notably less sex at every age.

In the end, what was true in high school remains true (theoretically) in the assisted living facility: it's about opportunity.

The Strange Politics of Sexual Desire

Plenty of young Americans are not in relationships that afford them sexual access. But many who are nevertheless report wanting more sex than they are currently having. This is hardly a new complaint, I realize. But since such a question is not asked on a large, population-based survey very often, we should take advantage of it and learn more about such persons and what might prompt some to say "enough" and others to say "I want more," and a few others to say "I'd actually prefer less."

Among the sexually discontented, men are overrepresented, as expected: 53 percent of men wish for more sex, compared with 35 percent of women. Baumeister notes the same in his book *Is There Anything Good about Men?* Therein he detects the persistent gender distinction in the pursuit of sex, despite contrarian claims that women's sex drives are just as intense as men's. He doesn't buy it. Nor has any population-based data of which I am aware ever revealed it. But that does not mean all sex drives are equal among men and women, either. While asking respondents about how content they are with the amount of sex they are having is not a perfect measure of sex drive, it is nevertheless illustrative.

For some reason, more politically liberal young-adult women report wanting more sex than they have been having.[41] Indeed, it is one of the strongest (non-sex-related) associations visible. No such political

correlation appears among men. Here are the estimates of which women
said yes, they would prefer to have more sex:

- 16 percent of "very conservative" women
- 30 percent of "conservative" women
- 38 percent of moderate women
- 44 percent of "liberal" women
- 53 percent of "very liberal" women

As you can see, the association is strong and quite linear. It is obvious that
more politically liberal women are apt to say they would prefer more sex.
Why? Here is where the plot thickens.

Remarkably, the association has little to do with how much sex women
have actually had recently. That is, while greater recent frequency of sex
understandably predicts less desire for more sex, accounting for it does
not erase—at all—the link between political liberalism and wanting more
sex. Moreover, there is only a modest correlation between political conservatism and greater frequency of sex. The mystery deepens. In regression
models (in Table A3.2), political liberalism remains significantly associated with the odds of wanting more sex even after controlling for the frequency of recent sex, women's age, marital status, education level, whether
they've masturbated recently, sexual orientation, race/ethnicity, depressive
symptoms, self-reported happiness, number of lifetime (male) partners,
and current pornography use. (A few of these are significant predictors of
wanting more sex.) And still personal politics matters. Perhaps this measure of political liberalism is reflecting more than just the respondent's
Democratic Party affiliation or voting habits. It would seem so. Rather,
political identity today likely captures embeddedness in distinctive world-
views, sets of meanings, and ideas about the self and relationships.

With regard to sex and sexuality in America, being politically liberal tends
to mean valuing sexual expression as a good-in-itself, not only as a means
to an end or contingent on the context (such as being in a relationship or
being married). Talk of "sexual health" is also more common among them
and typically takes acts of sexual expression for granted. In this perspective,
it is a moral good to express one's sexuality in actions of one's own free
choosing. Pleasure is reached for and should be. In keeping with this, liberal
women are more than twice as likely as conservative women to report past-
week and past-day masturbation. Sexual expression among liberal women
is perceived in personal terms at least as much as it is in relational ones.[42]

All this may be true, but I am still not sure it explains why liberal women want more sex, regardless of how much they are already having. I discussed this conundrum with others, and a plausible, four-part path explanation emerged:

1. More liberal women are less religious than conservative women. (True.)
2. More liberal women are therefore more likely to have a difficult time attributing transcendent value to aspects of life such as work, relationships, children, and daily tasks. Some psychologists speak of this attribution as "sanctifying daily life."[43] That is, liberal women are less apt to conceive of mundane, material life as somehow imbued with or reflecting the sacred. For them the world is, to use Max Weber's term, more disenchanted—predictable and safer, but emptier and less mysterious.
3. Nevertheless, most people experience sexual expression as, in some significant way, transcendent, or higher-than-other experiences. Giddens concurs: "Sexuality for us still carries an echo of the transcendent."[44]
4. More liberal women therefore desire more frequent sex because they feel poignantly the lack of sufficient transcendence in life. If sex is one of the few pathways to it, then it is sensible for them to desire more of it.

In essence, this line of reasoning asserts that the demand for transcendence in life is either stable across persons or at least reflects a normal curve. But liberal women are more apt to be less religious, and hence—so the argument goes—longing for sex serves as a replacement for religious transcendence.

So I added religious service attendance, importance of religion, and a unique measure of having become less religious in the past decade to the regression model predicting wanting more sex, and—as theorized— becoming less religious predicts wanting more sex. And what is more, political liberalism no longer matters for wanting more sex. This theory about replacing the loss of the sacred (with a quest for sex) is a plausible one, and it is not the first time this theory has been floated.[45]

In a world increasingly bereft of transcendence, sexual expression is emerging as an intrinsic value. Sex is the new opium of the masses, Baumeister and Vohs claim, a temporary heart in a heartless world.[46] Unfortunately, something so immanent as sex will not—and cannot— function in the manner in which religion can, has, and does. (To be sure, some replace it with an appreciation and devotion to nature.) Sex does not explain the world. It is not a master narrative. It has little to offer by way of convincing theodicy. But in a world increasingly missing transcendence, longing for sexual expression makes sense. It should not surprise us, however, that those who (unconsciously) demand sex function like religion will come up short. Maybe that is why very liberal women are also twice as likely to report being depressed or currently in psychotherapy than very conservative women.

Writer Anna Mussmann perceives the loss of nonsexual human touch in mundane social space, laments this, connects it to the loss of a compelling narrative, but refuses to turn it into yet more partisan politics:

> It might seem (to liberals) that by embracing sexuality we are simply freeing ourselves from the bonds of convention, or (to conservatives) that we are simply afflicted by the overly-sexualized, moral rot that accompanies the rejection of moral values. However, our obsession is something both more innocent and more desperate than that. We are uncomfortable with greater intimacy not because we don't like touch, but because most bodily contact has been so sexualized. Sex used to be a bit farther from people's minds. Before central heating, sharing a bed could be asexual.[47]

I like living in the twenty-first century as much as the next person, but I concur with Mussmann that our ancestors were simply better about this than we moderns are. And they were not sexless:

> They sang bawdy ballads, chased after girls, and produced offspring. However, sex was simply one part of bodily life—much like birth, aging, and death. Modern sex is different. Modern sex is not supposed to be part of the same cycle as aging and death. Instead, it is part of a strangely innocent, oddly desperate attempt to deny death's power over our sexy, tanned, and well-toned lives. We have wedded sex and youth in sacred union.

Sexual Economics and "Lesbian Bed Death"

Speaking of death, the unpleasant term "lesbian bed death" was coined by sociologists Philip Blumstein and Pepper Schwartz in their 1983 book *American Couples*, and refers to the empirical revelation that lesbian sexual relationships tend to be characterized by much-less-frequent sexual activity than gay or straight sexual relationships.[48] It is a finding that has been discussed and re-evaluated at considerable length in the decades since it was coined.[49] The contest over the veracity of the "bed death" claim continues unabated, though seldom assisted by random samples large enough to do more than speculate about whether the difference was real in the broader population of lesbians or just restricted to the nonrandom samples commonly employed to evaluate the hypothesis.[50]

In reality, the phrase indicates a process by which lesbian couples are thought to diminish the frequency of sexual activity within a relationship over time, until their baseline average is well under that of gay men's or straight couples. Estimates from respondents currently in a relationship reveal, in keeping with the stereotype and hypothesis, notably less recent experience of paired sexual behavior among lesbian women when compared with gay men and heterosexual men and women.[51] Table 3.1 notes that only 46 percent of women who identified as entirely homosexual in the *Relationships in America* data reported sexual activity in the past two weeks. "Bed death," however, is an overstatement: only 19 percent report no sex in the past three months. But the numbers do not lie—straight couples and gay men are far more likely to report recent sexual activity.

The reason for the disparity is, like many social science findings, disputed. Some scholars suggest lower sexual desire among women in same-sex relationships.[52] Others assert that women's sexual behavior preferences are simply different than men's, with women more apt to be satisfied with non-genital forms of sexual expression than men, regardless of sexual identity.[53] Both can be true at the same time, and both interpretations can make sense of the results in Table 3.1. And yet sexual desire is often out of step with actual sexual behavior. That is, many Americans report wanting more sex than they are currently having—44 percent in all. Just over 53 percent say they are content—61 percent of women and

Table 3.1 Percentage reporting sex in the past two weeks, among those currently in a relationship

	100% Heterosexual (Straight) (%)	100% Homosexual (Gay or Lesbian) (%)
Men	75	80
Women	71	46

Source: Relationships in America.

45 percent of men—while only 3 percent of adults report wishing they could have less sex.

Table 3.2 displays responses to the question about desire among gay and straight respondents currently in a relationship. While no more than 1 percent of men (and lesbian women) say they would prefer less sex, 4 percent of straight women said the same. So it is a rare American (in a relationship) who wishes for less sex. By contrast, 52 percent of self-identified lesbian women (in relationships) say they want more sex than they are having, signaling that self-reported desire for sex is not lacking among them. In fact, it is an estimate equivalent to that of straight men and well above that of heterosexual women (at 29 percent). Why the disparity in recent sexual activity among them, if the desire for more sex is as high as among gay and straight men?

Sexual economics provides an answer rooted in evolutionary psychology which suggests that just because someone self-identifies as something other than heterosexual does not mean they are able to just opt out of deeply embedded sex differences in socio-sexual behavior. The data clearly suggest that lower sexual frequency is not due to lower sexual desire, since their overall reports of unfulfilled sexual desire are not lower. No—the frequency is lower due to the fact that the couple is comprised of women, who are historically sexual gatekeepers. It is the very same reason that the other three estimates in Table 3.1—each of which involves a male component— are quite comparable. (They are not statistically significantly different from each other.) When women are in a relationship with a man, far fewer of them will be dissatisfied with the amount of sex in their relationship, as

Table 3.2 Contentment with amount of sex, among those currently in a relationship

		100% Heterosexual (Straight) (%)	100% Homosexual (Gay or Lesbian) (%)
Men	Content	47	51
	Wants More	52	49
	Wants Less	1	1
Women	Content	67	47
	Wants More	29	52
	Wants Less	4	1

Source: Relationships in America.

Table 3.2 indicates. Within many same-sex couples, one partner will often emerge as more consistently "interested" in sexual intimacy, such that they too will mimic the heterosexual exchange model. But mimicry it is, and the evidence in Table 3.1 suggests it is less successful among women, as the exchange model would lead us to expect.

Kara, a 24-year-old bisexual woman from near Washington, DC, illustrates this. She is currently in a long-distance (open) relationship with a woman who lives in Switzerland, where she herself hopes to move soon after securing a visa. We asked about aspects of their sexual relationship and were told that she has a higher sex drive than her girlfriend. We then posed the question of who tends to initiate sex. Her response is illuminating:

> She does for the most part in our relationship. Which isn't necessarily my preferred choice, but so it is what it is. [*Is most of the sex that you have mutual, sort of pretty equitable?*] For the most part. I have a higher sex drive. So if anything, I get off more than she does, um, just 'cause that's what she prefers, so.

Two gatekeepers, but one wishes to have more sex than the other; it's a common scenario, no doubt. But unlike in a typical heterosexual relationship, Kara—the one with the higher sex drive—awaits her partner's initiation rather than pursue it herself (as men would tend to do). She doesn't like it that way, and it's not hard to understand why.

It is not accurate, however, to claim that Tables 3.1 and 3.2 tell us the sexual behavior and desire levels of the same people. What of the 54 percent of coupled lesbians who report no sex at all in the past two weeks? Perhaps they also report much less sexual desire. In ancillary analyses (not shown), 59 percent of the sexless group reported wanting more sex than they are currently having. So no, the sexless among them do not exhibit lower reports of sexual desire.

Dietrich Klusmann, a noted German evolutionary psychologist, replicates gendered sexual motivational differences across data sets, age groups, and over the duration of partnerships, and observes the pattern that gives rise to the "bed death" claim:

> Female sexual motivation matches male sexual motivation in the first years of the partnership and then steadily decreases. ... This pattern is clearly evident for some measures of sexual motivation and less so or not at all for others.

Klusmann, like Baumeister, recognizes the hallmarks of "evolved design" differences that are "fine-tuned to the different conditions governing the reproductive success of males and females." Women's sexual motivations, they both hold, have evolved "to solve the adaptive problem of procuring male resources by establishing and maintaining a pair bond." It would be foolish to presume that our postmodern sexual identities will quickly and thoroughly do away with what are clearly old, biologically rooted realities.[54] While psychologists Jacqueline Cohen and Sandra Byers rightly observe that "the ideal sexual script for women has changed toward a great valuing of female sexual agency, especially with respect to sexual initiation," I would argue that the scope of such change is neither as wide nor as deep as many think it is.[55] Giddens may have held that gay and lesbian couples "have staked out new sexual ground well in advance of the more sexually 'orthodox,'" but historically stable sexual behavior patterns do not disappear in a generation or two (or three . . .).[56] As David Buss claims about the advent of online dating, so we can claim about the considerable advance in social acceptability of same-sex relationships.[57] Each are novel social environments, but "we come to those environments with the same evolved psychologies" as men and women have long held.[58] Very little about XX and XY are new.

Witnessing feminists commodifying relationships and making a consumer good out of sex seems like a lesson in futility. And yet Leslie Bell speaks openly and often of women's orgasms using language of consumption and acquisition, as if women's sexual agency is being put to use systematically and effectively in the same manner as that witnessed in men.[59] It will not work, at least not widely, and sexual economics tells us why. Even anecdotal accounts of lesbian attraction based on a "nesting" instinct (a desire to make a home with another woman) track with the estimates in Tables 3.1 and 3.2. That is, genital sexual desire is only one, and not likely the strongest, component of lesbian attraction. Bell herself sees it in her interview data and admits as much: "In relationships with women, for there to be any sex at all, desire must reside in women, not only in men."[60]

Among men, gay or straight, desire is a far more central and stable component. The sexual agency of women should not be measured in the manner that men tend to evaluate it, but rather in the ability to accomplish what one wishes in the domain of sex and relationships, and—as explained in Chapter 2—women are in a poorer position, on average, to do that with other women.

So are claims about lesbian "bed death" accurate? Yes and no. Yes—their reported recent frequency of sex remains notably below sexual relationships that involve men. And this is not because of diminished desire, as just articulated. But I could also answer "no," since the phrase itself is unnecessarily extreme, suggesting a complete cessation of sexual activity. That is untrue.

Sexual Partnering: Theories and Realities

Sarah's story, outlined at the beginning of the book, raises numerous questions about the sexual partnering practices of young adults today. Recall that Sarah delayed first sex until well after her adolescence was over, in step with a trend that the CDC data has long noted: from 1988 through 2013, the share of teenage girls who were sexually experienced declined from 51 to 43 percent, respectively.[61] And yet that did not seem to matter much about what happened next. Over the course of her twenties, Sarah slept with numerous men. Among the adults in our interview pool—not a random sample, I realize—many delayed first sex until age 20, 22, or even later, only to "make up for lost time" during the back half of their twenties. Many relationships I heard about track in the pathway of the "pure" relationship, which, to repeat, "refers to a situation where a social relation is entered into for its own sake, for what can be derived by each person from a sustained association with another; and which is continued only insofar as it is thought by both parties to deliver enough satisfactions for each individual to stay within it."[62] We should expect young Americans to be partnering with more people, and for shorter durations. Romance has given way, in part, to sheer desire.

The 20/80 Theory of Sexual Partners

But if sexual economics is right, the desires of some are more compelling than others. And even among men, there will be winners and losers, people whose wishes—for cheap sex, for lifelong love, or something in between—are more easily attained than others. Nick, whose story is featured in the *Vanity Fair* article discussed earlier in the chapter, told Nancy Jo Sales how he had "hooked up with three girls," thanks to the Internet and to Tinder, and that over the course of four nights, had spent a total of $80 between them. And he got what he came for with all three. Some observers of the (heterosexual) mating market hold that a small percentage of men like

Nick are monopolizing the market, circulating enough to prevent others from circulating at all, and functioning to prevent the mating market from "clearing," that is, from efficiently doing its job of helping people couple and get out (that is, off the market). If this is true, some fear, many singles could end up unhappily floating around the mating pool indefinitely—the women wondering why they cannot find someone who will stay and some men wondering why they can't find anyone at all.

The theory suggests a "20/80" split, namely, that 20 percent of men are responsible for 80 percent of the (female) sexual partners tallied across male respondents. This theory is an extension of the Pareto Principle, named after Italian economist Vilfredo Pareto's observation that 80 percent of the land in Italy was owned by 20 percent of the population. The idea is often extended to other observations of inequality in social behavior and economic status. For example, when I was more actively studying religious behavior in America, it was a rule of thumb among church leaders that 20 percent of congregational members were responsible for 80 percent of the volunteer hours expended.

I tested this theory using the *Relationships in America* data, focusing on men ages 25 to 50 years old in order to allow for more significant numbers of lifetime partners.[63] Pareto would be proud, or nearly so. It turns out that 20 percent of men (between the ages of 25 and 50) account for about 70 percent of all self-reported sexual partnerships with women in the United States. It is not 20/80, but it is not far off.

Some hold that the Pareto Principle, if it fits sexual partnering patterns in the United States, means that claims I have made about the wide availability of cheap sex are not true for the majority of young-adult men in the United States.[64] I understand their logic: sex may seem cheap, but it is only cheap for a minority of men. The rest do not share their experience. But I see no reason to conclude this. The thesis of cheaper sex in the era of wider contraceptive access assumes nothing in particular about a high average number of lifetime partners among men. It asserts, rather, that cheaper sex should lead to more sexual relationships overall, more one-night stands and "friends with benefits" relationships, and especially to the more rapid addition of sex within romantic relationships, to say nothing of making greater use of pornography and masturbation. Cheap sex is all of that. The fact that John has had 17 sexual partners by the time he turns 25 but Fred has only had two does not mean sex is "expensive" for Fred, extracting more from him than from John. It could be true, of course, but it may also be that Fred has simply not pursued more sexual relationships, and yet the two he reports became sexual quickly—within days. That, too, signals the ease of access to cheaper sex.

The Pareto Principle, applied here, would lead many to believe that the 20 percent is preventing the remaining 80 percent of men from having a stable partner. But it has little direct ramification for the marriage (or stable, long-term) portion of the mating market unless we have information about the strong preferences of marriage market participants. For example, if among the remaining 80 percent of men fidelity and a modest sexual history among their beloved are key values, then yes—the 20/70 phenomenon may well be dragging down marriage rates in the peak years of fertility (twenties to early thirties).

Moreover, for a man to have sex with a woman—or with many women—says little about his ability to "monopolize" the mating market indefinitely. Brief relationships of the sort Nick described are hardly monopolizing others' access to sex or relationships. What would constitute a more appropriate measure of monopolizing would be the prevalence of long-term overlapping sexual relationships.[65] Thus, modern polygyny is a better assessment of the monopoly theory. Establishing the duration of the 20/70 group's relationships would be helpful as well. Are the 20 percent of men stringing along one or more women for years against their wishes for security or commitment, or not? I don't have the data to say, but I doubt it in this era of increasingly confluent love.

Additionally, it is easy to misinterpret the 20/70 figure by assuming that 70 percent of all women are sleeping with 20 percent of men. That would be an understandable but incorrect interpretation. Rather, 20 percent of all men are reporting 70 percent of all relationships. We can get some clarity on this misinterpretation by assessing the same among women. When we do, we find that 20 percent of women in the *Relationships in America* data report 65 percent of the lifetime reported male sexual partners. So what do the two figures together tell us? That high numbers of sexual partners are largely concentrated among a minority of both men and women. Since men yield a 20/70 account and women a 20/65 account, it means that there is a great deal of coupling going on within 20 percent of the population. Nick, as well as his three women in four days, is almost certainly part of that 20 percent.

Is the smart cut-off at 20 percent? No. That is just the Pareto Principle's benchmark applied to the study of sexual partnering. When I trim the 20 to 10 percent, more interesting information is yielded. The most prolific 10 percent of men report 52 percent of all opposite-sex relationships, while the same share among women report 48 percent of the total male–female coupling reported in the data. So by shaving 10 percent, or half, from these baseline figures we have cut out 18 percent and 17 percent of opposite-sex relationships reported by men and women, respectively. It is a sensible move, revealing that this "second" 10 percent sleeps with far fewer partners than the top 10 percent.

Of more urgent sociological concern than the ratios cited here are the perceptions of the mating market and its monopolization. If young Americans perceive the market as dominated by a small cadre, then it is certainly real in its consequences, to borrow from early sociologist W. I. Thomas's claim about the social construction of reality. But from the numbers I can guess that there is little long-term monopolizing going on in what amounts to a very dynamic mating pool.

All this does not mean that no one is left out of the mating market. It only means that, over time, no one need be left out. But plenty are left out. Far more men than women come up empty in the mating market. An example of this is Matt, a 32-year-old from Johnson City, Tennessee. He's in a tough spot, no denying it: he's overweight, burdened by multiple insecurities, working a part-time job requiring modest skills, has nearly $100,000 in college loans, is living with his mother, and has never been in a romantic or sexual relationship in his life. A Christian, he wishes to save sex—something he'd very much like to have—for marriage, but marriage seems out of reach. (Even sex is out of reach for men like Matt in a way that it seldom is for women.) The whole situation depresses him, clinically, which compounds the problem. Matt's challenges are a reminder that the mating market—and especially the marriage part of it—has never been simple for someone in his situation. I spent the first 13 years of my life in rural Iowa, one of the most marriage-friendly locales in the nation, and can readily recall a handful of women—but always more men—who did not marry, not quite having fit in well enough to attract a suitor in spite of what may have been admirable character. But it takes more than character to bridge what the Irish rock band U2 dubbed the "mysterious distance between a man and a woman."

Predicting Partner Count

So what characterizes men and women (ages 18–60) who report having had lots of partners in their past? Here are several social and sexual characteristics that distinguish people with twenty or more sexual partners, a figure which—despite conventional wisdom to the contrary—is not often reached (yet). There is not enough information here to discern causality, but one can certainly speculate how the pathways are most apt to work. When compared with their peers who report fewer partners, those who self-report 20 or more in their lifetime are:

- Twice as likely to have ever been divorced (50 percent vs. 27 percent)
- Three times as likely to have cheated while married (32 percent vs. 10 percent)
- Substantially less happy with life ($p < 0.05$)
- Twice as likely to report having had an abortion (44 percent vs. 22 percent)
- More likely to be on medication for depression or anxiety (19 percent vs. 14 percent)
- Three times more likely to have been told they had a STI (38 percent vs. 13 percent)
- More likely to have tragic sexual histories: 23 percent reported having been forced to have sex against their will, compared with 13 percent of those with fewer than 20 sexual partners. They are also more likely to have been touched sexually by a parent or adult caregiver (16 percent vs. 9 percent)

To be sure, their appetite for sex is for more than just variety. They also have sex more often (about 2.4 times vs. 2.1 times in the past two weeks), and are less satisfied with the amount of sex they are having (55 percent "want more" vs. 45 percent of those with fewer partners).

Perhaps such persons are just not cut out for monogamy. Maybe they were not "born that way," as some polyamory proponents are now claiming. Writing in *Slate*—hardly an academic site but nevertheless a popular source of left-leaning conventional wisdom in this domain—Michael Carey poses the question of whether non-monogamy, like homosexuality, just might be innate in some people:

> There are some people whose innate personality traits make it very difficult to live happily in a monogamous relationship but relatively easy to be happy in an open one. . . . So, sure, there may be a larger fraction of non-monogamists for whom their unconventional relationship is "optional" or "a choice." But there are almost certainly also some "obligate" non-monogamists who would never feel emotionally satisfied and healthy in a monogamous relationship, any more than a gay man would be satisfied and healthy in a straight marriage.[66]

The patterns, however, suggest that non-monogamists are more apt to feel emotionally unsatisfied and unhappy, regardless.

Monogamish

Non-monogamy is a gentle mouthful of a word, a much politer replacement of sorts for terms like "adultery" and "infidelity." The same kind of transformation has already happened to "virginity loss" and "prostitute," terms no longer considered appropriate among sex-positive Americans. In their place, we now speak of sexual debut and sex worker, respectively. The lingo certainly tracks the emergence of the pure relationship model's relaxation of norms.

Most young Americans—but more women than men—remain invested in monogamy, at least in theory. But talk of "monogamish" has no doubt increased in frequency. It took a leap forward with Mark Oppenheimer's biography of sex columnist Dan Savage, which appeared in the *New York Times Magazine* on June 30, 2011.[67] In it Savage, who is gay and married with an adopted son, admits to having had nine extramarital partners, and spends considerable time outlining both the benefits and costs of monogamy, and concludes that monogamy simply does not fit very many people. The reality of monogamish—especially but not exclusively among gay men—is slowly emerging in scholarly circles as well.[68] It was once an open secret, since it was thought to be politically damaging to gay rights causes to admit it. But as support for same-sex marriage increased, however, so did this broader admission. It feels safer now in a post-Obergefell America. Even gay journalists are saying it's time to set the record straight here.[69] What does the data say about monogamish? That Dan Savage is hardly alone.

Table 3.3 reports estimates from the longitudinal Add Health study's fourth wave and reveals that bisexual women and gay men are the most likely to report having had another sexual partner during their current relationship, at 43 percent each. But the percentile gap in non-monogamy between men and women within a shared sexual orientation is worth highlighting.

Whereas only 9.1 percentage points separate straight men's and women's report of outside partners in their current relationship, a full 24.4 percentage points separate gay and lesbian admissions. In step with the data from Add Health, the National Survey of Family Growth reports a similar pattern: multiple partnerships are far more common among gay men than among lesbians. In the NSFG, 62 percent of gay men report having two or more same-sex partners in the past year, compared with only 21 percent of lesbians.

Table 3.3 Perceived and actual non-monogamy in current sexual relationship

	Hetero-sexual Women (%)	Hetero-sexual Men (%)	Bisexual Women (%)	Bisexual Men (%)	Homo-sexual Women (%)	Homo-sexual Men (%)
Respondent thinks partner has had another sexual partner	20.5	15.0	38.4	40.4	15.5	29.1
Respondent admits having had another sexual partner	17.3	26.4	43.2	17.4	18.5	42.9

Source: Add Health study, never-married 24- to 35-year-olds.

Table 3.3 also features a unique measure of suspicion about (or in some cases, open awareness of) their partner's outside sexual behavior. Only bisexual men, a small population, are more apt than these two groups to think their partner has had another sexual partner. And in keeping with sexual economics expectations, straight men and lesbian women are the least suspicious of their partners. Why? Because only their partners are reliably women.

These numbers exemplify the "monogamish" life. Gay men have more partners than straight men, as sexual economics would expect. It is not because of sexual orientation but rather due to stable male–female differences in relationship preferences and sex drive. Gay men do not wish to have more sexual partners than straight men. They are simply far more apt to be in relationships that permit non-monogamy because their relationships are with men, who tend—on average—to be more sexually permissive than women. "In almost every way," write online search analysts Ogas and Gaddam, "the brain software of gay men appears identical to that of straight men."[70] The difference is in the permissiveness of men. Early gay activist and journalist Randy Shilts remarked that among gay men there was "no moderating role like that a woman plays in the heterosexual milieu." The remark comes from Shilts's book *And the Band Played On*, in which he noted still more evidence favoring the interpretation of gay sexuality in line with sexual economics: "So much of the gay community's sexuality, right down to the cruising ritual, seemed more defined by gender than sexual orientation." Exactly. He continues:

> Some heterosexual males privately confided that they were enthralled with the idea of ... immediate, available, even anonymous sex ... if they could only find women who would agree.[71]

Vincent, a 32-year-old gay man, lives in Austin, works in finance, told me that he had had between 60 and 100 partners in his lifetime, and was very familiar with what Shilts had described:

> I don't know about the straight community but I think in the gay community there's a strong inclination towards people who are single and in a relationship to want to pursue the thrill, the hunt or the whole 'Catch me if you can,' let's go online and see how quickly we can get laid.

Many straight men—whether married or just in a relationship—wonder what that is like. We asked all interviewees about whether they keep in touch with previous partners on social media, and whether they'd like to get back with any of them, even if only for a night. Their answers ranged widely, but notably more men than women said yes, they were interested in a brief "reconnection." But such overlapping tends not to be so readily perceived as threatening to gay men's primary relationships as it typically remains among straights. Sociologist Judith Stacey concurs, in her interview with Mark Oppenheimer:

> "They are men," she [Stacey] said, and she believes it is easier for them—right down to the physiology of orgasm—to separate physical and emotional intimacy. Lesbians and straight women tend to be far less comfortable with nonmonogamy than gay men.[72]

The same conclusion was reached by my colleague Debra Umberson in her qualitative study of gay, lesbian, and straight couples:

> Men partnered with men were more likely ... to report sexual encounters outside their primary relationship and to indicate that such sexual encounters posed minimal threat to their long-term relationship, as long as emotional intimacy was absent.[73]

In other words, sex with someone else besides your primary partners is not the same as cheating.

The exchange model's hallmarks are all over this. When both partners are male and hence pursuers or "purchasers," two things are far more apt to occur: (1) one partner wishes for more sex than the other (given typical within-couple variation), and (2) bargaining about acceptable sex outside the relationship ensues, or—alternately—bargaining does not ensue but sex outside the relationship still takes place. Miguel, a 26-year-old gay man from Austin, articulated the reality of the first of these. When asked about initiating sex, Miguel said his partner initiates sex and wants to have sex more often than he does, a pattern consistent with those in his previous relationships.

The second thing we should expect—bargaining—is a pattern much less likely (though hardly unheard of) to be observed among two women or between a man and a woman, not because he doesn't wonder about it but because she will not stand for it and he has to navigate her wishes lest the relationship collapse. Seth, a 24-year-old gay man and computer engineer living in Austin with his 52-year-old partner, Bill, helps shed light on the bargaining process. He met Bill online when he was 19, hit it off, and moved south from upstate New York. They have been together five years now. His mother considers them married, something they were legally unable to do at the time of the interview (and for which they had made no impending plans). Unlike Miguel, Seth has not been in a sexual relationship with anyone else except Bill. Nor has Bill since they've been together, so far as Seth knows. He qualified the question we posed to him about it, noting that while some people may perceive outside relationships as cheating, "I guess I could frame that in a different way," at which point he mentioned open relationships. How common is that, I asked. Seth responded both with an estimate as well as a helpful illustration of how the subject is broached:

> Well, not in our relationship, but in the gay community, mmm, from what I've seen, maybe 50–50. [*So this is not characteristic of your relationship because you both wish for that to be true?*] Yeah. [*Okay. And you don't feel actively like cheating on him or having an open relationship?*] No. We've talked about it, but no need or desire at the moment. [*And how does a couple come to sort of say "Ok, we can try this," versus you guys have talked about it and didn't do it?*] Well, my partner more or less started it because he has sometimes trouble getting erections so, and he knows I'm younger so it's a lot more common. He went, "All right, since you're more active, if you want to we can talk about it, I'd be fine if we set some ground rules but . . ." [*So he offered it?*] Yeah. [*You said no. You said no because . . . ?*] Didn't need to.

In Seth's case, the one who commenced the discussion about an open relationship was not the one who wanted it. It beggars belief, however, to imagine very many women making such an offer to their husbands simply because they're aware of higher male sex drive. They still expect sexual and emotional monogamy, on average. And it is for that reason that even most coupled lesbians overwhelmingly disapprove of such "extradyadic" relationships. (Only 1.8 percent of cohabiting lesbians in the *Relationships in America* data agreed that "marital infidelity is sometimes OK.")

And yet Table 3.3 reveals that the most likely to have had another sexual partner on the side are bisexual women, at 43 percent.[74] If Kara, the 24-year-old bisexual from DC, had been in that random sample, she would certainly have been part of the 43 percent. Monogamish has been her trademark since the first time she had sex with a woman at age 18 and a man at 19. Since then it has been more women than men, but the future is uncertain. How did she figure out she had a problem with monogamy?

> It was with another guy. And that was kind of my first inkling. And after we broke up I was dating this other guy who wanted to be much more serious, and I remember thinking like, "God, I feel like I'm—he's my ball and chain." I really, I really hated that feeling. And that was definitely true then when I dated the woman that I lived with for two years. Towards the end I was just like, "I can't do this. Apparently I'm not made to be this way." Which was great when I found my current girlfriend who's, she was kind of in the same boat. And I was like, "Great, I don't have to worry." And it doesn't mean that I don't want a serious relationship, it just means I have a high sex drive and I like, I like that. [*And do your parents know about that?*] No. [*No, okay.*] Of course not (chuckles). My parents are actually pretty liberal, but not that liberal.

Speaking of liberal, Kara unwittingly identified a trend. In the *Relationships in America* survey, 64 percent of the pool of "very conservative" Americans who had ever had overlapping sexual experiences told us those relationships had occurred over 10 years ago. Only 3 percent said they were ongoing (or very recent). Not so among the most politically liberal: 17 percent of all self-reported overlapping partners among them were happening now.

The Timing of First Sex in Relationships

When a couple begins to have sex in their relationship is arguably the best indicator of the price of sex among them. The quicker sex begins in heterosexual relationships, the less women are "charging" for it: less time spent by men nurturing women's confidence in them, less romance, fewer signals of commitment and intention to remain with her. Remember, sex is her resource and in a consensual relationship she controls access to it. It doesn't happen if she doesn't permit it. And according to most observations, as well as Duke economist Peter Arcidiacano's research on "habit persistence," once sex commences it is very unusual for a couple to intentionally cease having sex without jeopardizing the relationship itself.[75] Arcidiacano distinguishes between the "fixed cost" of beginning to have sex and the "transition cost" of later discerning whether to continue to have sex or not. The fixed cost, he writes, typically appears as a moral or psychological barrier—whether they should have sex with someone or not. In Chapter 1, Sarah recounts this barrier as she described the logic by which she makes decisions about first sex. The barrier for her seemed less moral than psychological—attached to whether she really enjoyed her date or not (if she did, then she would delay sex for another date or two), as well as to her wishful thinking that ideally she would wait longer than she has. Other interviewees concurred. Cheryl, a 24-year-old African American from the DC area, signaled the same pattern as Sarah. If she didn't particularly like the men, she would have sex with them promptly because "it was just sex." Nothing else seemed at stake. What is hard is "to find quality people that you want to be with." Most of the male interviewees we spoke with did not recount lengthy waits. The most common refrain was after a second or third date, a week or two, "definitely" within a month. But nearly as frequently we heard of first-date encounters. Ben, a 28-year-old Denver-area man, noted the need to navigate "the subtleties of male/female interactions." Those skills, he suspects, "have been cheapened with the advent of uh, I guess you could call it information-age sex." He added economically, "I think it's made sexuality a commodity in a huge way."

Elizabeth is 25 and recently moved from Minnesota to Colorado. She works two jobs, one with developmentally disabled adults and the other in an alternative mental health center. She has a spirit of service and likes working with people. And she is interested in marrying someday but is in no hurry. When asked whether sex tends to precede the beginning of a defined relationship, her answer was not complicated. She and her current boyfriend had sex after their first meeting, and their relationship was clarified that night, by him:

> And it was kind of odd 'cause I know, for me, with dating, it's really kind of a gray area. Like you meet somebody, and it's like, "Okay, are we dating yet? Should I talk to this person . . . like, I don't, I don't really—it's very, very gray and I see that with a lot of young people. . . . I myself try to stay open about it and try to stay communicative about that, 'cause I don't like that whole gray area thing. I wanna know what's going on (sigh).

Other friends, Elizabeth asserts, struggle mightily with the matter of clarification, too. When asked why, she wanders in search of an answer:

> I really wish I knew. I think a lot of it has to do because relationships are more casual than they use to be. It used to be, even my mom told me when she was my age she didn't have friends that were guys. That didn't, that didn't happen. "Live with four guys? Pshhh, this girl's a hussy," you know? Like if you were hanging out with a guy, you were with him. It's like you didn't have (male) friends. So I think now that may, maybe it's because women have taken on a stronger role in both relationships and, and pretty much everywhere that that might have something to do with it.

Is she unique in holding this perspective? Hardly. When she was asked, "In the things that you observe, in your friends' and (in the lives of) other people your age, has sex entered the equation yet, before things get defined or not?" Sarah responds affirmatively, and asserts her normality in this:

> I would say . . . most of the time, yeah. . . . (At) my age it's uncommon though for somebody to wait a significant amount of time before they sleep with the person that they're seeing, you know it's, or I mean, but it's also not uncommon for them to do it right away. I mean me it's a case by case basis (chuckles). [*Okay. Um, how soon do you observe sex entering the relationships among people your age? Or when do most people expect it to begin?*] I would say at least in the first couple of weeks.

Figure 3.2 displays, using *Relationships in America* data, the time until sexual initiation in respondents' current (or most recent) sexual relationship.[76] It includes marriages but is not limited to them. Sarah's experience has now become the modal one in American relationships. That is, sex before a relationship begins is now the most common experience. (It is still a minority one, though.) Between 20 and 25 percent of men and women say they first had sex in their current relationship "after we met, but before we began to consider ourselves as being in a relationship." It may be the case, as it often was with Jennifer, that the introduction of sex is "the thing that makes it become a relationship."

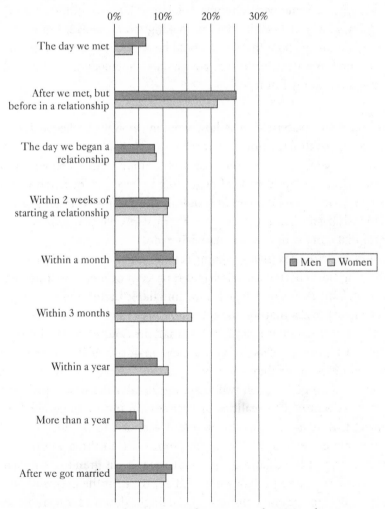

FIGURE 3.2 Time to sexual initiation with current (or last) sexual partner
Source: Relationships in America.

According to Figure 3.2, Sarah is quite normal: 45 percent of women said they first had sex with their current (or most recent) partner no later than the first two weeks of the relationship. Sarah estimated that she has had around 20 partners in her life. She professed a preference for seeing someone for a month before becoming sexually intimate with them, but that if marital material—vaguely defined as "some chance that we're gonna end up married"—is not obvious within six months, it's time to end the relationship:

> When I get to that point I think then "What am I doing here?" You know? . . . Some people might consider it kind of, um, oh I don't know what you'd call it, like I'm looking too far ahead, I'm worrying too much about that. . . . I would be perfectly happy not getting married, but I mean I'm not gonna date somebody if . . . I do not see them in my future.

This repetitive pattern signals how women, though gatekeepers, do not unilaterally control the price of sex. That is set socially as men and women do the work of perceiving the cost of sex among other couples around them. While the "fixed cost" of beginning to have sex for Sarah was psychological, for others it is certainly moral. The commencement of a sexual relationship still has much to do with what people perceive as morally appropriate, not simply what they wish to do.

First-meeting sex (in an ongoing relationship) remains less common, reflecting the reported experience of 6 percent of men and 4 percent of women. Waiting for marriage is rare, and likely increasingly so in an era of cheap sex and a mating market where men have more sexual options and women need their resources less than previous eras. The interviews reflected Figure 3.2 closely, with a clear majority of interviewees stating realities shorter than their preferences, the latter of which tended to hew to a range between two to six weeks after the first expression of mutual affection. The realities of first sex timing—a negotiated thing subject to the vagaries of the moment—tended to be notably earlier, commonly either just before, at, or within two to three weeks following the start of the relationship. Their great-great grandparents would have remarked, and probably not with approval, at the pace with which couples become sexual before commencing a slow and uncertain crawl toward the altar.

Waiting for Marriage?

Abstinence is increasingly out among the majority of young Americans, while speed is in. And the sexual impulse in developing relationships does not slow down with age, either. Figure 3.2 is largely impervious to age effects. Twenty-two percent of the youngest cohort (18–24) reported first sex after they met but before the relationship commenced, and so did 20 percent of 40- to 49-year-olds and 50- to 60-year-olds (results not shown).

So how many Americans wait until they are married to have sex? The answer is not nearly as simple to discern as it sounds. Several qualifiers have to be talked through first. Must their first experience of sexual intercourse be with their spouse, or not? That is, are we talking about virginity until marriage, or about a particular couple not having sex with each other before they marry? And what about other kinds of sexual experiences short of vaginal intercourse—do they count? Any estimate generated requires a host of qualifications. So how best to interpret Figure 3.2 here?

Figure 3.2 does not signal that 11–12 percent of Americans waited until marriage to ever have sex. It means that among all Americans currently in a sexual relationship, 11–12 percent of them waited until they married to do so.[77] If we reduce the sample to only currently married Americans, regardless of age, 17 percent reported first sex after marrying, an estimate comparable to the 18 percent of them who reported first sex after they met but before their relationship began. Again, this does not mean that 17 percent of married Americans were virgins when they got married, but that 17 percent of married Americans first experienced sex with their current spouse after marrying. (Both, one, or neither of them may have had previous sexual experience.) Confused? I don't blame you.

When I zero in on the 12 percent of men and 11 percent of women among all sexually coupled Americans who said they waited until marriage to have sex, and then look at the share of them who also reported only one lifetime sexual partner—presumably their spouse—we learn a little more. Fifty-five percent of those men reported only one lifetime partner, meaning 6.4 percent of all men currently in sexual relationships didn't have sex until they married their one and only lifetime partner. The same is true of 54 percent of women in the same scenario, meaning that 5.7 percent of women didn't have sex before they married their one and only partner. The closest we're going to get to a premarital virginity rate, then, is to call it about 6 percent, a finding comparable to other recent estimates.[78] It won't be higher than that, but it could be a point or two lower.

So who is most willing to pay, or charge, the highest price for sex? When I predict "waited until marriage" (in the respondent's current or most recent relationship), several robust predictors stand out:

· Attendance at religious services
· Political conservatism
· Higher age at first sex (remember, the respondent could have had previous partners)
· Self-rated happiness (which may be a result rather than a predictor)
· Holding more restrictive attitudes about sexual relationships (obviously)
· Married parents

This is after controlling for a variety of other measures, including age, race, sex, importance of religion (which didn't matter independently of attendance), education, evangelical self-identification, experiences with family of origin, and attractiveness. (Table A3.3 displays the results.)

Nothing in this list stands out as particularly novel or revealing. Beliefs about the prudence of waiting to have sex are largely channeled through religious behavior rather than subjective religiosity or particular religious affiliations or attitudes. That conclusion is not new, either; I discerned the same thing in my 2007 study of religious influence on the sexual behavior of American teenagers, drawing primarily on the Add Health project and the National Study of Youth and Religion.[79] And yet it is remarkable, when you think about it, that a factor like church attendance remains influential even after accounting for a key presumptive pathway of its influence—that of holding more restrictive attitudes about (and having less previous experience with) sexual relationships. There is clearly far more to "pricing" sex than just what people think about it.

Does Cheaper Sex = Better Sex? On the Elusiveness of Sexual Satisfaction

Cheap sex is having a tough time creating lasting love. Many relationships appear to burn passionately with a sexual spark, then flame out. But perhaps the trade-off is worth it. Perhaps cheaper sex can spell better, hotter sex, even at the cost of relational connection. What do we know about the sexual satisfaction of American adults in this era of easier sexual access?

One thing is clear—there has been a surge in research on sexual satisfaction since 2005.[80] It's a hip thing to study, and the concept itself is emerging as a key barometer of overall individual well-being.[81] That makes perfect sense, given the parallel emergence of the pure relationship model. After all, if a relationship isn't sexually satisfying, the standard script says it's time to get help or time to move on. Brent is a 24-year-old real estate agent from Austin and seemed to use our interview questions as a means to work out his thoughts about sex and the future of his three-year relationship with his girlfriend, Betsy. (This is an example of how researchers can unwittingly affect their subjects just by asking them questions.) While he definitely wants to get married someday, he was growing ambivalent about getting married to Betsy. We asked him if they would be together a year from now:

> You know, I don't know. We've been together for so long. We've been together for a long time, and like you asked me earlier, do you see yourself married to her, and since I can't say yes to that I don't—I am in the process of evaluating things. I don't understand why I can't say yes, or wouldn't want to say yes. I don't see myself wanting to marry her. ... I just don't picture it. I don't see it. I don't see the white picket fence; I just don't see that for some reason ... and I kind of feel perhaps like I am missing out on some things, I guess. [*Missing out on what? On marriage or being single?*] No, I guess, on being single. And I don't, I remember being single, being single stinks at least from my perspective. I like having someone around. I like having, you know, I like having a best friend because she truly is my best friend and maybe that's why it's so hard for me to take. I don't know. It's hard for me to imagine us together long term, and I don't know why. [*You're not sure why?*] No, I'm really not. You know, she is a bit of a prude still. And not actually a prude, she just has weird, (this) sounds weird, but she has a lower sex drive (claps hands). [*Tell me about that.*] So that's not fun. Yeah, I don't feel like we're compatible in that sense. I feel like we're compatible sexually, pretty much, but like I said her sex drive is pretty low which doesn't, you know, sometimes it can be a real bitch.

So how often do they have sex?

> It varies. Um, you know, there will be some weeks the max in a
> week probably would be three. And then it can go as bad as like once
> in two weeks. [*And what do you think about that?*] I think you can see
> (it in) my face about what I think about that.

Brent describes Betsy as "beautiful," tells us she is his best friend, but
wonders "if it's waned a little bit." (She's only 21.) It's clear that Brent
privileges sexual flow—the frequency of sex—to diversity, or new experiences with other partners. He doesn't have trouble with fidelity, but sexual
frequency is for him a key indicator of relationship health:

> You know this is the longest relationship I have ever been in, and
> so I am sure that probably happens but if, you know, like I said if
> she was ready to go (that is, have sex) every day I don't know if that
> would, you know what I mean—like the grass is always greener
> kind of thing. So yeah, I don't know. So not too frequent sexually,
> but like I said, I am wondering if I am ... I'm sorry I am all over
> the place.

After we turned off the microphone at the end of the interview, Brent asked
if we thought he and Betsy should break up. (We declined to respond.)

Sexual satisfaction is a big deal today, more pivotal than in the past
insofar as norms of confluent love increasingly characterize our relationships. It also raises the social science question of what exactly constitutes
sexual satisfaction. And that takes us quickly back to sex differences: men
and women may well perceive and measure it differently. For men, access
to consistent sex is a common priority: the more, the better. And if men
are in the driver's seat of how quickly relationships become more serious,
observers have no choice but to pay attention to how their partners navigate their interests. Men also desire diversity in sexual experiences more
than women do, on average. Meanwhile, plenty of research tells us that
women much prefer relationships to hookups.[82]

We shouldn't characterize Brent as a jerk just because he wants more
sex. He claims, after all, to be a relational guy (and seems to be so). And
he's on to something. Over half of *Relationships in America* respondents
who were in relationships and who reported sex more than 10 times in the
past two weeks told us they were at or near the top of the 1–10 relational

happiness scale, compared with 22 percent of those in relationships who reported no sex in the past two weeks (other results not shown). Table A3.4 (in the appendix) reveals that sexual frequency is associated with relational happiness independently of a good many other effects, including marital status, gender, age, race/ethnicity, self-rated happiness (the strongest predictor), pornography use, social media use, political liberalism, and religiosity.

Not all sex is equal, though. Sweden's Sexuality and Health Project found that although high rates of penile-vaginal intercourse (or PVI) were associated with better health and increased sexual and life satisfaction, high rates of masturbation were associated with decreased satisfaction with sexual life and with life in general.[83] Meanwhile, masturbation was negatively associated with satisfaction on all measures: sex life, relationship, mental health, and life in general. In other words, vaginal intercourse paid psychological benefits, but masturbation not only did not, it extracted costs. The study's authors point out how often we are led to believe that all sexual practices foster comparable effects. But the reality may well be otherwise.[84] Likewise, the *Relationships in America* survey data reveal that those who masturbated recently were less likely to be happy with life in general—and less happy with their current romantic relationship—than those who had not (results not shown).

When it comes to relational happiness, then, sexual frequency is neither necessary nor sufficient, but it is certainly a net positive for most.[85] And as Baumeister articulates, when men perceive a decline in their partner's sexual interest, it depresses them more than it does their partner. That was clearly the case with Brent.

There are other measures of sexual satisfaction, of course. But scholars and popular observers, however, are increasingly privileging one—orgasm—as a comparable way to measure sexual satisfaction for men and women alike. (It seems even in the study of sex men's interests dominate.) It may well be the only means by which to estimate equality in sexual pleasure, and we know how sociologists adore equality and standardized measures. It's not a perfect fit, though. When asked about it, Elizabeth, the 25-year-old transplant to Colorado, reported climaxing in her current relationship about half of the time, but says that the 50th percentile is not a problem: "Even if I don't orgasm, sex still feels really good. And I don't have to have orgasm to enjoy sex." I know few men who would agree, but plenty of women would, and do.

In a 2012 study in the flagship journal *American Sociological Review*, Elizabeth Armstrong and Paula England examined data from England's OCSLS study, a large survey of university students, supplemented with interview data from Armstrong's research project among female students at Indiana University and Stanford University.[86] They were chasing the mystery of women's sexual enjoyment, hoping to understand the role of orgasm in both long-term and hookup relationships. And they did a pretty thorough job. In the survey component of the study, they asked whether the respondent experienced orgasm in four different scenarios—their most recent (1) hookup, (2) hookup with intercourse, (3) relationship sexual event, and (4) relationship sexual event with intercourse. What did they find? That familiarity and relationship matters. Orgasm rates for women were as follows:

1. Most recent hookup, no previous hookups with this partner: 11 percent
2. Most recent hookup, one to two previous hookups with this partner: 16 percent
3. Most recent hookup, three or more previous hookups with this partner: 34 percent
4. Most recent sexual event in relationship lasting more than six months: 67 percent

While there is a linear association visible here, the study authors also asked respondents how much they enjoyed their (respective) experience, regardless of orgasm. In keeping with the gendered nature of sexual satisfaction, reported rates of enjoyment hovered well above those of orgasm and signaled the importance of relationship: recent hookups yielded self-reported enjoyment around 50 percent of the time, while enjoyment of relationship sex exceeded 80 percent.

Moreover, it's not just the presence of the relationship that matters. It's also the hope of one. In their regression models predicting orgasm, the authors found that even if the respondent was only interested in being in a relationship (prior to hooking up), their odds of experiencing orgasm increased by 30–40 percent, and the odds of enjoying the hookup by around 2.4 times, controlling for a variety of other factors. Meanwhile, among those women in relationships already, those having experienced another (that is, simultaneous) partner reported diminished enjoyment of their current experience, while being interested in marrying their current partner created a surge in enjoyment, boosting the odds of such by 4–5 times.

There is far more to their study than I will mention here, but what shouts at me from it is the importance of relationship security (or even the hope of it), and with it, a sense of romance, mutuality, and desire for marital commitment. Women were (1) far more apt to enjoy hookup sex if they thought there was the possibility of a relationship, and (2) far more apt to enjoy relationship sex if they hoped to marry their boyfriend. (Not exactly a vote in favor of the pure relationship model.) And yet Armstrong and England elect to focus mostly on sexual technique, something they note was more apt to occur when sex partners liked each other enough to be in a relationship. Indeed, they seem to characterize relationships as means to an end: "[t]he benefit of a relationship is that you can tweak your skills."[87]

Their illustrative study suggests that cheap sex is not satisfying sex to very many women. Instead, it shows women prefer (and enjoy) costlier sex—in the form of closed relationships with high expectations for a secure future together. That is the kind of sex in which they are most apt to experience orgasm and that they claim they enjoy most. So while cheaper sex may spell more sex for many young Americans, it does not promise better sex. Better sex costs more.

Conclusion

Online dating, now normative, is a cheap sex delivery system. It can be used in the ways in which it is often advertised—as a means of meeting a mate—but on the way to lasting love it makes efficient the cycling of short-term relationships and the commodification of sex and persons. It brings into stark relief the economics of mating as well as highlights the average differences in men's and women's preferences. That something like Tinder has caught on among women, however, signals their weak position in the mating market. Opportunistic men are pressing women to operate more like men by privileging the physical over all other traits, and women—to mate at all—feel like they must play along. Most Tinder "swipes," of course, lead to nowhere—because of her wishes, not his. Comparing the sexual desire and behavior patterns of gay and straight Americans reinforce claims about the elevated sexual interests of men. And yet the actual sex lives of average young Americans are not as glamorous—or as frequent—as the media makes them out to be. Just like in high school, opportunity matters: cohabiting and married Americans report notably more sex than singles. And although an elite of men and women—between 10 and 20 percent—exhibit most of the sexual partnerships—they neither dominate nor monopolize the mating market. No, cheap sex is democratized and more widely available to the masses, who report—on average—short waits for sex in their relationships. In fact, the modal romantic relationship in America becomes sexual before it becomes "official," that is, before a couple even acknowledges that they're in a relationship.

4

The Cheapest Sex

TRENDS IN PORNOGRAPHY USE AND MASTURBATION

PORNOGRAPHY AND MASTURBATION are nothing if not the cheapest forms of sex. Men, as Roy Baumeister notes, used to toil for days, weeks, months, even years, in order to earn a glimpse of a shapely woman naked in front of him.[1] Now they can do that in seconds in a way unanticipated by their genetic material. Men can see more flesh in five minutes than their great-grandfathers could in a lifetime. In other words, humans are not evolutionarily familiar with the accessibility, affordability, and anonymity that Internet pornography offers. Men especially seem to have been unprepared to navigate the advent of cheap (or free) online pornography that commenced in the early 1990s but received a big leap forward with "streaming" content in the mid-2000s. Glimpsing a topless pinup on a garage wall is not really equivalent to today's video sex on a 42-inch monitor with surround sound. Both appeal to men's greater interest in cheap sex, but the former depicts a potential sex object, whereas the latter mimics real sexual interaction. The difference matters. The distinction between private, solitary sexual activity and paired sex is eroding, and the resulting abundance of real and imagined sex has transformed what Illouz calls the "ecology of choice" such that the explosion in sexual options has begun to inhibit real commitment. Imagination, in this case, tries to imitate, augment, replace (if necessary), and shape reality.[2]

Many have welcomed porn. Others view it with regularity but wish they did not. And while some couples utilize pornography as part of paired sexual activity, most of us think of pornography as a largely solitary activity, but one with potential social and sexual consequences. Baumeister suggests that we would best understand pornography as reflecting the basic observation that men have elevated levels of interest in sex. And given that pornography is essentially a cheap form of sex, it stands to reason that many men, and certainly more men than women, will gravitate toward it. Other scholars, he notes, perceive darker forces at work here, including ideas of male domination of women. Giddens himself shares this latter perspective, asserting that in it "rage, blame, and awe of women are unmistakably mixed."[3] Baumeister dismisses them and thinks the simplest explanation is the best one: excess sexual desire meets modern technology delivery systems. "Craving for sex is precisely what is behind those acts," he holds.[4]

Masturbation, meanwhile, is as old as humanity. But there is good reason to believe it has gotten a significant boost in popularity from pornography's explosion into the digital world. Compare for a moment sexual intercourse before the wide availability of pornography with music before the advent of Edison's phonograph. You simply had to be there, meaning coupled sex and music were going to be live performances if they were going to be experienced at all. Not so anymore. Many people prefer recordings to a live concert. (How many prefer porn and masturbation to actual intercourse?) And yet listening to my own tailored Pandora.com algorithm as I write this has not affected me—or anyone else—in quite the same way that pornography affects nearly everyone, even those who do not give it a second look. Online music is simply a more efficient vehicle than a cassette or a concert for a comparable experience—listening to desired sounds. Digital pornography is not just a more efficient delivery system, though it is that. It replaces sex (for some), augments it (for others), and alters real sexual connection with real persons. It has changed sex and altered relationships in ways that iTunes has not changed music.

Modern pornography is distinctive in that it not only supplies cheap sex but stimulates interest in it, too. That is not how supply-and-demand curves typically work. Instead, porn creates—then meets—demand with a near-infinite supply kept afloat by a propensity toward compulsion. Even the market in actual sex work (that is, prostitution) does not function like that.

Naomi Wolf Was Right: "A Vagina . . . Used to Have a Pretty High Exchange Value"

I am well acquainted with the criticisms of sexual economics by sociologists of gender, many of whom dislike its roots in evolutionary psychology, its assertions about robust male–female differences, and its aversion to the idea that gender is socially constructed. So it is unusual to witness a liberal feminist author eloquently criticize pornography using economic language, but Naomi Wolf unabashedly did so.[5] Wolf captures the sentiments of many women who came of age before Internet pornography really began to surge in supply and popularity:

> For two decades, I have watched young women experience the continual "mission creep" of how pornography—and now Internet pornography—has lowered their sense of their own sexual value and their actual sexual value. When I came of age in the seventies, it was still pretty cool to be able to offer a young man the actual presence of a naked, willing young woman. There were more young men who wanted to be with naked women than there were naked women on the market. If there was nothing actively alarming about you, you could get a pretty enthusiastic response by just showing up. ... Well, I am 40, and mine is the last female generation to experience that sense of sexual confidence and security in what we had to offer.[6]

The fact that she wrote this in 2003—and nothing has changed since, at least in terms of what Wolf would label as improvement—reinforces the gravity of the situation. It is difficult for those of us who grew up before the Internet to truly identify with how sexual education and assumptions about relationships have changed because it exists. While there are many aspects of the "pure relationship" that Naomi Wolf would applaud—including its being made possible by fertility control—there have been unintended consequences, and she is not alone in either discerning or disliking them.

Women are entirely correct when they perceive, as Wolf does, that pornography creates competition. It lowers the price of sex among sexual gatekeepers:

> The young women who talk to me on campuses about the effect of pornography on their intimate lives speak of feeling that they can never measure up, that they can never ask for what *they* want; and that if they do not offer what porn offers, they cannot expect to hold a guy.[7]

Jonathan, a 24-year-old from Austin, described his experience of using pornography while he was in a relationship with someone: "It's just an unfulfilling cycle. It's stressful, um, it, you become dissatisfied sexually with the person you're with. How can you not?" He echoed the sentiments of Anthony, a 26-year-old from the same city: "If you're, you know, looking at porn every single day, you're gonna want something else. You're not gonna want what you've got. There's no way you could be happy with it."

When Academy Award-winning actress Jennifer Lawrence found herself the victim of hackers who illegally downloaded nude photos she had taken of herself (and sent to her boyfriend who was living elsewhere at the time), she explained why she snapped the photos in the first place with this remarkable concession: "Either your boyfriend is going to look at porn or he's going to look at you."[8] If even the most desirable, high-status (and thus "expensive") of women—Hollywood actresses—take the men-and-porn association for granted, what does that say about the relationship and behavior assumptions among average American young adults?

Men are apt to disagree with Wolf here and assert that there is no competition. But what men fail to understand is that the competition is for their monogamous attentions. Men do not perceive competition between women and porn because many men are content to have both a real and virtual partners. It is this distinction that leads many women to perceive porn as a form of cheating—the transgression of monogamous intentions. Men tend to disagree, suggesting that cheating is only when it is with a real (other) person having real sex, not a virtual one and masturbation.

Carlos is a 24-year-old from Austin, a college graduate whose parents are assisting financially until he can do better than the last job he had (which paid $8.25 an hour). He's been with Melina, his girlfriend and fellow college graduate, for nine months. She's the first woman he has not cheated on (yet), unless you count virtual partners and old memories. "I'm happy with her," Carlos claims, "and okay, sure I'll get married, but with Theresa (an ex), like, she's exactly what I want in a girl, like sexually, physically, you know."[9] Carlos keeps videos of his sexual escapades with exes. What does Melina think of that?

Yeah, she knows I watch, that's why she hates touching my computer cuz (if) she like types anything, I have everything bookmarked, I guess, and like it just comes up. .... She knows and she doesn't, she doesn't like to use my laptop, but what bothers her is not the porn, but the pictures I have of my ex-girlfriends naked and videos of them, of us. Like videos of me and my ex-girlfriends having sex, and just pictures of them, like that's the only porn that she doesn't, pornographic material that she just cannot stand and hates. [*How many of those do you have?*] You know, pretty much every girl, you know every relationship I've been in, you know.

We asked Carlos what Melina thought of masturbation, which he does at least daily.

(S)he knows. Um, she doesn't like it. She doesn't like that I masturbate because then when it comes to her like I'm not 100%, you know, so she'd rather me not, but I mean then I'll tell her, "Well, have more sex with me," but she just doesn't have a high sex drive, like she, you know, she never masturbates and you know we're completely honest with each other. . . . She finds it repulsive, you know to touch herself, you know, so she doesn't understand why I do it a lot. [*And, um, has that caused any tension in your relationship?*] No, just sometimes when I can't function just cuz I'm too desensitized, you know, I can't get it up. You know there's some, of course, there's some disappointment, but you know it's okay. But the one time where it was a problem was when my laptop was broken temporarily and I was with Serena (another ex) and I asked her, "Hey, can I use your laptop, I need to like write a report" while she went off to class or work, and um, like I used it to watch porn but she like checked the history and she got so pissed off at me. But I don't know, I didn't give a shit, so.

There may have been an era in which Carlos would have had trouble retaining the sexual interest of a woman, but that era is no more. In its place has grown a culture of tolerating pornography among men's sexual partners—the interviews confirm this—including those that vehemently dislike it. Like Wolf observes, it's the new cost of doing business with men.

Wolf's withering criticism, which has gone unheeded, could easily be aimed at Giddens's claims that modern sexuality has been liberated by the pure relationship. The advances of technology in one sexual domain—fertility control—are not unrelated to the advances of technology in another sexual domain—the explosion in online pornography. Each in their own way seek to "purify" sexual relationships, the Pill from the exigencies of reproduction, and porn from the exigencies of self-control and the challenges that come from navigating relationships and the real-time wishes of real people. Wolf would like the former but bemoans the latter:

> But does all this sexual imagery in the air mean that sex has been liberated—or is it the case that the relationship between the multi-billion-dollar porn industry, compulsiveness, and sexual appetite has become like the relationship between agribusiness, processed foods, supersize portions, and obesity?[10]

Not only have Americans witnessed the increasing standardization of expectations about women's physical appearance, creating a hierarchy of sexual attractiveness. The same has also occurred to the sexual encounter itself. Pornography has not variegated sexual experience; on the contrary, it has fixed it in predictable sequences. Critics—rightly, in my view—suggest that the "capitalist cultural grammar has massively penetrated the realm of heterosexual romantic relationships," and this is one way it has done so.[11] It is the most obvious way in which sex has been commodified. Eva Illouz identifies pornographic culture as having dismantled any sense of "sexual honor" or norms of monogamous commitment.[12] It is difficult to disagree, after listening to so many interviewees answer our blunt questions. Even Christopher Ryan, the author of *Sex at Dawn* and a proponent of non-monogamy, sees reason for concern. Speaking about Tinder to writer Nancy Jo Sales in her *Vanity Fair* article on the death of dating, Ryan admits there can be problems with sexualized technology:

> "It's the same pattern manifested in porn use," he says. "The appetite has always been there, but it had restricted availability; with new technologies the restrictions are being stripped away and we see people sort of going crazy with it. I think the same thing is happening with this unlimited access to sex partners. People are gorging. That's why it's not intimate. You could call it a kind of psychosexual obesity."[13]

Pornography and Compulsive Sexual Behavior

Psychosexual obesity. Gorging. Supersize portions. Industrialized sex. The effect of pornography on the market in relationships—whether short-term or long-term—sounds deleterious. And all that from authors who are openly and firmly committed to aspects of liberalized sexuality. But pornography, they hold, sows the seeds of compulsive behavior. This too

Giddens anticipated in 1992, writing just before the popular advent of the Internet. The sexual and technological shifts that he described (and that I recounted in previous chapters) should lead us, he asserted, to "expect male sexuality to become troubled and, very often, compulsive . . . acting out of routines that have become detached from their erstwhile supports."[14] About pornography, in particular, Giddens was even more specific, asserting that it "easily becomes addictive because of its substitutive character."[15] That substitutive character quietly bespeaks the exchange model, for what is substituted is access to real sexual behavior, the part of the equation to which women hold the key (in heterosexual relationships).

Pornography is also unique among sexual behaviors today in that segments of both Left and Right are now openly expressing concern about it. Conservatives, of course, have long fretted about it (hamstrung only by their higher allegiance to free speech), but they are no longer alone.[16] Liberals who otherwise loathe appearing restrictive here are nevertheless increasingly concerned that indulging porn has gotten out of control and is now harming persons and their relationships. And since "protection from harm" is a fundamental principle that liberals care deeply about—more so than conservatives—it should not surprise us that figures like Naomi Wolf and Christopher Ryan (and Noam Chomsky and Andrea Dworkin) are concerned.[17]

But liberal concern about pornography has not yet been consolidated or organized, and it has failed to make inroads in scholarly circles.[18] For example, sex addiction is widely presumed to exist. The same is true of addiction to pornography. Celebrities have sought in-patient counseling for what has been medically labeled "hypersexual disorder." Yet none of these is given much space in the DSM-V, the newest edition of the bible of psychological and psychiatric problems. In fact, sex addiction was in the DSM-III, but was removed from the 1994 edition and remains that way today—out.[19] It is a matter of mild controversy, too.[20] "Sexuality, with its moral ties, is handled much less objectively in scientific debate," suggest a pair of neurosurgeons in a commentary on how researchers fail to evaluate pornography:

> This is no casual, inconsequential phenomenon, yet there is a tendency to trivialize the possible social and biologic effects of pornography. The sex industry has successfully characterized any objection to pornography as being from the religious/moral perspective; they then dismiss these objections as First Amendment infringements. If pornography addiction is viewed objectively, evidence indicates that it does indeed cause harm in humans with regard to pair-bonding.[21]

But when Utah governor Gary Herbert signed a resolution in April 2016 declaring pornography a public health hazard, the move was met with more guffaws and LOLs than serious consideration.

Meanwhile, hypoactive sexual desire disorder, or the unwanted experience of low sexual desire, remains squarely in the DSM-V.

Getting a Best Estimate of Pornography Use

But perhaps we are overestimating the problem. As with most data on sex, we only have quality information going back a few decades. There are not a plethora of population-based surveys that ask about porn use, either, so we have had limited options. Health surveys seldom include it, given little conceptual link between pornography and physical health markers. (Public funding for research on this subject is scarce.) The old standby General Social Survey asks only about annual use, which is not very helpful.[22] The result has been wide variation in estimates of pornography use—not ideal.

So a pair of colleagues and I explored the reasons for the variation in such estimates using data from four recent nationally representative samples—each of which asked a different type of question about pornography use and each of which came up with quite different estimates.[23] We attributed the variation to differences in question wording and answer options, and argued that the "general use" approach to asking about pornography lends itself to a few standard problems. First, there is social desirability: for many, pornography use is unpleasant to admit. Second, there is a tendency to regress toward a lower mean when asked about "average" use. That is, someone who looked at pornography several days in a row might think such a bender was uncharacteristic of their average use patterns and instead report "once a week" or "a few times a month." Third, people are prone to recall bias: who remembers what one was doing "on average" six or eight months ago?[24] One otherwise-fine survey asked the number of times the respondent looked at pornography in a year, as if people keep a diary of such things.

We concluded that a survey question asking respondents about their most recent use of pornography is the best way to assess the overall prevalence of pornography in a population. That is what the *Relationships in America* survey did. Everyone was asked, "When did you last intentionally look at pornography?"[25] The results reveal just how gendered (and just how frequent) pornography use is: 43 percent of men and 9 percent of women report watching pornography in the past week. If I limit it to 18- to

39-year-olds, the estimates shift upward, to 46 percent of men and 16 percent of women. In a manner unlike women's estimates, men's porn use clusters around the most recent options, hinting at possible compulsive behavior: 24 percent of American men reported their most recent use of pornography as either today or yesterday. When expanded out to encompass the past month, the estimate barely doubles—to 53 percent.

Many cultural critics and parents associate porn with teenage boys or young adult men, but Figure 4.1 reveals that assumption is inaccurate. Weekly pornography use (by group) peaks among men in their midtwenties, remains elevated until the late thirties, then exhibits a very gradual decline. But 60-year-old men are still only slightly less likely to have viewed pornography within the past week than men in their twenties and thirties, and remain more likely to do so than women ever are. Cheap sex is not an idea that is lost on men as they age. There is certainly demand that has been stimulated among older Americans as well. While only people born before the early 1980s can be said to remember a world absent of Internet pornography, by the looks of it they have caught up, making up for lost time. Porn attracts both those who never knew a world without it, and those who did. Hence, porn use in America is common among men, and that has occurred not because attitudes toward it have eased entirely but because access to its attractions has.[26]

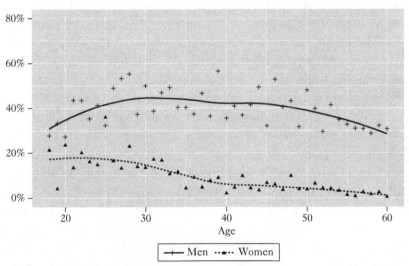

FIGURE 4.1 Percent reporting pornography use in the past week, by age and sex
Source: Relationships in America.

Women and Porn: A Growing Trend?

Minutes after I finished a talk about the contemporary mating market at a mainstream religious college in the mid-South, a conversation ensued with two female students and a male administrator about how pornography shaped the experience of dating. One of the women declared that she knew more women than men who watched porn. While her anecdotal claim does not hold at a population level, it was true in her world and she was convinced that the sex drive of women thus exceeded that of men. (That observation won't hold, either.) But social scientists know better than to shrug off her statement as simply incorrect. She was telling me something: women her age were into porn at rates that people around her underestimated. I heard a similar story at a more conservative college several months before.

She is on to something: a second look at Figure 4.1 confirms the narrowest phase of the gender gap in porn use occurs early—among late adolescents and young adults. Among women, there is a more linear (but slow) downward trend in pornography use with age. While 19 percent of 18- to 29-year-old women report viewing pornography in the past week, only 3 percent of women in their fifties report doing so, meaning that—unlike among men—the youngest women are over six times as likely to have viewed pornography recently as the oldest women.

Might this signal a new and more enduring openness to pornography among women? While it is possible, it pays to be skeptical. While porn use remains subject to greater-than-average risk of biased estimates, and such bias may be more pronounced among women than men, it stretches the imagination to suggest that social desirability bias entirely accounts for—explains away—the gender gap in porn use.

Porn use is not exclusively tied to sex drive among women. If it were, we should see greater use among older women than we actually observe. In fact, when asked whether they were "content with the amount of sex you are having," the youngest women (ages 18–23) were the least likely to say "no, I want more" (30 percent vs. 39 percent among 24- to 32-year-olds). However, the correlation between wanting more sex and looking at porn recently was highest among the youngest group (0.19). In other words, there is a stronger connection between unmet sexual desire and pornography use among younger women than older women. (It is still far weaker than the same link among men.) The correlation between actual reported frequency of sex and porn use is highest (but still modest, at 0.11) among the oldest group of women (ages 50–60), reinforcing the standard explanation that—unlike men—those women who use porn are augmenting sex rather than replacing it. Recent sexual frequency and past-week porn use are altogether unrelated among the sample's youngest women.

That pattern doesn't characterize everyone, though. Alyssa, the 27-year-old from Milwaukee, is not where she wanted to be in life at this age. She wants stability and permanence—she wants to be married by 30 and have children shortly thereafter—but they've been elusive from the beginning (her parents split before she was born). She narrated a history of multiple relationships, three different colleges, and a series of job transitions. Most recently she was fired from a public accounting firm for not progressing amply in job performance. She is currently unemployed and defaulting on three different college loans (totaling $40,000). But a ray of hope for her lies in a new relationship—started online seven months ago—about which she is optimistic. They slid into cohabiting after five months of spending most of the time at his apartment. They waited two months to have sex, at his request, which was unusual for Alyssa and made her "frustrated as hell." "I'm not used to waiting. That's not my preference," she explained, which was closer to two or three weeks. She initiates sex more than he does, a fact she attributes to an elevated libido that she describes as "annoying."

In her adult relationships, she has been "interested in rough sex," something not all of her partners have taken to. The trajectory of Alyssa's sexual development made it unsurprising when she revealed a proclivity for pornography. Indeed, her sexual behavior and interest pattern reflect a more traditionally masculine form. She is reflective and insightful about her unusual relationship with pornography. The thought of her boyfriend looking at it "makes me feel icky," but she considers herself having been an addict in college. "It's definitely a double standard," she admits. She first saw it at age 9; her older brother left a trail of it: "I remember finding pictures in the shower and, just, all over. It was omnipresent." Porn "was a daily habit all the way through college, and it didn't really slow down until maybe my, my last long-term relationship." What about it attracted her? "It was definitely a sexual outlet . . . there's an inverse relationship to if I'm in a sexual relationship or not. . . . For a long time I was really attracted to a very rough and very, um, like power-play, dominant and submissive sort of things, and um, rape fantasy and things like that," an interest that has diminished as she's gotten older but a pattern clearly shaped by events that occurred when she was younger. "Being older," she deduced, "I'm a lot less interested in a lot of things that are seemingly self-destructive, and I think that there was part of my brain that saw that as like, a projection of personal, sort of debasement that was on some level psychologically attractive. That's my guess." The effect of porn, she holds, is not just a personal thing. It's social:

> I have come to believe that people from my generation, anyone who grew up with the Internet, get a lot of their ideas about sex from porn, and I think that sex didn't used to be the way it is now, and we are emulating porn currently. [*Describe how you think sex is now, how you think it was before, and how do you think you're emulating it.*] Sex today in my experience, from me personally, and from knowing other people, talking about this, seeing other people have sex, [it's] a lot less romantic. I mean it's much more mechanical, and um, you don't necessarily have to be connected to that person in any way. That seems slightly unnatural and out of line with my idea of kind of purpose and function of romantic sex in a traditional relationship. I feel like even within the context of relationships, even when it's not casual sex, people are still, I mean the act of sex is, it's not about . . . like the concept of making love, people think is cliché, and weird and silly, and sex is just very, um, physically serving, and it's much less of an emotional and a loving act.

Alyssa does not exempt herself from its effects, about which she is ambivalent:

> I can see in myself the effect that watching porn has had on me. [*Describe that a little bit for me.*] Um, I think that uh . . . I guess I can't say for sure how I would have turned out, or what I would have liked if I had never seen it before I did it. [*Okay.*] But I know that I feel a little bit sexier when I'm having sex like a porn star. [*Okay, how does a porn star have it?*] Um, porn sex is not, like I said, not romantic and it's not, like, it's not slow. It's not seductive, it's much more about um, like the thrusting and the grunting than the touching and the sighing, you know. The gentle loving aspect is not hot. The hot, sexy, um, like really exciting part of sex, is like porn sex, where it's just fast, and hard, and loud, and all that. . . . I just know that, um, the feelings that I'm feeling and the things

that I am choosing to do will, when I'm engaging in sexual activity, I am recalling in my mind things that I have seen before, so I know that there's an effect on it.

She became sexually active with a boyfriend at 15 after a year of "foreplay activities," has had nearly 20 partners (most of them brief), and reported several instances of touching or making out with a woman. She struggles with monogamy and is "on kind of the border line of identifying as bisexual," but "given the nature of how much easier it is to find male partners, and just comfortable, and like I know what I'm doing, and there's just sort of this fear of the unknown with female partners, I really haven't explored it too much."

Despite all the sex-related problems she has endured and, in some cases (by her own admission) provoked, Alyssa has remarkable insight on sexual influence, and, at age 27, hopes the future is more stable. She can even envision marriage, something she has seldom witnessed:

> I used to think that marriage was ridiculous and that everyone was just forcing themselves into it, but, as I've gotten older, just, I've lost my interest for partner hopping and for experiencing you know, new people and new styles and lifestyles and it's just, I want to settle down. I want to stay put.

That impulse was simply not present in years past. In keeping with Alyssa's observations, younger adults are less likely to object to pornography (and to no-strings-attached sex, etc.) than older adults. This, however, has always been the case.[27] What has changed for all, however, is access to this form of cheap sex. By their uptake of modern pornography young women are acting more like men—certainly more so than women only 10–12 years older than them. But they are not more or less permissive in their attitudes about uncommitted sex than women in their upper twenties and low thirties. And their frequency of sexual behavior does not seem strikingly different. But among the youngest adult women, the correlation (or connection) between past-week porn use and past-week masturbation is more than twice as strong as it is among the oldest group of women in the survey (0.61 vs. 0.26, respectively). This is not a function of non-heterosexuality, either, since the correlations remain comparable when I limit the sample of women to only those who profess to be "100 percent heterosexual." For men, the association between recent porn and masturbation is strong across all age groups (ranging from 0.64 to 0.55). What I see in the data is that the youngest women mirror men here far more than do women not much older than them. While overall porn use is much lower among women than among men, its connection with masturbation is tighter than I expected. Will they "grow out of it," as the saying goes, since women in their upper twenties do not display a close association between pornography and masturbation? It's hard to say. We need to revisit that one in a decade.

All these observations do nothing to answer the why question: Why the greater attraction to pornography among younger women? Speculation is difficult to avoid. The simplest suspect is that they have had more long-term exposure to digital porn's availability—this is Alyssa's hunch—or perhaps feel less embarrassment about saying so on a survey than have women just a few years older than them. Porn may simply be more normal for them than for others 5, 10, or 20 years older than they are. But exposure need not mean attraction and uptake.

Have younger women always glimpsed more porn than older women? Yes. Data from the General Social Survey reveals that the youngest women in nearly every survey iteration since 1972 have reported being more apt to "watch an X-rated movie" in the past year than women older than them. And yet the delivery system has changed, and we do not have a good sense of how much pornography young women were actually consuming (or how often) in the past. An "annual" rate tells us something, but not much.

Does this mean that women who report weekly porn use are somehow more sexually jaded—however defined—than men who do the same, simply because it is more uncommon among women than men? Not necessarily. Some speculate that women's porn use is not the solitary thing that it often is for men, who typically use it as an aid in masturbation. But here too, the conventional wisdom is beginning to crumble: whereas 80 percent of men who said they watched porn within the past day also said they had masturbated within the past day, 74 percent of women who did so reported the same.

What can be known with confidence, however, is the basic message: regular porn use is notably higher among the youngest adult women than among women in their upper twenties or thirties. Is this consequential? Very likely, in ways Alyssa eloquently spelled out. If porn use undermines long-standing ideas about marriage—such as the expectation of sexual fidelity/monogamy and relationship permanence—then it stands to reason that greater porn use among women should undermine those marital values. That much is true: women who say they never watch porn are the least likely to report having cheated on a romantic partner and the most likely to express disagreement when asked whether "traditional marriage is outdated" (results not shown). It makes sense. Porn use thus appears to constitute a liberalizing force, at least when it comes to support for traditional institutions and arrangements.

To suggest—as some critics do—that pornography lacks the ability to alter desire or behavior does not make sense. Of course it can. Pornography is not like the passive consumption of any given movie. Instead, it is as if you were watching the same movie over and over again, with minimal variations. It is a repetitive and powerful narrative about sex that certainly contains the capacity to shape us.

Plastic Sexuality and Pornography

We tend to equate porn use with straight men ogling women online, and it is true—most pornography is consumed by heterosexual men. But that is only because they comprise the vast majority of American men. Their porn consumption patterns, however, are eclipsed—dramatically so—by the rates visible among sexual minorities. Table 4.1 displays pornography use rates both in the past day (today or yesterday) and in the past week, among men and women ages 18–60 in the *Relationships in America* data. I thought about displaying only those ages 18–39, but the additional cases provide more robust estimates and the two tables do not look radically different.

Over half of gay and bisexual men self-report pornography use in the past day, and between 71 and 76 percent in the past week, respectively. That is well above the 20 and 38 percent rates, respectively, reported among heterosexual men. This is not new news, either. In their study of billions of web searches, analysts Odi Ogas and Sai Gaddam found that when compared with straight men, gay men watched more porn, had larger porn stashes, searched for more porn online, and subscribed to more pornographic websites.[28]

But the same pattern is visible among women. Whereas only 2 percent of straight women reported past-day pornography use, 17 percent of bisexual women did so, 11 percent of "mostly heterosexual" women said so, as well as 8 percent of lesbian women. In most estimates displayed here, the pornography use rates of sexual minority women are three times that of straight women.[29] Bisexual women even give straight men a run for their money. (In fact, their past-week use rates are higher than among heterosexual men.)

Why the clear link between sexual minorities and more frequent pornography use? This really should not surprise us. Back to
Giddens: "plastic" sexuality is a precursor to the development and pop-
ularization of the "pure relationship," of which sexual minorities represent the vanguard. What does the pure relationship model have to do
with porn use, which tends to be a solitary activity? Plenty. Remember
what the pure relationship involves—concern for the personal satisfactions that can be derived from it. And recall the new mentality around
sexuality that Giddens describes: (1) it becomes the property of the individual, (2) it is open to being explored and cultivated (or shaped) in
diverse ways, and (3) the generation of sexual pleasure now far eclipses
any concern for what Giddens called the "exigencies of reproduction"
(that is, the connection of sex with baby-making.) Sex is for fun and
experimentation, and if pleasure can be derived from pornography,
then those most apt to seek it out are not simply men—due to their
elevated sex drive—but especially those men (and women) in the vanguard of this new model.

What this explanation does not leave, however, is any room for alternative causation. Leaning on Giddens, we are left to conclude that either
non-heterosexual orientations cause elevated pornography use or else
something else causes both. An altogether different hypothesis is that we
may be shaping or molding our sexuality, at least in part, through interaction with pornography.

How, after all, do people learn about different sexual positions, sex toys,
fetishes, and different kinds of partners—tall, blond, short, hairy, masculine,
multiple, etc.? They are certainly not apt to be immutable preferences—as
if a person was born to find brunettes more attractive than blondes or was

Table 4.1 Pornography use in past day and past week,
by self-reported sexual orientation

	Today or Yesterday		Within Past Six Days	
	Men (%)	Women (%)	Men (%)	Women (%)
100% Heterosexual	20.3	2.3	38.0	6.7
Mostly Heterosexual	43.1	11.2	69.4	23.9
Bisexual	54.5	16.6	70.6	43.8
Mostly Homosexual	42.2	6.5	62.6	18.3
100% Homosexual	54.1	8.4	75.6	21.4

Source: Relationships in America.

hard-wired to prefer bondage or big breasts. No, they are largely learned. Learned where—from a partner? Perhaps, but even partners learn from someone, or somewhere. It is no longer a leap to assert that pornography is not just a response to demand, but is itself an influential teacher. Some of its lessons are learned, attempted, and rejected—of the "been there, done that, don't wish to try that again" sort—while others are learned, liked, and repeated.

As an example of the hypothesis I am posing, straight men are glimpsing other men having sex (with women) in pornography—the "cumshot" scenario in porn is not just common but listed as popular and desirable by straight men when queried about their own pornography preferences.[30] In reality, then, straight men are attracted to the sexual pleasure of other aroused men. I am not suggesting here that porn use leads straight men to "turn" gay. No. What I think is a reasonable interpretation, however, is that pornography is indirectly shaping (and increasing) the sexualization of situations, what people are willing to try, and what they come to desire sexually. Sociologist Jane Ward's evaluation of men who have sex with other men—but consider themselves straight—is hence not an oxymoron.[31] To be gay, in her perspective, is not simply about sexual attraction or behavior patterns, but about the (additional) adoption of a community and culture. Pornography, then, is blurring the lines between sexual orientations, contributing to the growth of what is sexually attractive. This may be why bisexuals' porn use rates are among the highest in America. As pornography increasingly saturates American private life, it is becoming scientifically untenable to maintain that porn doesn't matter.

The Politics of Porn

In surveys, most sex-related variables are correlated with political affiliation, with liberals more apt to back the sexually permissive response. Support for pornography is certainly an example. In the *Relationships in America* study, agreement with the statement "Viewing pornographic material is OK" hews closely to political lines:

- 63 percent among very liberal respondents
- 60 percent among liberal respondents
- 38 percent among moderate or "middle-of-the-road" respondents
- 25 percent among conservative respondents
- 19 percent among very conservative respondents

Moreover, support for the statement "Viewing pornographic material is OK" is nearly as strong among liberal women as it is among liberal men.[32] For them sexual freedom is a principle, a freedom to back, even if the expression of that freedom via porn use is utilized far more by men of all political persuasions than women. Fifty-four percent of "very liberal" and 57 percent of "liberal" 24- to 35-year-old men in the *Relationships in America* data reported porn use in the past week, compared with 31 percent of "very conservative" and 43 percent of "conservative" men of the same age. (Past-week porn use ranged among young women from 10 percent among very conservative women to 19 percent among the most liberal.)

How do we account for such politico-sexual distinctions? Is there consonance between political liberalism and a pornographic vision of sexuality (e.g., as no-strings-attached)? Or are the conservatives lying hypocrites— saying one thing and doing another?[33] Or is it possible that pornographic technology is actually helping turn America "blue" (that is, more politically liberal) by socializing attitudes toward committed sexual relationships that are more consonant with a liberal vision than a conservative one? Sound crazy? It may not be.

Does Porn Shape LGBT Support?

Take, for example, same-sex marriage, an idea that garners far greater support from political liberals than conservatives. Not so long ago—a blink of an eye in the study of social behavior—the majority of Americans felt differently. Today, many have changed their mind. Does heightened porn use matter for fashioning political attitudes about marriage?[34] It does among men.

Data analyses from *Relationships in America*—fielded just about 18 months before the US Supreme Court ruled in favor of a constitutional right to same-sex marriage—reveal that when young adult Americans ages 23–39 are asked about their level of agreement with the statement "It should be legal for gays and lesbians to marry in America," a modest gender difference emerges, just as expected and consonant with most polls: 41 percent of men agreed or strongly agreed, compared with 45 percent of women.[35] But of the men who view pornographic material "every day or almost every day," 43 percent "strongly agreed" that gay and lesbian marriage should be legal, compared with around 12 percent of those whose porn-use patterns were either monthly or less often than that. Regression analyses (in Table A4.1) confirm that last pornography use is a (very) significant predictor of men's support for same-sex marriage in the full sample, displaying a linear association even after controlling for other obvious factors that might influence one's perspective, such as political affiliation, religiosity, relationship status, age, education, sexual orientation, and social media use. It's even significant after I control for their attitude about pornography (which is also very influential).

The same pattern emerged when I considered the statement "Gay and lesbian couples do just as good a job raising children as heterosexual couples," a question I asked on the NFSS survey. Only 26 percent of the lightest porn users agree, compared with 63 percent of the heaviest consumers. It is a linear association for men: the more porn they consume, the more they affirm this statement.

Of course, correlation doesn't mean causation. On the other hand, I am pretty confident a causal arrow wouldn't run in the other direction. (Why would supporting same-sex marriage prompt men to look at porn?) Still, we should consider alternative explanations. What might predict both porn use and support for new family forms? Religion? Politics? Perhaps a general rise in permissive sexual norms predicts both porn use and LGBT rights. While religiosity matters for perceiving marriage as outdated, it does little to alter the stable link between porn use and same-sex marriage support. The same is true of political affiliation. And recall I already controlled for permissive attitudes toward pornography. These all matter; they just don't explain the association between porn use and supporting nontraditional family forms.

Why might this association exist? Given that I study sexual behavior, I cannot help but note the contrast between classic descriptions of marital sexuality and how sex is portrayed in modern pornography. The latter redirects sex away from any sense of it as involving relationships of permanence, exclusivity, or expectations of fertility. On the contrary, pornography typically treats gazers to a veritable fire-hose dousing of sex-act diversity, and presses its consumers away from thinking of sex as having anything to do with love, monogamy, or childbearing—all traits that most Americans long equated with marriage.[36] So, add to the sharing of bodies temporarily and nonexclusively a significant dose of alternative sexual activities—different positions, roles, genders, and varying numbers of participants—and that is basically where porn leads today: away from sex as having anything approaching a classic marital sense or structure.

In the end, contrary to what very many people might wish to think, men's support for redefining marriage may not be the product of actively adopting ideals about expansive freedoms, rights, liberties, and a noble commitment to fairness. It may be, at least in part, a passive byproduct of regular exposure to the diversity of sex found in contemporary porn.

I'm not alone in seeing the connection, either. Other scholars are documenting the same pattern in their data sets, too.[37] When asked to explain the link he found between pornography use and same-sex marriage support, Indiana University media professor Paul Wright remarked that "pornography adopts an individualistic, nonjudgmental stance on all kinds of nontraditional sexual behaviors" and added that "since a portion of individuals' sexual attitudes come from the media they consume, it makes sense that pornography viewers would have more positive attitudes towards same-sex marriage."[38] It's not just about same-sex marriage. Researchers cannot locate empirical support for claims that pornography is anti-feminist, something it has long been accused of. In a 2016 study appearing in the *Journal of Sex Research*, social scientists found that porn users are more apt to identify as feminists and hold more egalitarian attitudes—toward women in positions of power, women working outside the home, as well as toward abortion—than are nonusers.[39] You think technology cannot change people's minds? It may be time to reconsider.

First Porn, then Sexual Violence?

While Giddens noted the addictive nature of pornography in 1992, he and others suspected pornography to be associated with sexual violence. But the link, he held, would not be obvious. The connection between the two would be through the "episodic" nature of male sexuality. It is not a simple logic Giddens traces, but some forms of sexual violence (like rape) display by their nature an episodic form of sexuality. Pornography, he holds, typically portrays not intimate, relational sex but instances (or episodes) of sex characterized by a man's conquest of the complicit, overcome woman. Giddens is right about pornography—that it fosters the episodic sexuality he describes. It is corrosive to the decidedly non-episodic rhythm of relationships, especially settled married life. So it is that men often "compartmentalize their sexual activity from the parts of their lives in which they are able to find stability and integrity of direction."[40]

But Wolf is more right than Giddens in her claim that "far from having to fend off porn-crazed young men, young women are worrying that as mere flesh and blood, they can scarcely get, let alone hold, their attention."[41] Pornography use has not, as many suspected, led to a surge in interpersonal sexual violence.[42] If porn use expresses an underlying penchant for dominating women, as Giddens suspects, it is certainly a virtual rather than real form of such.[43]

Futurist George Gilder, who wrote an interesting book of sexual predictions in the early 1990s, similarly feared for the sexual violence that he believed was close at hand.[44] What a society cannot handle for long, he held, is a culture of the "unmarried male," that is, when long-term commitments are undermined by short-term opportunistic philosophies. For men, marriage combats that. But Gilder's prediction of violence in the wake of this has not materialized, at least not in the West. Ease of sexual access—real or virtual—has, if anything, deadened men.

Our in-person interviews, which posed several questions about pornography use, reinforce this conclusion. My research team found men consistently inarticulate about the subject. It is as if they themselves do not know what to make of their own penchant for spending hours online gazing and ejaculating. "You don't have to look at it," one experienced looker reminded us. While true, his is a remarkably unhelpful statement about a behavior that has a track record of tracking toward compulsivity. Just like the psychiatrists debating the matter, these men are seldom prepared to label it a problem, but they also clearly display enough halting conversation about it that neither are they prepared to suggest that nothing is wrong or off-kilter. Their porn use certainly seems to make them less, rather than more, confident in their interactions with women.

Porn use also deadens religious impulses as well. Duke University theologian Reinhard Hütter makes a compelling case for the connection between pornography and what was once called "acedia," a listlessness or apathy more often found in solitary acts that yield boredom, sadness, and a rejection of the personal and social goods typically located and experienced within relationships (and, by extension, within sexual intercourse).[45] Acedia was labeled a vice by the ancients, who associated it with the subsequent development of malice, spite, sluggishness, and faintheartedness. Others, like the economist Tim Reichert, identify it as ennui or apathy. The end result is spiritual passivity. And the empirical evidence supports

this claim. Using two waves of survey data collected from the same people, University of Oklahoma sociologist Samuel Perry notes that pornography use predicted subsequent growth in religious doubts and declining
personal importance of religion.[46] Even being prompted to recall sexual
experiences was found to diminish subsequent religious/spiritual aspira-
tions in a series of controlled experiments conducted by researchers at
Belgium's University of Louvain.[47]

Into Porn and Off the Market

So 46 percent of American adult men below age 40 are weekly porn
watchers, and one in four of them stared at it yesterday or today. It is
possible that a significant shift has occurred, a barrier breached, and
we didn't even notice it. That is, the quality of porn-and-masturbation
may well have reached a level significant enough to satisfy many men,
such that the pursuit of real sex with real women—heretofore considered
worth it in comparison with masturbation—seems no longer a benefit
worth the costs of wooing. Fake sex is closer to real sex than ever before,
and the dopamine hit along the way extends foreplay. Now men can ogle
and stare at the women they (almost) have sex with. They ejaculate at her,
rather than in her. They may not declare virtual sex great sex, but they
may conclude that it's "good enough." A key concern about pornography,
at least from a sexual economics perspective, involves its effects on the
mating market. Does pornography use—together with masturbation—
satisfy enough of the male sex drive that it has prompted some share of
men to actively or passively remove themselves from the mating market?
If so, how many?

While it is probably a rare woman who would be interested in commencing a serious relationship with a man she knows to be hopelessly
hooked on pornography and masturbation, this scenario—if repeated
among enough men and women—threatens to exacerbate the gender
imbalance in the mating market. The threat, in the form of fewer men
seeking a committed sexual relationship with a real woman, further undermines women's power in the market—that is, their ability to get what they
want. (I explained the outlines of this in Chapter 2.) A sex-ratio imbalance created by men retreating from relationships with real women would
then boost the power of the remaining men to navigate the mating market
to their advantage. This means women who have no interest or experience with pornography—but are seeking a committed relationship—can

be harmed by porn's effects on the mating market if enough men retreat from it because they have decided that porn is "good enough."

Provocateur and gay British writer Milo Yiannopoulis summarizes the basic argument here in a two-part article entitled "The Sexodus," a frank discussion of his perspective on the market that generated much popular commentary when it was published in December 2014. He writes, some-what presumptively (at least about academics and scientists, who tend to reserve judgment until the evidence warrants it):

> Social commentators, journalists, academics, scientists and young men themselves have all spotted the trend: among men of about 15 to 30 years old, ever-increasing numbers are checking out of society altogether, giving up on women, sex and relationships and retreat-ing into pornography, sexual fetishes, chemical addictions, video games and, in some cases, boorish lad culture, all of which insu-late them from a hostile, debilitating social environment. . . . Why bother trying to work out what a woman wants, when you can play sports, masturbate or just play video games from the comfort of your bedroom?[48]

Other men actively exit the market because they feel that they themselves—not women—have a problem with pornography that first requires a solution before they can engage in a healthy relationship. Jonathan, the 24-year-old quoted earlier, would like to marry someday, exhibits realis-tic ideas about its challenges and gratifications, but deduces that he's not marriage material yet. He's working at Chick-fil-A, is scoping out a woman at his church, but thinks his penchant for pornography will get in the way. So he's stopping short:

> If I'm not capable of doing that (quitting porn), then I shouldn't be in a relationship with her. And honestly I shouldn't be in a relation-ship at all because that's not, um, gonna set me up for any healthy relationship. . . . I can always go back to having sex, you know, when I want. Um, that's always on the table. Um, but, I don't want to wait forever to find out if I'm even capable of doing it right, you know? (But) porn is one that uh, that I can't get away from. It's always an option. Sex you have to go look for, usually. Where I mean once I get out of the bar scene, now that I'm not there to get it I have to look for it. So that's easier to resist. But porn is something that if you're

bored or alone, like it's always an option, and that's why it's so hard. Um, so I mean, I was um, I'm kind of using her in a sense for uh, just some kind of encouragement or motivation that, that there is a chance, or there is still hope for me, because there's someone who's still willing, that someone's who's still waiting, or, uh, there's a possibility on the table.

The question is not whether some men have exited the market, courtesy of porn. The question is how many. Sociologically, is it enough to make a difference in the mating market? It is going to be difficult to tell, since participation in the mating market requires no application or certification, and people are more or less active in it with regularity. Being "off the market" can go unrecognized even among those of whom it is true, and anyone can get back on the market without acknowledging or realizing it. So if market participation is not simple to document, how can we tell if there is a porn-fueled retreat from it by a substantial share of men? Indirectly.

The *Relationships in America* survey asked a variety of questions about respondents' marital status, their dating behavior, their pornography use, etc.—enough to make a guesstimate of the share of men who are off the mating market due (in part, perhaps) to their porn use habits. In the data are 1,170 men and 1,206 women under the age of 50 who reported having never been married, and who were asked a question about their recent dating behavior: "What's been your experience of the 'dating scene' in the past year?" Respondents could select one of five responses:

1. I've dated some in the past year, and it's been fairly easy to navigate
2. I've dated some in the past year, but the dating scene is more challenging than I expected
3. I haven't really dated in the past year because I'm not interested in it
4. I haven't really dated in the past year because no one has exhibited interest in me
5. None of these answers fits my experience

That last response was selected by 34 percent of all men and women who were eligible to answer it. (There was less than 1 percent variation by sex.) So clearly the other four answer options are only resonating with two-thirds of the respondents. Be that as it may, we can still learn about the respondents who explicitly identify as off-market. Among men, I honed in on the 29 percent who said they had not dated in the past year, either because they were not interested in it or because no one exhibited interest in them. I have to consider the rest of the men "on the market." Among that off-market group, 33 percent reported pornography use in the past day and 53 percent within the past 2–4 days (a figure which includes the past-day reporters). It may be too much of an assumption to hold that such frequent pornography consumers who report no dating in the past year because they don't want to or they think they're uninviting are off the mating market because of their pornography use, but I hold that their porn use may be undermining their participation. When extrapolated to the share of all never-married heterosexual men under 50, I estimate that between 9 and 15 percent of them are frequent pornography users and have seemingly exited the mating market (at least temporarily). That's a hefty share of unmarried men.

However, men are not the only ones who exit the mating market. Seventeen percent of never-married women under 50 (who identify as heterosexual) said they had not dated in the past year because they were uninterested in doing so (for reasons I could only speculate about). So while I suspect a not insignificant share of men are off the market and entertaining themselves with pornography, it is no larger a group than that share of women who do not wish to date. Perhaps it's a wash, in terms of mating market dynamics.

The Pornographic Double Bind

Another mating-market casualty of pornography is the relationship that begins but fails to thrive, done in by revelation of pornography use.[49] That is, porn use prompts an end to an unknown number of relationships.[50] Breaking off a relationship because of pornography use can be a rational and moral reaction to someone's predilection for peering at nudity online—but few recognize that such actions contribute in ways not often noted to the broader retreat from marriage and significant relationships about which many claim to be concerned.

I recently observed an online dispute over the matter of men, marrying, and pornography. A crestfallen young woman discovered her boyfriend "struggled" with pornography. I am never quite sure what "struggling" actually means, since it can be code for anything from shame at taking pleasure in women's unclothed beauty all the way up to addiction to hardcore porn. (There is a difference. Without the former, the human race is doomed.) This young woman elected to remain in her relationship, but she was counseling other women to consider the "path of least resistance," that is, leaving. Departing, she suggested, is the best option.

It was not the first time I had encountered this. Not long before that, I sat around a campfire with a couple dozen enthusiastic young adults, listening to the women recount their list of relationship deal-breakers—porn use was a common one—while the men sat by sheepishly. Although I am sympathetic to the women's concerns, the numbers just cited on porn use suggest widespread departures would likely backfire on women (as many things tend to do in the domain of relationships), who would leave for pastures that may well not be any greener.

I would never dream of telling anyone—devoid as I am of information about particular situations—what they ought to do in such a situation. However, I have no trouble or qualms in declaring that collectively a categorical call to leave relationships because of the other partner's pornography use makes little sense if you value a social world marked by the normative presence of committed relationships. By the numbers—41 percent of never-married 18- to 39-year-old heterosexual men report past-week pornography use—this would rule out a great many men as unworthy marriage material for women. Heck, one in three married men age 60 or under said they'd looked at pornography in the past week. (What are their wives supposed to do?) If so many men are off limits, a comparable number of women will not find themselves in a committed relationship at all. (And, of course, the remaining men would seize the advantageous position, as outlined in Chapter 2.) This is the pornographic "double bind," wherein women find themselves stuck between unhappy scenarios—the unwanted porn use of the man they are with, the elevated odds of the same among the men they might leave him for, and the risk of being alone. On the matter of men and pornography, the data suggest you may not be able to flee far enough.

Masturbation: Are Americans Increasingly Going Solo?

It is impossible to talk sensibly about pornography today without also talking about masturbation. Historically, masturbation has been considered an even more embarrassing or invasive subject to study than pornography, despite its common occurrence in human experience and its far older history. Giddens, however, tells us to pay heed. He directs our attention back to the dramatic social shifts in sexual expression that have taken root: "Such changes (in sexuality) are nowhere better demonstrated than in the case of masturbation."[51]

Survey administrators didn't get the memo, though. Few large, population-based survey projects have included measures of masturbation in their inventory of sexual behaviors. While the Kinsey reports were the first to collect and publish figures on masturbation in the US population, Kinsey's study was far from nationally representative. It was not until the NHSLS of 1992 that a population-based data set documented Americans' masturbation practices. Drawing upon their probability sample of 18- to 60-year-olds, the NHSLS reported that 61 percent of men and 38 percent of women masturbated in the past year.[52] This figure was comparable to reported rates of masturbation in other countries.[53] But here again annual rates are just not helpful, since for many masturbation is—or has become—a far more regular behavior. Nor does it make sense to lump 20-year-old men together with 60-year-olds, given testosterone levels diminish with age.

So in an era of cheap sex and shifting norms about sexual expression, who masturbates more? Who masturbates less? Is the practice increasing in frequency over time? What—besides its popular association with pornography—predicts variation in it? Does having a stable sexual partner diminish masturbation, or not really? Does social media usage (e.g., time on Facebook) stimulate it? These are all answerable questions.

The Numbers on Masturbation

The two most unsurprising things we know about masturbation are its association with age and sex (that is, male/female). Rates of masturbation increase during adolescence, peak in young adulthood, and then decrease throughout the rest of the life course. And in analyses of sex differences in sexual behaviors, significant distinctions are consistently observed here, exceeded only by pornography use.[54] In the 2010 National Survey of Sexual Health and Behavior (NSSHB), the cohort with the highest overall rates of masturbation (25- to 29-year-old men and women) still display obvious sex distinctions, with 44 percent of men reporting masturbating two or more times per week while only 13 percent of women say the same.[55] While these trends are occasionally offered as evidence of repressive societal sexual scripts that constrain women's pursuit of physical pleasure, or social stigmas that hinder women from reporting their actual (higher) rates of masturbation, others critique such arguments as unnecessarily cumbersome and instead consider the data simply evidence for a higher male sex drive.[56] (That's my preferred explanation as well.)

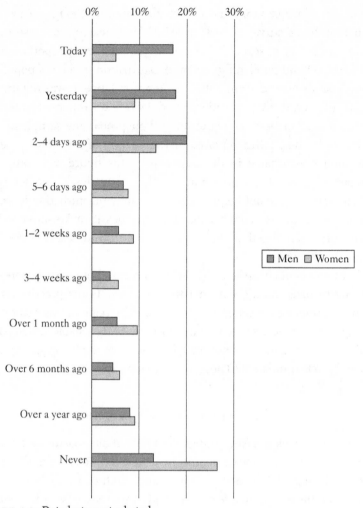

FIGURE 4.2 Date last masturbated
Source: Relationships in America, 24- to 35-year-olds.

The 2010 NSSHB sex study included a measure of masturbation that assessed how often the respondent masturbates, on average. The 2014 *Relationships in America* survey, however, measured frequency the same way it did pornography use, by asking the respondent, "When did you last masturbate?"[57] While this approach may not be preferable as a measure of *average* masturbation frequency among individuals, I argue that it is a more valid measure—and one subject to considerably less social desirability bias—given that the question is specific rather than general, and makes no attempt to solicit an average from the respondent. (A respondent who typically masturbates about once every six months is not likely—on average—to have done so yesterday.) So what does the data say about masturbation among 24- to 35-year-olds, an age group assumed to be in the peak period for sex drive?

Sorted by sex of respondent, 24 percent of young-adult women report never having masturbated, while the same was reported by 9 percent of men. A few characteristics are worth noting about this population. They are more likely to be:

- Pentecostal (30 percent of whom said they had never masturbated)
- "Traditional" Catholics (25 percent)
- Politically "very conservative" (36 percent)
- Sexually inexperienced (i.e., no sexual intercourse) (33 percent)

You may call them deceptive—some may well be—but that is the sample who say they have never masturbated, and certainly some significant share of them are telling the truth.

Figure 4.2 displays the percentage of 24- to 35-year-old Americans who report last masturbating on given dates, sorted by sex. Predictably, men report higher levels of very recent masturbation, with the modal answer (20 percent) being "2–4 days ago," followed closely by both "yesterday" and "today" (at 17 percent each). Fully 54 percent of young-adult men report masturbating within the past four days. For women, the distribution of answers is more even, but with a modal answer of "never." But while the data suggests notable sex differences, they are not quite as dramatic as at first glance. Just over one in four female respondents said they had masturbated within the past four days.[58] When you contrast that with the 27 percent who report "never," it suggests a bimodal distribution—fairly recently or not at all.

Figure 4.3 expands the age range and displays the percent of Americans ages 18–60 that report masturbating at least once in the past week (or rather, as the survey language states, in the past six days). More than Figure 4.2, this graph gives us a sense of how many men and women of varying ages tend to masturbate regularly. The numbers reinforce the gendered nature of regular masturbation. The trend lines (which minimize fluctuation) indicate women's regular masturbation peaks in the early twenties, whereas men's peaks in the late twenties (just below 70 percent) but remains above 60 percent until after age 40. The gap between male and female trend lines here is smallest in the early twenties and widest in

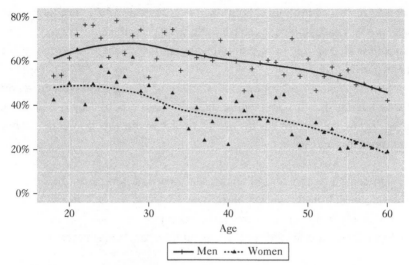

FIGURE 4.3 Percent who report masturbating in the past week, by age and sex
Source: Relationships in America.

the late thirties and forties. Even the oldest men in the sample report more regular masturbation than virtually all ages of women except for early to mid-twenties, where the two lines are statistically comparable.

The interviews we conducted reinforce these estimates rather remarkably, and even though we had already cycled through a variety of questions about sexual relationships and behavior, the question on masturbation still tended to catch men off guard; most quickly recovered. Answers followed the survey estimates, with the caveat that men seemed more apt to round down (or further back) for masturbation in contrast with their tendency to round up (that is, more) on sexual partners. Masturbation is not as masculine as sexual "conquests," it seems. When asked the last time they masturbated, a sample of male interviewees responded:

· I don't know, probably like a week ago, or a week and a half ago.
· Last night.
· Three days ago.
· Gosh, probably a month ago.
· Earlier this month?
· Twice a day.
· It has been awhile.
· Probably like six or seven weeks ago.

- I would probably say yesterday. It was yesterday.
- About a year ago.
- Last night.
- Um, this morning.

Women's self-reports similarly reflect Figure 4.2, especially the bimodal distribution visible there. It was either pretty recently or well back in the past, with several who reported none. A sampling includes:

- Probably like a week ago.
- Probably in the last couple days?
- Back in, like, January (six months ago).
- Like, the day before yesterday.
- Six years ago maybe.
- Two days ago.
- I think maybe it's been about five months ago.
- It's been probably about a month.
- Never have.
- Two weeks ago, about.
- I would say, six months ago, maybe.

Such ranging answers and guesstimates make the 1992 NHSLS's question about annual masturbation seem profoundly unhelpful in light of the high frequencies we heard about in the interviews as well as in the 2014 *Relationships in America* survey. If in fact masturbation is the cheapest sex, and the purest measure of excess sexual interest, it is fair to say that there is more than ample sexual interest in the American population below age 40, and—from the looks of Figure 4.3—above it as well.

While the estimates on masturbation are notable in their own right, they are dominated by the fact that most Americans identify as heterosexual. But heterosexual Americans, it turns out, are the least likely to self-report recent masturbation. The differences (not displayed) are not only significant, they are stark. Over three times as many lesbian women (25 percent) and five times as many bisexual women (36 percent) report masturbating in the past day, when compared with straight women (7 percent).[59] The pattern holds when I push out the time horizon to the past week. Just over one in five straight women (22 percent) report masturbating, compared with 51 percent of lesbian women, 65 percent of bisexuals, and 53 percent of women who perceive themselves in between straight and bisexual. Men, whose overall levels of masturbation eclipse those of women, display a comparable—if slightly less dramatic—pattern. One in four straight men reports masturbating in the past day, whereas 56 percent of bisexual men and 59 percent of gay men do. Pushed out to one week, the figure for straight men doubles to 52 percent, while bisexual and gay men's estimates climb to 78 and 89 percent, respectively. Interestingly, straight men's past-day and past-week masturbation estimates track lesbian women's closely and actually lag behind those of bisexual women.

Why the difference? Giddens, who noted that masturbation has "come out" as openly as homosexuality, argued that being gay (or lesbian) is to live in the vanguard of the Western shift toward a lifeworld more focused on sexual pleasure. This is not at all exclusive to gay men, as the estimates of other men and women signal. It is just more pronounced among them. This lifeworld is glimpsed in part by the elevated estimates of masturbation—the frequent practice of which serves to reinforce an embodied narrative that genital pleasure, solitary or otherwise, is close to the heart of what it means to be human. Plenty of straight men would concur. But they are not in the forefront of the movement.

Is Masturbation Increasing in Prevalence?

Is it fair to say that young adults are masturbating more than, say, their parents did at their age? Or is masturbation simply easier to admit on a survey than it was 20 or 30 years ago? While it is impossible to say for sure, the existing evidence supports the notion that masturbation has increased in frequency—recently—and is arguably at an all-time high. (This is not to say that it hasn't become easier to admit, too; it certainly has.) What sort of evidence favors such a claim, especially since the practice itself is as old as humanity?

To help us here we have to look around the neighborhood—at other data collection projects and what they reported in the recent past. When I do that, there emerges plenty of reason to believe that the frequency of masturbation is increasing. Here's why I say that: the 1992 NHSLS data noted that 29 percent of men aged 18–24 reported masturbating, on average, at least once a week.[60] The 2014 *Relationships in America* data, meanwhile, finds that 25 percent of 18- to 24-year-old men report having masturbated in the past day—either today or yesterday. When expanded to encompass the past six days, that figure rises to 49 percent.

Although the measures are not directly comparable—and social desirability concerns may have diminished some over the past 20 years—the gap in estimates nevertheless suggests not a minor uptick in masturbation but rather a potential surge in its frequency among men. In 1992, there simply was no online pornography to (further) stimulate sexual desire. While genuine demand for masturbation could have naturally increased in 20 years, there's no reason to think it would at this point in history, unless the technological and social fostering of sexual desire (and hence demand) has increased. And it has, revealing that male desire and arousal is not fixed; it is malleable and can and is being stimulated. The same may be happening to women, too.

Frequent porn use has come to be equated with masturbation, and the data reinforce this. Among 24- to 35-year-old men who said they have never intentionally viewed pornographic material, a mere 4.4 percent reported masturbating in the past day (that is, yesterday or today). But as frequency of porn use increased, so did masturbation. The two track along a diagonal: 74 percent of such men who said they looked at pornography today also reported having masturbated today; 79 percent who said "yesterday" to the former also said "yesterday" to the latter; 66 percent of those who said "2–4 days ago" to the question about last pornography use also said "2–4 days ago" to the last masturbation question.[61] The causal order here is not complicated, and given the refractory period after male orgasm, it would be ridiculous and nonsensical to suggest that masturbation leads to porn use.

Ian Kerner, a popular New York City sex therapist often featured on CNN and NBC's *The Today Show*, concurs: "By my estimate, men are masturbating 50 to 500 percent more than they would normally without Internet porn."[62] Kerner's dramatic guesstimate is of the range of growth in frequency because of pornography. That is, he thinks some men masturbate 50 percent more frequently than they would if porn didn't exist, while others masturbate six times as often because of the same (accounting for variation within men). I'm unable to tell, given I don't have data that can map someone's masturbation history. The contrast of *Relationships in America* data with that of the 1992 NHSLS, however, suggests something not far below 100 percent growth in the share of men who masturbate weekly or more often.

Something similar has likely occurred among women as well. Whereas 9 percent of 18- to 24-year-old women reported masturbating an average of once a week in the 1992 NHSLS, past-week masturbation was reported by 32 percent of same-age women in the *Relationships in America* survey. To be sure, some portion of this may be due to increasing comfort in admitting masturbation, but to suggest that a nearly 275 percent increase in just over 20 years is due solely to ease of admission seems pretty unlikely.

The same diagonal pattern—or alignment—between last pornography use and last masturbation appears for 24- to 35-year-old women as well. Whereas 2.5 percent of women in this age range who report never looking intentionally at pornography also reported masturbating "today," that number leaps to 57 percent among those whose last pornography use was "today." (Keep in mind, however, that less than 5 percent of all women reported masturbating "today.") Sixty-nine percent of women who reported last pornography use "yesterday" also reported "yesterday" as the date of their last masturbation experience. And although I'm analyzing 1,779 women ages 24–35, numerous cells are empty. For example, no women at all reported pornography use "today" and last masturbation either 2–4 days ago or 5–6 days ago.

What's my point? It's this: although overall pornography and masturbation self-reports are notably lower for women than men, the effect of pornography on masturbation seems comparable for women and men. The story here is not just about simple access to pornography, though. It is about the unprecedented exponential multiplication of sexual memories and the fostering of a more erotic imagination (in the brain). In other words, modern pornography use contributes to a more sexualized existence. In an earlier era where adult magazines were perused by fewer men (and far fewer women), had to be hidden (in most cases), and were a fixed, finite product, the effect on men's and women's erotic memory was far more modest than in an era of high-definition video pornography accessible from every web-access portal. Basically, use rates suggest we are making far more sexual memories than our grandparents did, on average. Porn comes with strings attached.

This, too, is sexual malleability. It is also about developing new sexual interests, proclivities, and preferences.[63] Newfound interests in particular sexual practices do not arise from nowhere. It would be untrue to assert that the forms our sexual expressions take today are either fixed or random. Aspects of sexuality are malleable for everyone, though some experience or nurture these more than others.

Is Masturbation a Satisfactory Substitute for Sex?

If masturbation is, at bottom, a form of cheap sex, then it stands to reason that some may use it to altogether replace coupled sexual behavior. This is difficult to discern, though, since uncoupled persons may use masturbation to replace the coupled sex they cannot (or do not) have. What exactly is the relationship between masturbation and real sex?[64]

A pair of popular theories is thought to explain it. In the *compensatory* model, masturbation and coupled sexual activity are believed to be inversely associated. Masturbation is seen as an (inferior but better-than-nothing) outlet for sexual energy when paired sexual activity is unavailable, either because of the lack of a partner or the unwillingness or inability of a partner to engage in sex as often as desired. In this way, masturbation is considered a substitute.[65] Darren, a 30-year-old man from northern Virginia, characterizes this model succinctly from observing his own history: "I hardly ever masturbate when I am in a relationship. If I am in a sexually-active relationship with somebody, almost never."

The *complementary* model holds that masturbation supplements paired sexual activity, enhancing the sex life of sexually active adults. Sociologist Ed Laumann, who oversaw the NHSLS in 1992, saw more evidence for this than for the compensatory theory (but in a data set that didn't map frequent masturbation very well at all).[66]

If masturbation and paired sex are linked in a compensatory relationship, then the following should be true: access to a sexual partner and recent sexual frequency will decrease masturbation. If the complementary theory is true, we ought to expect the opposite results. (It is also conceivable that the two are unrelated. Very few scholars suspect this, however.)

What do the *Relationships in America* data say? It appears to depend on an altogether different factor—sexual contentment. (It makes sense.) For women who are content with their sexual frequency—whatever that is—those who report sex four or more times in the past two weeks are 36 percent more likely to report recent masturbation than those who had no sex in the past two weeks. For women, then, masturbation appears to augment rather than replace sex. Sexually discontented women are more apt to masturbate in general, but their recent frequency of sex seems not to matter much. For men, the evidence points toward the compensatory model, a substitution of sorts—in keeping with the claims I have been making throughout this book. Those who are not content with the amount of sex they are having are 29 percent more likely to masturbate recently if they have not had sex in the past two weeks than if they have had sex twice a week. But the link between the two—masturbation and sex—is largely contingent on subjective sexual contentment. More frequent sex— but only in the context of contentment—predicts recent masturbation among men. This conclusion flies in the face of long-standing popular assumptions (embedded in the compensatory theory) that men simply or mechanically replace a lack of partnered sexual access with masturbation. For women, on the other hand, the strong, linear baseline association between sexual frequency and greater likelihood of recent masturbation appears after closer scrutiny entirely contingent or dependent upon sexual contentment.

One storyline often goes unspoken but is evident in more complicated models (not shown): men and (especially) women who report contentedness with no recent sex are comparatively unlikely to have reported recent masturbation, net of other effects (including their partnered status, etc.). Contentedly sexless persons are less apt to masturbate. Thus masturbation seems to have much more to do with subjective contentment and unmet desire rather than any fixed need for periodic sexual release. All this reinforces the claim I made earlier that whatever shapes subjective perceptions of desire or discontentment—media and pornography both come to mind—are powerful forces in shaping solo sexual behavior.

Conclusion

Pornography and masturbation—the cheapest forms of sexual experience— are surging in popularity among both men and women, though the baseline level of interest in the former remains well above that of the latter. For most women, pornography remains uninteresting—if not revolting. The supply of realistic sexual alternatives lowers the price of real sex, access to which real women still control (as gatekeepers). Hence, Wolf is right to lament that a vagina used to have higher exchange value. Women correctly perceive in porn competition for the sexual attention of men and are increasingly finding themselves in a bind—annoyed with their partner's use but uncertain that future partners will avoid it. A minority of men may have even opted out of the mating market due to porn's satisfactions. But given the latent character of mating market behavior, it's difficult to tell for sure. Like porn, masturbation is far less common among women than men. Having been stimulated by the explosion in porn, the share of American men masturbating weekly appears to have doubled over the past few decades, and surged even more among women, who started from a lower baseline. Porn is shaping Americans' sexual tastes, and perhaps even pressing their political ideals in liberal directions. Rates of both pornography use and masturbation are notably higher among sexual minorities, in keeping with Giddens's portrayal of them as in the leading edge of the "pure" relationship system.

5

The Transformation of Men, Marriage, and Monogamy

RECENTLY I WITNESSED an odd online exchange. A New Yorker temporarily residing in France had discovered his girlfriend had participated in some salacious photography (as a model). Disturbed, he was seeking more information about the circumstances of the shoot, the photographer, and whether there were other (i.e., more revealing) photos of which he was not aware. While I am not sure why he elected to air his concerns and efforts so publicly, it was one of the many terse and unsympathetic responses he subsequently received that caught my eye. It read, "She doesn't belong to you." This blunt claim opened a window onto modern dating and mating mentalities, and prompted me to reflect on the place of belongingness in a "pure relationship" era. Do people belong to other people? At face value, the idea sounds archaic, implying a chattel arrangement from which moderns recoil.

And yet to be married (which admittedly this man and woman were not) was long understood to mean that the spouses belonged to each other. Even family law long treated marriages as a unit of consequence. But something tells me that the online critic would have said the same thing—she doesn't belong to you—even if the desperate man was writing about his wife. I say this because it is consonant with the rise of confluent love and the circulation patterns in the mating market. To belong to another is to have somehow opted out of this new regime, a path that is becoming more difficult. "Opting out" is a good way of putting it because it means that the default mode is the pure relationship—no one belongs to anyone else and agreements are temporary and can be voided. We participate in romantic and sexual relationships (including marriage) for so long as we are discerning ample satisfaction. To opt out of this model is to assert brashly (and oddly) that a relationship between two persons can have a sacred, binding quality to it.

That such a description now sounds pre-modern signals that marriage is in the throes of deinstitutionalization, as sociologist Andrew Cherlin has detailed. It is a capstone now rather than a foundation. It is an achievement attained by two independent individuals, not a shelter ducked into wherein two are dependent upon each other. Understood in this way, it is not surprising that many recoil at the thought of a person belonging to another person. What marriage means, what it entails and what it does not, public perceptions about it, and optimal timing for it and behavior within it—everything about marriage seems in flux today. Marriage, and perhaps even monogamy, is being transformed. Westerners are increasingly privileging the idea of marrying, if at all, after peak fertility has begun to wane, or of embracing the child-free life. Giddens asserted that marriage too "has veered increasingly towards the form of a pure relationship, with many ensuing consequences."[1]

And yet at the same time Americans' marriages have never been stronger or happier. This is true largely because Americans are far more selective about their marriages than they have ever been. They are slower to enter them and quicker to leave poor-quality ones. This is especially true of women, who are apt to be choosier today than ever before. Why? Because they can (literally) afford to be and because most women perceive a poor-quality marriage as worse than remaining unmarried. Our great-grandmothers were not in such a position.

Figure 5.1 reveals the basic story of Americans' very recent flight from marriage (on the front end). The X depicted there is a really big deal. There was, at the turn of the millennium, a 21-percentage point gap difference between married and never-married 25- to 34-year-olds in the United States. As recently as 2000, during that period when people tended to get married (after education but before peak fertility waned), most people were doing exactly that. Less than 10 years later, that gap had not only vanished, but reversed: by 2014 there was an 11-percentage point gap between never-married and married young Americans, with the former now more numerous than the latter. Thus, in an unbelievably short period of time— 15 years—the share of young adults in the United States who have never been married has eclipsed those who are married, with little evidence that the trend will dissipate anytime soon. The lines continue their march in opposite directions. Americans are slowly but surely giving up on marriage.[2] Why now? Perhaps because "cultural lag" is nearing its end.

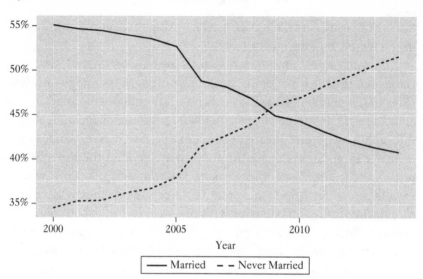

FIGURE 5.1 Share of married and never-married Americans ages 25–34, by year
Source: American Community Survey, 2000–2014.

Contraception and Cultural Lag

Cultural lag is a term coined by early American sociologist William Ogburn, who theorized that a period of "maladjustment" often follows in the wake of a significant material change. That is, people fail, for a time, to synchronize their attitudes and behavior to the new reality.[3] Cultural lag occurs when one part of culture—typically the development of technology—changes faster than another, with normative behavior struggling to catch up. For a simple example, think about how cell phone etiquette has changed in just the past 10 years. A line full of adults all individually staring down at their smart phones is now considered normal rather than odd or pathetic. Meanwhile, talking on the phone while driving (remember they were once called car phones) is not only illegal in my own city but is increasingly treated socially like failing to buckle your children in their seats—a mark of poor character. First comes the technology-driven change, then new norms slowly begin to emerge, then we wonder how we could have ever thought and acted differently.

We are now more than 50 years removed from the advent of artificial, hormonal contraception. But contraception is not just another technology. It is different than the uptake of cellular and smart phones. Smart phones enable persons to call others almost anywhere, check personal correspondence, read the news, update their calendar, and map their travels. They make more efficient common actions people have long undertaken.

The Pill, on the other hand, is a technology characterized not by its efficient delivery of the mundane—like online dating—but by its novel physiological ability to prevent something personally and socially seismic (pregnancy) from happening. It did something new and unheard of in the realm of the private—easing access to desired pleasures without the historic anxiety (welcomed or unwanted) over whether an orgasm might have unwittingly generated a pregnancy. Sexual access, before contraception's wide uptake, was simply rarer for most men. The Pill did not deliver efficiency. Nor did it undo the exchange model of sexual relationships. But it helped create new felt needs and altered how we interact, and what we say we want (and when).[4]

Applied to marriage, cultural lag here has become quite visible. Indeed, many people are marrying because they are still following the cultural practices of their parents and grandparents, even though historically compelling reasons—like babies, financial and physical security, or the desire for a "socially legitimate" sexual relationship—no longer hold. As an example, my wife recently attended a wedding and was caught up in a conversation. The mother of the bride had married at age 19, shortly followed by two children and—13 years later—a divorce. The bride herself was marrying at age 30, after several years cohabiting. A younger friend of the groom, sitting next to my wife, declared that she would create her own wealth, her own provision, and perceived any dependence on a man as risky, despite the fact that she was in a long-term relationship herself. Here is the cultural lag in full view. Mom marries young and regrets it. Daughter marries at the conclusion of "peak" fertility and years of co-residential coupling. The next generation, today no older than teenagers, will wonder why they should marry at all.

All this occurs comparatively slowly, over decades and generations, because normative behavior in the domain of marriage, family, and childbearing is saturated with meanings, hopes, and expectations that will not respond quickly to shifting material conditions around them, according to demographer Jennifer Johnson-Hanks and her colleagues.[5] To use the example above, marriage is simply much less necessary in an era like ours today. But marriage contains a long-standing package of norms and values that doesn't just transform overnight. Although the mother of the bride married in 1978, the erosion of the "companionate marriage" normative package was far from complete. What followed was a tumultuous pair of decades for the institution as behaviors and attitudes began to catch up and adjust to the new realities—described earlier—that fertility technology now enabled. Hence, the bride married at a far older age than her mother did, and after years of taking advantage of access to the Pill. What is worth noting, however, is that she still wanted to marry. Marriage was, to her, the sign of a successful and desirable adulthood and the context into which she wanted (optional) children to be born. The normative package in which marriage is now embedded has changed with the advance of the "pure" relationship model, but the marrying part—and the hope for permanence—has not yet disappeared from it. Will it ever?

Marriage is very old, but it's hard to see how it could survive solely on its symbolic and desirable merits. It will survive because it works. It's functional, even if the meaning of marriage has become far more a symbol of consumption than of production. Poorer Americans would benefit profoundly from marriage's functionality, but they too have adopted marriage as a status marker and seem unlikely to reverse course on the matter anytime soon. Marriage is in the throes of "deinstitutionalization." Not disappearance, but deinstitutionalization; it is losing, or perhaps has already lost, its foundational status. But it will not disappear.

Cheap Sex and the Declining Marriageability of Men

One reason that men are proposing marriage less often these days (as Figure 5.1 implies) is that they are increasingly considered unfit for the long run. Have sex with him? Sure. Marry him? Not so fast. And many men, too, perceive that they are not prepared for marriage.

Marriageability is an old but powerful idea. What does it mean? In his landmark book *The Truly Disadvantaged*, Harvard sociologist William Julius Wilson defined it as the ratio of employed men to all women (of comparable age), and concluded that declining marriage rates among African Americans could be attributed to poor economic opportunities among men.[6] But there are other ways of defining marriageability, such as the ratio of employed men to employed women, a measure more sensitive to the reality that very many women are in the workforce today.[7]

Marriageability resonates as an individual concept as well, not just as a contextual one like Wilson's. The fact that so many women work today has certainly altered the criterion of marriageability to include not just the economic prospects of men but other latent traits as well. Since women can now be pickier about a spouse, personal traits like affability, flexibility, "personality," social support, and ideological homogeneity matter more than they once did.

Meanwhile, men are seemingly becoming less marriageable, not more. They have faltered in adapting to obvious labor market shifts, both that toward work requiring more specialized education and away from work that is readily (and typically) outsourced or automated. And it has befuddled economists, as *New York Times* writer Binyamin Appelbaum details:

> "I think the greatest, most astonishing fact that I am aware of in social science right now is that women have been able to hear the labor market screaming out 'You need more education' and have been able to respond to that, and men have not," said Michael Greenstone, an M.I.T. economics professor. . . . "And it's very, very scary for economists because people should be responding to price signals. And men are not. It's a fact in need of an explanation."[8]

Men, mysteriously and in contradiction to economists' expectations, have not responded as expected. Might cheap sex—ease of access to desirable sexual experiences—have anything to do with this failure to adapt? Baumeister thinks so. Building upon the proposition that a key priority for young men is sex, the social psychologist and his colleague Kathleen Vohs observe the ramifications of simplified sexual access:

> Nowadays young men can skip the wearying detour of getting education and career prospects to qualify for sex. Nor does he have to get married and accept all those costs, including promising to share his lifetime earnings and forego other women forever. Female sex partners are available without all that. . . . Sex has become free and easy. This is today's version of the opiate of the (male) masses. . . . Climbing the corporate ladder for its own sake may still hold some appeal, but undoubtedly it was more compelling when it was vital for obtaining sex.[9]

Wide economic growth is taking a sustained hit in the wake of the Great Recession, entrepreneurship levels—long dominated by men's efforts—are way down, and all of it is prompting long-term bearish outlooks.[10] Is cheap sex due any blame for this? Is men's far greater compulsive porn use pattern part of the equation—sapping their motivation? Perhaps. It's certainly true that women seem better suited than men to effectively navigate not only this economy but this era of cheap sex as well. Political economist Nicholas Eberstadt notes in his 2016 book entitled *Men Without Work* that 25- to 54-year-old men who are neither in the labor force nor seeking work watch 5.5 hours of television and movies per day. His assessment of them is grim:

> To a distressing degree, these men appear to have relinquished what we think of ordinarily as adult responsibilities not only as breadwinners but as parents, family members, community members, and citizens. Having largely freed themselves of such obligations, they fill their days in the pursuit of more immediate sources of gratification.[11]

How do they get by? With the help of parents—and girlfriends.

Wen, a bubbly 28-year-old Asian American from Austin, is in her fourth year of a relationship with Jeff, whom she claims she intends to marry someday. When? "Whenever he feels confident enough, because I make a lot more (money) than he does," Wen holds. Jeff was unemployed for the past year and a half—in a city known for its low unemployment rate—until recently landing a job as a warehouse associate. "I don't know if that job's gonna last or not, 'cause he says it's mindless and boring," she relays. The better money he once made as a commercial fisherman is out because "if he does, he loses me, yeah," due to the long-distance relationship to which she objects and because "he said every moment he spent on that boat made him dumber. [*Dumber?*] Yeah, 'cause it's just the crowd on the boat and, um . . . just a very mindless job."

The two met (online) when Jeff came to Austin from New Orleans on his time off. They began a sexual relationship on their second date—one date earlier than her average experience with previous partners—and moved in together a year later. Like many accounts of cohabitation decisions—the most common scenario, in fact—Jeff's lease ran out and it "made more sense for him to just move his stuff into my condo." (Another interviewee described it this way: "My lease is ending. Your lease is ending. Let's move in together.")

Wen is more liberal than the average Asian American young woman and knows it. She has HPV, which she monitors closely following a cervical cancer scare at age 23. Her boyfriend watches porn, and it doesn't bother her. And about the prospect of marriage, she has concerns:

> I don't have any successful marriage in my family, either side. Like none that lasted, like none. All my uncles divorced, every one of

them. [*Even though Taiwan is kind of traditional?*] Umm, yeah but, yeah their marriages were so bad that in the traditional society like that they still all divorced, so. Um, and the ones that are not divorced I know they cheat for a fact, like I know my dad cheated on his current wife now, and I know my dad cheated on my mom before and I was a mistress myself for five years all because of the stupid idea in Asia that you're not supposed to get divorced, so people cheat and people get married too early. It's a stupid thing that they do there.

But on other matters she recognizes the value in tradition. Wen relayed the practical inconvenience of "reversed" gender expectations; she has had notably more sex partners than he has, and makes more money than he does. It has made for an awkward status quo. But she has been a tradition-buster in other domains of life, having started college early and having preferred the sciences to humanities. She thinks she will eventually marry Jeff, anyway. But not yet:

I'm not gonna marry him while he doesn't have a job . . . just because I know it's not gonna work. He's not gonna be happy that way, I mean. I told him if he's happy being my wife, you know, taking care of kids at home, I would happily marry him as my wife, but like he found that very offensive. Apparently I said it when I was drunk, like two years ago and he didn't talk to me for a whole day the next day so. [*That is not his anticipated role?*] No, he's very like a macho person; he's a body builder.

But what would marriage alter about their existing relationship? Not much. "Tax deductions," she deduces, and perhaps a better environment for having children.

Because Wen, too, likes sex, she questioned whether men should work to get it. Many (though not most) women balked at the notion of men "earning" sex. On the pill since she was 16, Wen reported that she and Jeff have sex (on average) two or three times a week. Both initiate. In an unusually effective account of signaling, Wen said "he kicks the couch, which is our signal to go upstairs and do it." I asked, "And this is like a stimulus-response thing?" Yes:

It's a code for get off of the couch (laughs) and let's go. [*OK. And do you always go up?*] Yeah. [*Because that's what you want, too, or do you ever like sigh and say, 'Please don't kick the couch!'*] Occasionally yes, but 95 percent of the time I'll happily go up.

It would be difficult to establish whether ease of access to sex in the contemporary mating market aggravates men's marriageability, and if so, by how much. It is, in the end, a chicken-and-egg conundrum: when more and more men are considered less and less marriageable, the resulting sex-ratio disparity in the pool of marriageable men tends to spell greater and greater problems for women in how they conduct their relationships. *Atlantic* writer Hanna Rosin is aware of all this, but seems unconcerned by any of it. The author of *The End of Men* holds that:

> [W]omen benefit greatly from living in a world where they can have sexual adventure without commitment or all that much shame, and where they can enter into temporary relationships that don't derail their careers.[12]

Perspective may be in the eyes of the beholder. What Rosin calls a "long sexual arc" through which many emerging adults now move, I am more apt to label as a boulder-strewn pathway or a history of relational wreckage that most women would prefer to avoid if they could. It is decreasingly possible; Rosin asserts that "feminist progress (now) is largely dependent on hook-up culture." The longer pathway to marriage, however, will pose a problem. Economist Marina Adshade describes what to expect:

> When marriage markets do not clear efficiently, the end result can be lower overall fertility rates, a higher percentage of births to unmarried women, and higher expenditure on fertility treatments as men and women delay marriage into their 30s and 40s, or never marry at all.[13]

Fertility is at its lowest in US history. But from the looks of it, young men and women don't seem to mind. The greater likelihood is that plenty find the marriage market frustrating but feel constrained and helpless.

One thing is clear and not just from Wen's account: cheap sex does not make men more productive. And it will not contribute to their marriageability in an era in which marriage rates are tumbling. Baumeister and Vohs hold that "giving young men easy access to abundant sexual satisfaction deprives society of one of its ways to motivate them to contribute valuable achievements to the culture."[14] It is not a new theory. And it need not hold for all men for it to make a profound impact on the American marriage system. (Indeed, it does not hold for all men.) Even Christopher Ryan, no fan of monogamy himself, recognizes this principle, noting Sigmund Freud's observation that "civilization is built largely on erotic energy that has been blocked, concentrated, accumulated, and redirected." Ryan and his *Sex at Dawn* co-author claim (accurately, it seems) that "societies in which women have lots of autonomy and authority tend to be decidedly male-friendly, relaxed, tolerant, and plenty sexy."

Sex, of course, is not the only male motivator and perhaps not even the most important one, but it is an underestimated one. (For example, men are powerfully motivated by competition in sports and business, but seldom over women anymore.) Baumeister and Vohs (and Freud) are on to something, and human civilization is no mean accomplishment. Many Americans still profess their admiration for what has been dubbed "The Greatest Generation," that cohort of men who liberated Europe and the Pacific, and the women who played a critical supply-chain role in making it all possible. But perhaps a key reason why today's young men could not replicate their great-grandfathers' accomplishment is because of diminished or dulled motivation.

Technology has created still other anti-marriage forces to contend with. Educational debt delays plans to marry.[15] Disappearing work and shrinking living wages go hand in hand with technology and increasing mechanization. We are living in a globalized era wherein companies can outsource work, move operations, find cheaper labor, and replace people with machines.[16] Demographic historian Steven Ruggles speculates optimistically that our "silicon servants" (that is, automated assistance) will free us "to pursue our dreams and passions."[17] I agree, but when it comes to men, their dreams and passions are pretty predictable.

Compulsive Sexuality and the Collapse of Traditional Structures

"Men are the laggards in the transitions now occurring," observed Giddens in *The Transformation of Intimacy*.[18] Virtually everyone is in agreement. What is seldom considered, I just observed, is whether men are increasingly the unwitting victim of their newfound sexual successes. Some will counter that most men are not so sexually successful—that the cornucopia of flesh is available only to more desirable men, among whom the "good times" are better than ever. That is, they can poach short-term sexual partners from across the spectrum of female attractiveness, something less-attractive men are not readily able to do. But this, however, presumes that cheap sex is only about real sex. It's not. It's virtual, too. High-definition pornography functions similarly, and Chapter 4 detailed its popularity. A laptop never says no.

Cheap sex, regardless of the delivery system, does little to stimulate the "laggards" of our modern economy toward those historic institutions—education, a settled job, and marriage—that created opportunity for them and their families. In its place is an increasingly compulsive sexuality uprooted from familiar narratives:

> Addiction has to be understood in terms of a society in which tradition has more thoroughly been swept away than ever before and in which the reflexive project of self correspondingly assumes an especial importance.[19]

I have not said much about this "reflexive project of self" (nor will I), but Giddens is asserting here that more than ever what we become is up to us today. And he's not just talking about one's educational or career achievements. The self, Giddens suggests, is more tightly connected to matters sexual than ever before, a reality which has a dark side:

> Compulsive sexuality has to be understood against the backdrop of circumstances in which sexual experience has become more freely available than ever before, and where sexual identity forms a core part of the narrative of self.[20]

I could not agree more. Margaret Archer, a British social theorist quite familiar with Giddens's work, labels this idea of personal identity "Homo inconstantus" (or serially reinvented man), a widely held (but seldom recognized) perspective on personhood and identity that has replaced the "burden of conformity" to, say, traditionally masculine roles of worker, husband, and father, and replaced it with the imperative of "do-it-yourself biographies . . . in short, inventing and reinventing their personal identities."[21] It is the lack of social structure, Archer notes, that characterizes moderns' exhausting concern with status. And it is doomed to failure, since in our postmodern era one's personal identity "is ultimately an ideational self-construct rather than a seat of action."[22] In other words, the identities we are chattering about today tend to be more rootless and directionless than those of the past. They do not instruct us in how we ought to live. In turn, this lack of social structure, as well as a dearth of tradition, means a lack of constraints, leaving people vulnerable. Chronic "ontological insecurity," Eva Illouz detects.[23] This is neither flourishing nor diversity, Archer holds, at least not in any appreciable sense of the terms.

Even my own academic discipline—sociology—now seems rooted and united in pre-commitments to resisting the historic encroachments of strong social obligations. Archer would agree. But all we have done is replaced the burden of conformity to traditions (like marriage, religious community, or ethnic heritage) with the imperative—at least as burdensome—of creating, sustaining, and expressing a "personal culture," as Archer calls it.

The solidarity people once felt toward each other as women or men, or as friends, or neighbors, or fellow Catholics, or as Irish—and that formed the subject matter of many sociological classics—is in rapid retreat in the United States. In its place is an emergent genre of self-help and self-identity, since kinship, marriage, neighborhood, faith, and common culture can no longer be counted upon, whether you live in Boston, Billings, or Baton Rouge. No wonder anomy and desperation are rising and suicide rates among men are inching upward.[24] We lack social solidarity.[25] There is no dignity—and no notable accomplishment, either—in being faithful to one's preferences or to one's own amorphous, shifting identity.[26] *New York Magazine's* Elizabeth Wurtzel understands this. In reflecting upon a series of relationships that failed and matrimony that never launched, she waxes wistfully on the social point of marriage:

> Convention serves a purpose: It gives life meaning, and without it, one is in a constant existential crisis. If you don't have the imposition of family to remind you of what is at stake, something else will.

Instead of resting, if even uncomfortably, in social structures (like marriage) not of our own making, moderns cannot seem to rest at all, for the self—the new primal unit of postmodern society—requires renewal and remaking and, most important, the dogged pursuit of acceptance and love. Hence, identity politics have emerged as pivotal narratives in the United States in a way they have not in much of the Western world.[27] It makes sense, since the collapse of traditional social structures has left a vacuum of legitimacy, and the social conflicts over new statuses is as yet far from settled.

The Fragile Future of the "Pure" Relationship

In step with fragile identities, confluent love relationships are evaluated more critically, and more often, than spouses have historically evaluated their own marriages. Even today marriage—though influenced by the pure relationship and modeling aspects of it—is still considered more robust than it. Elizabeth, the 25-year-old Minnesotan living near Denver who we first met in Chapter 3, speaks of marriage with trademark serious-ness and selectivity: "I'm only gonna do it once and I'm not gonna divorce so I'm gonna be damn sure before I do." So why does she want to marry in the first place?

> I don't know, I guess it's, I don't know. That's a good question. Like, kind of like to know that this person, like I belong with this person and they're mine and I'm theirs and we're like bonded together in that way, that's like, you know, that's really significant and that's, that's something that I'd like to experience.

This sounds different from Giddens's description of the pure relationship. It has high boundaries for entrance and exit. That may be why Elizabeth said she would need to be in a relationship for at least two years before she could know. So far, she has never been in a relationship for more than a year.

American young adults profess to desire a variety of fine-but-dissimilar things for their relationships. They want security and freedom, fidelity and good sex, predictability and fun. And most still wish to add children to a marriage. Is it all too much? Can relationships in an era of radical amounts of choice, fueled by persistent discontent fostered by social media and real-time marketing, possibly meet the high expectations people set for them? Or have we entered the era of the "suffocation model" of marriage without realizing it—one in which some couples hit the jackpot but far more find themselves frustrated and eyeing the exit?[28] And how long do the rela-tionships of unmarried persons like Elizabeth last? The pure relationship model is believed to shorten the duration of romantic and sexual relation-ships. Has it?

Yes. Demographer Michael Rosenfeld explored over 3,000 persons through three waves of data collection (2009–2012) in his *How Couples Meet and Stay Together* survey and notes a variety of interesting findings about modern couple longevity. First, most wash out early:

> Of the unmarried couples whose relationship duration was shorter than two months at Wave 1, 60 percent had broken up by the next yearly wave of the survey.

That's remarkable: three out of five new relationships were over in little more than a year. But getting past the initial hurdles reveals more longevity. Over 20 years, unmarried (heterosexual) couples witness a decline in their annual breakup rate from 60 percent down to about 10 percent. But those are unmarried couples, whose security remains more precarious than married couples, whose annual breakup rate begins at 10 percent but dwindles down to 1 percent as their marriage lengthens. These are dramatic differences. What else, besides time and getting married, predicts a breakup? A few obvious factors emerged, like money and relationship quality. Most other factors, however, did not matter, including education, presence of children, meeting their partner when they were teenagers, race (and being an interracial couple), and parental approval. It's all rather surprising.

One that did matter, however, was self-reporting a lesbian orientation. Even after controlling for a host of other measures, lesbian respondents were more likely to break up than straight or gay respondents.[29] If Giddens is right that same-sex relationships are in the vanguard of the pure or "confluent" relationship model, then perhaps we should expect this. He did.[30] Other studies, including both random and nonrandom samples, likewise reveal that two women are significantly more apt to break up than other pair combinations.[31] Are such differences a function of lack of access to marriage? While it is possible—and we will soon find out now that same-sex marriage is legal in the United States—there is reason to doubt. Sociologist Tim Biblarz and his co-author Judith Stacey (quoted earlier about male orgasms) noted this phenomenon in their review of research on lesbian couples who are parents, asserting that they face a "somewhat greater risk of splitting up," due in part, they argue, to "their high standards of equality."[32] A decade earlier the two, having discerned the same patterns, wrote that same-sex parents (which typically meant lesbian parents)

tend to embrace comparatively high standards of emotional intimacy and satisfaction.... The decision to pursue a socially ostra-
cized domain of intimacy implies an investment in the emotional
regime that Giddens (1992) terms "the pure relationship" and "confluent love." Such relationships confront the inherent instabilities
of modern or postmodern intimacy.[33]

In other words, being in the vanguard of egalitarianism and high standards for relational satisfaction is tough, especially under conditions of
homophobia. And so it takes its toll. And yet Biblarz and Stacey held that
the differential dissolution rate was not causally related to sexual orientation and would erode "were homophobia to disappear and legal marriage
be made available to lesbians and gay men."[34]

They are half right. The dissolution rates are not caused by sexual orientation. They're wrong, however, to think that lesbians have distinctively
higher standards of emotional and relational satisfaction. No—it's women
in general. Men and women tend to conduct their relationships differently
and exhibit different preferences in their relationships. When the partnership diverges from sexual complementarity—that is, a man and woman in
relationship—decidedly sex-typed preferences are consolidated, not mod-
erated. It means that same-sex couples are ironically more subject to deep-
rooted gendered relationship patterns and habits, their stated egalitarian
attitudes aside. There is nothing political about this; it is just the empirical
reality, one that sexual economics makes ready sense of. If the sexes were
a simple social construction, utterly malleable, we should see very little
distinction in how men and women pursue relationships, how they act
within them, how they act apart from them, what they prioritize about
them, and how they conclude them. But we see all of that.

Demand for Divorce in an Era of Confluent Love

You may have heard that divorce rates are dropping.[35] Is it true? It depends
on which segment of the population you are looking at. Keep in mind
that divorce rates are very sensitive to marriage rates. (When fewer people marry, fewer will get divorced.) Younger Americans are finding their
unions more stable today, due to greater "social selectivity," that is, their
reticence to marry in the first place. Caution no doubt nixes some subop-
timal matches.

While Elizabeth's high hopes for enduring marriage seem noble, her disdain for dependence upon a husband and her knee-jerk criteria for leaving nevertheless suggest the pure relationship mentality has profoundly altered how she understands marriage:

> I see this with women a lot too, um, that they rely so much on the guy for their happiness and their well-being and their financial support, you know, that they like either they wanna leave this person or they can't or this person leaves them and they're left with nothing. I don't wanna do that. . . . [*So is that like a fear of divorce, you mean, or separation?*] Yeah, I mean I'm still, like I said, I don't wanna divorce like my parents [did], but I don't know what's gonna happen. Maybe one day my husband will fall in love with somebody else. What am I gonna do? Or he cheats on me or he hits me. You know, then I'm gonna have to get out.

Amid a sea of parental divorce experiences, risk aversion and anticipation of marital regret has become a far more significant feature of the ecology of choice for young adults today.[36] That is, the specter of divorce haunts their relationship decision-making. In turn, Elizabeth demands an exit option, and in that she is not at all unusual. Economist Tim Reichert details how the split mating market I described in Chapter 2 now wars against settled relationships, forcing women to build a hedge of protection against their collapse before they even marry:

> Because of the lower relative bargaining power that women wield relative to men in the marriage market, at the margin more women will simply strike "bad deals" and will want a way out of the marital covenant ex post. In the era before contraception, roughly equal numbers of women and men in the marriage market meant that men and women roughly split the gains from trade that stem from marriage. By contrast, in the postcontraceptive era women give away many, indeed most, of these gains to men.[37]

What Reichert means is that in the exchange relationship, which is intended to produce more together than they could create separately, women sense they are now putting in more than their fair share, both before and during marriage. American parents are (ironically) tacitly encouraging this pattern, perceiving it as the safer path. They prefer a higher age at marriage for their children and diminished importance of marriage as a life goal.[38] They would like their daughters to marry eventually but they want their daughters to never need marriage. And while no one wishes to watch their child go through a divorce, most Americans want the option. Older Americans, meanwhile, are increasingly exercising that option, having become just as skeptical about their marital futures as their unmarried children. Divorces have doubled over the past 20 years among Americans over age 35.

It nevertheless remains true that women tend to like the idea of marriage more than men. Among Americans who are either cohabiting or in a non-marital (romantic) relationship, women remain more than twice as likely as men to say that they are more interested in marrying their current partner. Men, meanwhile, are more likely than women to report that their partner wants to get married more than they do. This is nothing new; no transformation here.

But the contemporary mating system now openly wars against the kind of marriage that economist and Nobel laureate Gary Becker evaluated in his landmark 1973 article entitled "A Theory of Marriage."[39] There Becker asserted not simply the existence of a marriage market but the distinctive "gains from trade" that men and women each made by exiting the market through marriage. Such a theory assumes men and women bring their differences—strengths and weaknesses, skills and needs—into marriage. But that is not how most marrying men and women tend to perceive the matter anymore. And it's the kind of marriage most parents now warn against. In a marriage market wherein men and women look more similar than ever, Reichert holds women's net gain from marriage declines:

> This lower level of "surplus," or marital benefit, for women means that there is precious little room in the course of their marriages for downside. In other words, when things go wrong relative to what was expected, women who expected to be somewhat better off because of the gains from marriage now find themselves in a position of being worse off within marriage than they would have been as single persons. This, in turn, leads quite naturally to an increase in the demand for divorce ex post.[40]

Others agree.[41] Reichert notes that women are the strongest supporters of access to divorce. Is he right? Absolutely. In the NFSS, among those respondents most at risk for splitting up—that is, the share that ranked themselves as being in the bottom 40 percent of relational happiness—women are 48 percent more likely than men to disagree (or strongly disagree) with the statement "Society would be better off if divorces were hard to get." Among over-30-year-olds in the *Relationships in America* survey, 48 percent of women (but only 32 percent of men) disagree with the statement "If a couple has children, they should stay married unless there is physical or emotional abuse" (and another 30 percent of women report being unsure about it). Mediocre marriages have long existed; women are simply in a better position to leave them than ever before. So are women more apt than men to actually leave?

Yes. But since many states now permit cooperative divorce, it has become unhelpful to ask divorced survey respondents whether they or their spouse filed for it. That had been, until recently, the go-to method for discerning sex distinctions in the pursuit of divorce. Figure 5.2 displays results from a question posed to just under 3,900 ever-divorced respondents (about their first, and for most their only, divorce) in the *Relationships in America* study. It asked respondents who wanted the marriage to end (more). Women are far more likely to want out of their marriages than men. Among divorcees, 55 percent of women said they wanted their marriages to end more than their spouses, while only 29 percent of men reported the same. (These figures come from combining the percentages displayed in the first two pairs of columns in Figure 5.2, where the respondent is talking about their own

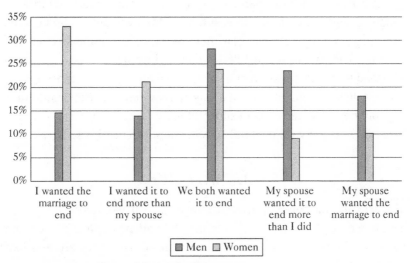

FIGURE 5.2 Perceptions of desire for divorce
Source: Relationships in America, ever-divorced respondents.

desire for a divorce.) The gap is not due to sex differences in perception, either: 42 percent of men report that their spouse wanted the marriage to end more than they did, but fewer than 20 percent of women said the same. Both men and women's perceptions converge here; they agree that the majority of the time the wife wanted a divorce more than the husband.

Demographer Michael Rosenfeld, assessing longitudinal data he collected in his "How Couples Meet and Stay Together" project, claims that his analyses point to marriage as "an anti-feminist trap," since he documents a gendered breakup effect only among marriages.[42] (It is not present among cohabitations.) He found that among marital breakups, 69 percent were sought after by women, compared with 56 percent of cohabiting breakups and 53 percent of non-marital, non-cohabiting relationships. I see it differently: first, 56 percent (vs. 44 percent) may not be statistically significant when you are assessing only 76 cases (of cohabitation dissolution), but if that were a presidential vote, it'd be a landslide. I think this is a statistical power problem.[43] But even if it was not, men and women approach cohabitation and marriage decisions differently, as I articulated in Chapter 2. (Rosenfeld's hypothesis does not presume so.) That is, women, who are generally more interested in marriage than men, tend to perceive in a tough mating market that cohabitation is a solid step toward marriage and often are the protagonists of moving in together.

Men, on the other hand, perceive a much stronger divide between cohabitation and marriage. Committing to marriage signals a greater willingness to sacrifice and invest in a particular woman, a decision more significant in a mating market that favors their interests. Men will be less prone to end a marriage because they were far more serious about nuptials than about moving in together. Meanwhile, divorce is incentivized among women, who tend to lose less than men from the legal dissolution of marriage than from a collapsed cohabitation. Marriage may or may not be an anti-feminist trap, but neither entering nor exiting different kinds of unions is commensurate and cannot yield the kind of evaluation Rosenfeld is seeking.

Are MGTOW?

Men actually enjoy their marriages more today than women do. Economists have noted this for years now.[44] And men tolerate poorer-quality marriages more readily (and for longer) than women do. And they are less likely to think about separating than women are, whether they are married or cohabiting. Table 5.1 documents this, as well as makes clear the far more precarious state of cohabitation in America.

But this pattern entails risk. Given (1) heightened economic egalitarianism, (2) women's diminished need for what men historically offered in marriage, (3) women's support of easier and more generous (to them) divorce laws, and (4) ease of access (for men) to premarital sex and pornography, some popular observers hold that men rather than women will ultimately—and imminently—opt out of marriage altogether. It even has an acronym: MGTOW (Men Going Their Own Way). To be sure, the MGTOW phenomenon is real, and there are plenty of men who feel marriage is a bad deal for them, and that cheap sex is a welcome shift from expensive promises that can, in the end, leave them alone and with a child-support tab to pay.

So are men done with commitment? So far as I can tell, no, or at least not yet. They may be slower to marry than before, but that doesn't mean that M are GTOW. Brian, a 27-year-old carpenter from Milwaukee, grieved the loss of his live-in girlfriend of eight years (who he nevertheless had cheated on several times when she was away in college). After she left him,

> I always just wanted her back. I was like, you know, like "Dude, I love you," you know, "I don't really understand this all. I mean, I'm happy with you. Like I don't need ... I'm not looking for the perfect woman or anything. I'm content."

Perhaps too content. They were going nowhere, by his admission. The child of divorce, Brian was skeptical of going too fast and wondered aloud to her about the real difference between marriage and cohabitation. So he didn't rush it:

> I mean we'd always talk about it (marriage), and I'd, I mean, I don't know, I don't feel like I need to be married at the age of, you know, before 23, 24, 25, and you know I would tell her like, just, I mean, "Give it a little more time, I mean, we don't ... this is nothing to really rush, (or) to worry about."

Hence, there were no markers of time or relationship maturation, save for her moving in, which wasn't even a decision. It just happened when she finished college. In a manner consistent with numerous interviewee accounts of dying relationships, the sex slowed, then the breakup occurred—slowly, over several weeks—but with enough post-breakup sex to confuse the two of them about what exactly was going on. Finally even Brian had had enough.

Table 5.1 **Percent of respondents who thought about separation, talked about it but didn't separate, and talked about it and did separate, by sex and relationship status**

Sex/Gender	Thought about leaving in the past year (%)	Talked about it but didn't separate (%)	Talked and did separate (%)
Married men	13.4	9.6	0.6
Cohabiting men	25.6	19.2	1.8
Married women	19.5	12.0	1.1
Cohabiting women	40.9	27.6	3.3

Source: Relationships in America, married and cohabiting respondents ages 25–60.

For both men and women, cohabitation doubles the likelihood of thinking and talking about separating, as well as actually doing so (see Table 5.1). To be sure, there is selectivity at work, meaning that more relationally confident people are more apt to get married in lieu of, or following, a spell of cohabitation. (And thoughts about separating—or conversations with one's spouse or partner about it—do not signify that a relationship is over.) My point is more basic: men like their significant relationships more than women and are less apt to think about leaving them.

The NFSS survey posed a series of questions about the significant romantic relationships in which many respondents are embedded. When I restrict the sample to only those who are currently married, more women than men disagreed with each of these statements, sometimes by a 3-to-1 margin:

· We have a good relationship.
· My relationship with my partner is very healthy.
· Our relationship is strong.
· My relationship with my partner makes me happy.
· I really feel like part of a team with my partner.
· Our relationship is pretty much perfect.

Married women were also more likely than married men to report "numerous times" that they thought their relationship "might be in trouble" and that they and their husband discussed ending their relationship. Gratefully, those were not the modal responses from either husband or wife, but the point remains—women are typically quicker than men to sense dissatisfaction in their significant relationships.

So why would anyone conclude that men are done with marriage and are going their own way? MGTOW rightly notes that the terms for marriage are becoming less and less attractive to men. When things are not working out well within marriage, the exit has become legally more appealing to her than to him: loss of access to one's children, half of all savings and retirement accounts, and a share of present earnings. Hence, marriage is more expensive. And in an era wherein more and more marital horror stories are accessible online (which is itself an echo chamber of self-selectivity), more men are thinking twice about it and concluding that cohabitation or the bachelor life may better represents their interests than marriage.

And yet M are not GTOW. Why not? Because the Becker model of marriage has not disappeared in lived reality. The trade-offs of marriage still work for them, if less optimally than before. This is when it pays to keep in mind that marriage is a massive social structure spanning ages, eras, cultures, and nations. It is inextricably linked to the exchange model. It may be in the throes of deinstitutionalization in the West, and it may not represent men's interests so well anymore, but this hardly means that people in 2050 or 2100 will not marry. Marriage may well shrink significantly—I think it will—but it will not disappear. It is not that malleable.

Putting the Brakes on Marriage

It is not just in demand for divorce that the influence of confluent love is felt. It is also recognizable in the brakes applied to marriage like never before. One in every three persons now in their early twenties will never marry, claims one noted demographer.[45] It's a startling statistic. Until recently the share of women who never married had fluctuated between 5 and 10 percent since data recording began with women born in 1825. Among those that do marry, median age at marriage continues to rise, to the current 27 for women and 29 for men. (Canada and much of Europe exhibit older median ages.) While neither 27 nor 29 are strikingly high, they should be juxtaposed with Figure 5.1, which indicates the concurrent flight from marriage altogether, age aside.

The collective valuing of a higher age at first marriage has become pronounced, itself reflecting a shift from being marriage "naturalists" (more characteristic of marrying in the early twenties) to marriage "planners" (late twenties to mid-thirties) and from the idea of marriage as a foundational signal of adulthood to that of marriage as an achievement, a status symbol of a young adulthood lived shrewdly and wisely.[46] The Becker model of marriage is fading. The marriages Americans are fashioning today seldom emphasize the idea of marriage as a functional form, enabling two people to accomplish things they otherwise could not alone. Now we can accomplish a great deal—certainly enough—on our own.[47] Hence, marriage in America has shifted away from being a populist institution—a social phenomenon in which most adults participated and benefited—to becoming an elite, individualist, voluntary, consumption-oriented arrangement.

The "pure" relationship system underwrites this shift, providing ample time in Americans' twenties and early thirties to sexually experiment, love, leave, and date around before "getting serious" about marriage. Accounts like that of Sarah (in Chapter 1), who abstained from sex through her teen years but exhibited a series of partners in her twenties, are consonant with this mentality and norm. The pattern is also a response to the painful experience of parental divorces and the resulting sincere desire for young adults to avoid marital breakdown.

Melinda is a 32-year-old editor for a publisher in Austin and is a textbook case of anxiety about marriage and its seeming finality. The men in her past were more interested in her than she was in them:

> I have a problem committing. Um, yeah it's frightening. I don't, you know, um, my parents are divorced. They fought a lot, you know . . . during the times when they had to have contact which was you know, all the time until I turned 18 and left . . . I'm not worried about it, I know that I won't, (but) I'm afraid that I could let this happen to me.

Declining marriage rates and a rising median age at first marriage do not necessarily tell us that women are newly uninterested in marriage, but perhaps that they—together with many men—simply prefer to marry later. It is an empirical question, and an important one at that: Are women still interested in marrying? Figure 5.3 displays a fitted curve outlining the share of unmarried women (by age) in the *Relationships in America* data who said yes to a very basic question posed to them: "Would you prefer to be married?"[48] It is a different question than one like "Would you like to get married someday?" It is more specific, and responses to it are

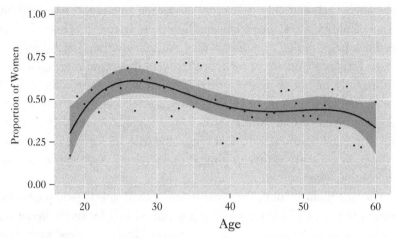

FIGURE 5.3 Unmarried women who want to be married, by age
Source: Relationships in America.

certainly more sensitive to the particular relationship context of those who are answering the question. So what does Figure 5.3 tell us? Several things stand out:

1. Preference for being married rarely eclipses 60 percent.
2. Peak interest coincides with median age at first marriage (ages 26–28).
3. Interest in marriage is nearly as high among 50- to 60-year-olds as among 18- to 23-year-olds.
4. While odds of marrying are believed to decline with age, interest in it never dips sharply.

There are other interesting items of note: 55 percent of currently cohabiting women said they preferred to be married, compared with 47 percent of never-married women who were not cohabiting. (That is less of a difference than I anticipated.) Church attendance is largely unrelated to wanting to be married (among those who are not), but self-rated importance of religion is a good predictor of it—ranging from 38 percent among the least religious women to 57 percent among the most. Yet even many very religious women say they prefer their (current) unmarried status, in contrast with the prevailing conventional wisdom about them.

Being on public assistance—in this case, receiving only one form of it—is associated with desiring marriage (56 percent of women), but that figure declines in a linear manner with each additional report of public assistance, such that only 36 percent of women who report receiving four forms of public assistance wish that they were married. (The more they need the help, the less confident they are that marriage will deliver it.) Heavy Facebook and social media users wish they were married at rates significantly higher than non-users. Women who report being sexually dissatisfied are much more likely (58 to 43 percent, respectively) to wish they were married than women who were sexually content.[49] The same is true with masturbation. Indeed, it seems the wish for a settled sexual partner is behind a share of this longing. It makes sense. And yet the marriage rate continues to tumble.

The vast majority of our (mostly heterosexual) interviewee pool—who were in the crest of Figure 5.3 by age—still wished to marry. What was stopping those who were already in relationships? The three most common scenarios among them could be characterized as follows:

1. They are cohabiting, but their union is not stable and trusting enough yet to bet on it.
2. They are financially insecure, especially if his employment trajectory was iffy.
3. They have few successful exemplars or no clear narrative about marriage to follow.

On average, most interviewees exhibited at least two—and some all three— of these scenarios concurrently. Only 41 of the 100 interviewees' parents were still together, leaving many no obvious or optimal immediate exemplar to help them navigate how to stay married and surmount difficulties. Like Kathryn Edin and Maria Kefalas's interviews in *Promises I Can Keep*, many interviewees with whom we spoke wanted to marry, liked the idea of it, were not yet ready, often were not sure when they would be ready, and inadvertently relayed a variety of reasons for us to believe that—in spite of their stated interests—they would not actually marry the person they are currently (living) with. Why? Because marriage remains a big deal—most seem to get that—and their situations seemed too risky to them.

Scholars talk plenty today about the concept of resilience, that is, faring better than expected given the high odds against success. But it is an idea commonly applied to individuals, not relationships. I could not help but pore over the transcripts of our 100 interviews and come to the conclusion that the men and women we listened to displayed plenty of admirable, resilient traits. But their unions? Not so much.

I first mentioned Jennifer in Chapter 3, where she detailed the dating scene in and around Bristol. Following a variety of retail sales positions and a stint as a coffee shop barista, she had been hired recently by Verizon to work as a sales representative in a local retail outlet, making around $12 an hour. A high school graduate, she would like to go to college someday but isn't sure she has what it takes. In love as in work, she has met with only modest success. She's had 10 sexual partners in her lifetime, but wishes there were fewer. Like many women following a popular cultural script, Jennifer did not want that number to be in double digits. She had been in a relationship with four of them; the rest were casual or brief, or both. At age 19, Jennifer began a four-year relationship with Nick. Halfway through it, and without warning or signals, Nick became physically abusive, including holding her head underwater. At one point she was trying to escape him, and a neighbor saw him chase her and drag her; he threatened Nick with a gun (and called the police). The end result was a temporary restraining order. The abuse, she related, occurred when he drank too much. Nick's addiction to pain pills, so common in that region of Tennessee and in the accounts of our interviewees there, didn't seem as pertinent to her. For others, it mattered. In a twist on the exchange relationship, Jennifer relayed how area men use opioids in order to ease access to sex:

> It's called the Appalachian mating call. . . . It's so true that it's a mating call, you know, the sound of pills in the bottle. . . . Basically giving girls things, I mean they still know what's going on, but they know it too. It's like a two-way thing, I guess, like giving girls drugs in exchange for sex, but not in the way that you're whoring, [since] it's unspoken.

Nevertheless, they continued dating and even became engaged. She broke it off after three months. She didn't breathe a word of the violence to her friends or her parents (who split when she was three). The reach of old flames—even troubled ones—can be long, however. When asked if she would ever like to reconnect sexually with any previous partner, if only for a night, Jennifer said yes. With whom? Just one—Nick, "if it was just for a night."

For the past year, Jennifer has been dating someone different, a man named Trevor. Although he pressed for sex, she held out—by her account—for two months, after which they had sex and a conversation in which they clarified they were, in fact, in a relationship. The two moved in together (out of convenience) after six months. Nevertheless, Jennifer has grown unhappy in the relationship and plans to end it soon. But as with many relationship sagas, this one is easy neither to continue nor to conclude. Jennifer lapsed in taking her birth control and got pregnant four months before we interviewed her. She didn't want to have a baby with Trevor, so she got an abortion. Jennifer reported no regrets about the decision, but told us she struggled a great deal emotionally when it happened. Since then her libido has plunged; she and Trevor have only had sex a few times in the past three months. If the pregnancy had occurred with someone else, someone "who is gonna take action and who's gonna do something," then she would not have gone through with the abortion. Trevor, however, is financially irresponsible, younger than Jennifer, is not seeking a better-paying job—he's a short-order cook at a restaurant—and does not do his fair share at home. He doesn't even split the rent equally. Marriage was out of the question.

Every Woman for Herself: The Collapse of the Cartel and the Rise of Career Trade-Offs

One obvious conclusion to be drawn from the explosion in women's labor force participation (and hence their rising standards for the marriage-ability of men) that followed upon the uptake of artificial contraception and the concomitant drop in the price of sex is the collapse of the "cartel" of women. That is, the patterned behavior by which unmarried women would police—sometimes subtly, other times bluntly—each other's publicly discernible sexual behavior for the purpose of fostering an elevated price of sex within the community. It simply no longer made sense to artificially withhold sex from men in an era of effective contraception, since pregnancy was no longer a predictable outcome and the threat of STIs too private and often manageable or ameliorable with antibiotics. I say "artificially" because the restriction was seldom because women didn't like sex and wished to hold out until they simply must agree to it. Women have appreciated sex for a very long time. (That ought to go without saying.) But a woman's precocious behavior threatened her peers' ability to command (and receive) a high price for sex—relationship commitment in the form of engagement or marriage, together with its accompanying resources. That remains the case today, though few women recognize it and fewer still attempt to proscribe their peers' sexual choices. It is a social conundrum. That is, proscriptions do not work unless deviance is socially—not just personally—sanctioned. But I cannot see it happening. Instead, they seldom even recognize the quandary they are in or how they unwittingly contribute to it.

A former graduate student of mine relayed a conversation she had with a friend of hers, a woman 31 years of age, who was in a serious (and sexual) relationship with a man several years her senior—both well above the mean age at first marriage. My student's friend said she was going to have a conversation with him about engagement, in the hopes that it would move things along toward that goal. "Wish me luck," she texted my student. A day later, another text came from her discouraged friend. It read: "Marriage is not around the corner." I told my student that her friend ought to consider a sex strike (not unlike the plot of Spike Lee's 2015 film *Chi-Raq*). That won't happen, she said. No wonder women have so little authority to make their relationships move forward in the manner in which they prefer. The sex may be good. It may be great. But it does not cost enough. We know where this relationship will most likely go: nowhere fast. Why? Because her boyfriend said so, and she has invested too much time to risk leaving a man she loves in order to start over. So long as she stays, he controls the pace.

Success in the marketplace has cost women in relationships. It has not harmed all women, of course—that is never the case—but enough of them for the new challenges to be widely discernible. Some object to this claim, citing statistics that marriage is still reliably experienced by college-educated women. It is true, at least for now, unless you're African American. (I could make other qualifications as well.) There are enough success stories to (erroneously) convince most women that any problems they experience here must be their own fault.[50] But the profound sex-ratio imbalance in college graduates spells the coming doom of educational homogamy, or the common practice of women marrying men who are at least as educated and well-compensated as they are.[51] If educational homogamy is a key measure of marriageability—I am not convinced it is—then the institution is in even more dire straits.

Women have begun responding to these challenges in the way a sexual economics approach would expect them to. In a series of experiments, social psychologists conveyed impressions of local sex-ratio disparities (via photographs and newspaper articles) to different sets of undergraduate women, seeking to assess the effects of "sex ratio manipulation" on the participants' reported relative desire for a satisfying career versus a happy and well-adjusted family life.[52] Perceptions of scarcity of men in the local area led women to believe it would be difficult to attract a mate, led a different research pool to prioritize starting a career over starting a family, and prompted still another set to prefer a lucrative career to family—but especially if women perceived themselves as less desirable (that is, less attractive) to men. Three different studies, three identical results, each issuing in the same, predictable response to emerging sex-ratio challenges confronting women today.

Education and careers are good things. And they are hedges against relationship failure (or failure to launch). Young women understand it, as do their parents. So marriage waits. But many years spent on the mating market can yield the unintended consequence of extending market mentalities—notions like cost-benefit estimates, risk assessments, and concern about settling—into the marriage itself, if only by force of repetition or habit. It is not that marriages cannot survive market mentalities; they can. But they are not optimally designed for it, since marriage is not an instrumental good, a means to meet some individual preference or end. Instead, marriage optimally leads us to "mint our own non-convertible 'currencies' of love, caring, and concern," something "entirely alien to the market exchange" model.[53] Agreed. Perhaps this is why sociologists of the family continue to note the existence of a "sweet spot" for age-at-marriage that rests between the ages of 23 and 27, a social age range characterized neither by too little maturity nor too much long-term independence.[54]

So it is that the market-savvy (or weary), who experience extended exposure to the bluntest realities of the mating market, can find their confidence in men, women, and marriage waning. That was the case for Debra, a 30-year-old nurse and Austin transplant from California who, during an exchange with me about her experiences with men in the two years she had lived in Austin, declared "the men here (in Austin) are all douchebags." She elected not to expand in greater detail, other than to remark that the men were skilled at feigning interest in order to more readily access sex. It was not an unusual experience: "I have given them numerous opportunities (to prove otherwise)." Like many other women, the road to marriage was more circuitous than she expected, leaving her wondering whether it would ever happen, and—increasingly—whether she should even continue to hope for it. Cheap sex has a way of doing that.

Critics retort that most who wish to marry still do. Yes, but the pathway to marriage is lengthening, and the journey there increasingly circuitous. And more than ever no longer arrive at a destination they were aiming for.[55] Other patterns accompany this: more living alone, more dual-earner families (and with that, higher cost of living in urban cores and greater relative poverty among those living by themselves), more infertility concerns, more solitary sex. All of these patterns are not, I hold, because the average woman prefers it to be this way. Even the average man is not a fan of many of these developments. They need not be because that is how trade-offs work: a desire is sought and acquired, but comes seeded with unintended consequences. In the end, the sky is not falling. But it is time we acknowledged the reality of cheap sex and its consequences, instead of recasting all of it in only positive light.

Was Gary Becker Wrong?

So was Gary Becker wrong on marriage, or is he just hopelessly behind the times if taken seriously today? Neither. On the contrary, he was prescient. Becker's model, rooted in the concept of social and sexual exchange described earlier, predicts—accurately—that the benefits of getting married decline as women's earning power rises. For a key decade (1973–1983) young women's wages climbed steadily while men's fell, never to recover. As a result, marriage rates dropped, as you should expect.

And yet many scholars act as if contraceptive technology, a desired fait accompli, played only a bit part in the transformation of family behavior and attitudes that we are witnessing, rather than the starring role that it actually occupied. Ruggles, quoted earlier, asserts that "the decline of young men's wages since 1975 is the main reason for the retreat from marriage in that period," but then treats that decline as if it were an exogenous, uncaused force.[56] The most he admits in his otherwise excellent article on marital shifts is that, with regard to young men's declining wages, "One factor was doubtless the mass entry of married women into the labor force."[57]

Give credit where credit is due—the world would be a rather different place without artificial hormonal contraception.[58] It was a quiet but monumental grand bargain that has resulted in some unintended fallout in the domain of marriage and relationship formation and continuity. Previous cohorts of men who did not make ample wages were simply not considered marriageable and hence were unable to access sex with the regularity they craved. They worked for it, and some became marriageable. The reality for men today is quite different. This matters in ways that sociologists unfortunately dismiss and economists have difficulty mapping.

Marriage Prep in an Era of Confluent Love

Like Jennifer and Debra, nearly all of the women—and a solid majority of the men—with whom we spoke in person want to marry. But many of them do not know how to make it happen. Marriage as it has been conventionally understood—faithful, closed (to others), enduring, kids, the whole package deal—is a desired state into which very many young Americans hope someday to naturally and passively find themselves. They do not think of it as a pathway requiring their present-time discipline, discernment, sacrifice, self-control, and prudent judgment, together with ample amounts of the same from their peers. Young Americans are not practicing to be married, but rather hoping to someday wake up in it. I realize that the in-person interviews we conducted are not a random sample of young Americans, but this theme recurred so consistently that it demands sustained attention. An example will help.

Nina is a 25-year-old transplant from South Florida to Denver, Jewish by birth but presently "more spiritual than religious," and is emblematic of many of her peers' quests for settled love. She is petite in stature, attractive, and faring well professionally in her position with an insurance company. But Nina is struggling emotionally. She weaned herself off Zoloft, an antidepressant, a couple years ago after a decade on it. But then she lost her mother late last year. (She had a good relationship with her, which typically eases the experience of loss.) Her father died when she was 5. She is young for being an adult orphan. But it is obvious that the pain in Nina's life ranges well beyond the death of her parents and stands in contrast to her educational and professional successes.[59]

Nina historically sequestered particular men as good friends—confidantes—with whom sex would be "too risky," that is, it could screw up a good relationship. Other men were for sex. That was the pattern she had witnessed in herself and in other women, a pattern that led her to develop a "cynicism for dating." When we asked her if she ever felt guilty about having sex—a question which yielded a wide variety of responses across the interviewee pool—she said yes. When asked to describe an instance, she didn't mince words:

> Um, when I knew that I wouldn't have [had sex] if I had used my better judgment, you know, or followed my intuition knowing that this probably wasn't a good idea, or um, whenever I've gotten involved with somebody too quickly and I regretted it. Um, particularly like

if I ended up hurt afterwards. [*How often would that happen, that you would end up hurt afterwards?*] I think my cynicism for dating has a lot to do with that. Um, I think that even though I know the guy's a loser and he sucks, I stopped realizing that I need to care too. . . . [*How would you say your cynicism for dating developed?*] Um, just one shitty thing after another. One bad guy after another. Like I said, I think particularly after my last relationship in college, the one where I had the abortion and he cheated on me and I think that just totally skewed my perspective on guys and what's the point of dating, you know? I think even my guy friends that are in relationships lie to their girlfriends and I think that makes me sick. It turns my stomach. I don't wanna be with anybody who lies or cheats or manipulates, or an abusive relationship.

And yet Nina had experienced all of that. She is not old, 25, and has not given up on love or marriage or children, but confessed "I was raised by a single parent and I don't want my kids to have to go through that." When will marriage happen for her? "When I was a kid I used to say 27, and now, now that I'm 25 I'm thinking maybe 32 (laughs)." She believes that a marriage ought to develop differently—as friendships first—than most of the relationships she has been in. She feels very protective about David, a man from Florida whom she once dated and with whom she remains in contact.

He's the only guy I've ever dated that I would consider marrying. Um, he's getting his masters in neuroscience now, and um . . . [*And what happened to that?*] Oh, we're still really good friends, but he lives in Florida and I live here. We're gonna see each other in six weeks and . . . [*Is that a deal breaker, long distance?*] No, he had already gone to medical school in Georgia and he had started dating some other girl after we started dating because he thought that I was still talking to my ex-boyfriend or something like that. And this was in college, and we haven't seen each other for three years, but um, we're gonna get together in six weeks. [*Do you think you'll have sex?*] My goal is not to. [*Okay.*] Because I've already told him, like I joke around with him, I'm like "Oh, don't worry, we're gonna get married one day, you'll see," and I, uh, and I told him, I was like, 'cuz he tells me about all, because now he's back at where we went for undergrad, but he's getting his masters there now, and um, and

I told him, I was like, "You can date all these dumb little girls, just tell 'em you've got a wife in mind," you know (chuckles) and just kind of joking with him. [*But you're being serious?*] I'm dead serious. [*Would you . . .*] I would marry him, I would raise his kids, raise a family.

Nina thinks it could work with David. It's ideal, in fact. It's how she imagines marriage happening: "Yeah, I think I'd wanna be best friends first, and fall in love with my best friend." It would be for keeps, too:

I don't really believe in divorce. I feel that the person that you married, and I don't think anybody ever goes into marriage planning on divorcing them, but I still, I think that if I can marry you then we can, we can work anything out. Because you're supposed to be that one that's above the rest. You're the one that I married, not the one I dated.

It's hard not to admire Nina's ideals, ambitions, and wishes. But her "I hope not" response to our question about whether she'd have sex with David when they see each other in a few weeks reminded me of Sarah's admission about men and first-date sex in Chapter 1. Both Sarah and Nina "waste" sex on men they willingly identify as poor quality:

These days we give in too easily and I think that, you know, oh, because he's nice and he's cute and he's sweet and I really wanna be with him. We think that sex might kind of lure them into being more attracted, or, I don't know, you know? And it just doesn't work out. [*Um, what does it usually take then for a guy to end up getting sex with some girl?*] I don't know. [*Does he . . .*] I think for me it's just different, though. Like for me I'd rather, I think the sexual chemistry is the most important and if I really want to I will.

What Nina and Sarah (and numerous others) do not realize, however, is that even wasted sex is priced—cheaply—and contributes to the socially discernible cost of sex in the surrounding mating market. It matters. Kristin, a 29-year-old from Austin, betrays a naivety about this when we asked her whether men should work to access sex, or not: "Yes. Sometimes. Not always. I mean, I don't think it should necessarily be given out by women, but I do think it's okay if a woman does just give it out. Just not all the time." Nina justifiably wishes to be treated better, to not be cheated on, to be sacrificed for, to be wooed, but she and so many women are in the unenviable position of simply *hoping* that some man will someday do those things for them, even while they are unwittingly teaching the men in their lives that such things are noble and nice but just not required in order to be with them. It reminds me of how Cheryl (from Chapter 3) struggled "to find quality people that you want to be with," but perceived no connection between this and her habit of having sex promptly with men if she didn't particularly like them, since "it was just sex." She wishes to be a free rider—in this case, to find a good man—without contributing to the kinds of normative relationship behavior that make men better. It won't work. It can't work. Good husband material doesn't occur naturally, but is instead the product (in part) of socialization, development, and social control. The same is true of the "douchebags" Debra keeps meeting. They too are made, not born. In the domain of sex and relationships men will act as nobly as women collectively demand.

This is an aggravating statement for women to read, no doubt. They do not want to be responsible for "raising" men. But it is realistic. To be sure, I could put on an altogether different set of lenses through which to understand Nina's life and relationship choices. I could truthfully assert that she is exhibiting control over her body, pursuing consensual pleasures when and with whom she pleases. I could admit that she is old enough to own her own troubles and fashion new ways of dealing with men so that they are not able to hurt her. I could counsel her to be patient about marriage—that the right man may be just around the corner. And that she doesn't even need marriage to enjoy a successful life. It would all be the truth, of a sort. But it would be a short-sighted truth, one that mistakenly equates elective decision-making about sexual and reproductive health with signals of deep human flourishing. Nina's choices contribute to an obvious share of her suffering. She does not know how to get what she wants. When she looks around her, she knows something is wrong while perceiving normative (but problematic) behavior patterns in others and in herself. She is one of the countless victims of cheap sex and the transition toward the pure relationship system, which delivers orgasms with a side of loneliness. It's the "confluent love plate" at the Pure Relationship Diner. Even Giddens recognizes that more loneliness is part of the deal.

What if Non-Monogamy Became the Norm?

Perhaps loneliness can be solved by spreading love around. Monogamy's critics seem to be growing in number and visibility, lining up to take their turn punching the idea of committing to one person for life, or even for a while. Maybe we all just have to get used to a more individualistic world in which adults form relationships for a season. Perhaps this is the shrewdest way to make the best of a difficult situation.[60] After all, assuming stability or monogamy is no longer central to the Western way of relationships, right? Giddens alerted us:

> Unlike romantic love, confluent love is not necessarily monogamous, in the sense of sexual exclusiveness. What holds the pure relationship together is the acceptance on the part of each partner, "until further notice," that each gains sufficient benefit from the relation to make its continuance worthwhile. Sexual exclusiveness here has a role in the relationship to the degree to which the partners mutually deem it desirable or essential.[61]

Non-monogamy—the practice of supplementing a primary sexual partner with one or more others—has even became hip in some corners of the United States, and I'm not talking about rural Utah.[62] Our interviewees brought up the subject of monogamy with a good deal of regularity in our interviews: 27 percent of them used the word, even though it was not a term or theme that we directly inquired about. Something is afoot.

Note the terminology. Polyamory is different than polygamy. Polygamy is still off limits, but it is so not because of the poly part but because marriage is out of vogue in places where polyamory has emerged as a minority practice. For polyamorists to think of marrying more than one person is laughable—it would esteem marriage far too much. The distinction between the two, however, may be splitting hairs: NYU sociologist Dalton Conley labels Americans' sexual behavior patterns "dynamic polygamy."[63] It doesn't look like "old school" polygamy, with multiple marriage partners at once. But multiple it is. Divorce, he reminds us, does not actually sever a relationship. It just concludes the marriage part of it. Financial and other obligations can long linger. And when children are involved, you remain in contact—even if on acerbic terms—with your ex for years. And remarriage compounds it. Conley thinks we tend to overlook all this. He's right.

Instead, contemporary polyamory or non-monogamy is popularly presumed to refer to the negotiated practice of consensual sex outside of a primary relationship. That is, when both partners in a relationship have agreed to allow one or the other or both to experience sexual activity—and possibly form ongoing sexual relationships—apart from their primary union. This new version includes women forming such relationships, too. (The old school version did not.) The lack of commitment that characterizes modern cohabitation, together with the sexual malleability outlined in Chapter 2, has enabled the emergence of polyamory. Monogamy, it is increasingly held, is unnatural. But, of course, people "need" multiple partners like they need four houses or six automobiles. These are wants, not needs. And when seemingly reasonable people argue that in previous eras people didn't live so long, such that the death of a spouse functioned as a way for humans to fulfill their "need for sexual variety" it pays to be skeptical.[64] (Since when did golden anniversaries become something to pity rather than something to celebrate?)

No, the new turn away from monogamy was made possible not because we figured out that we were still animals but because we figured out how to effectively prevent pregnancies or end them prematurely, freeing us up to pursue the art of sexuality—the body as a tool of consumption rather than production. Giddens called it.

So what if non-monogamy became more popular? Private choices wouldn't harm anyone else's way of life, right? Wrong. As poly becomes more popular, marriage retreats even quicker. Sociologists Yoosik Youm and Anthony Paik helpfully demonstrate what non-monogamy does to the marriage rate even when the sex ratio remains stable.[65] Figure 5.4, reproduced from their analysis of the implications of sex market patterns for family formation, details how expectations of monogamous sex are apt to issue in more marrying than when polyamorous sex is available. They are identical sex ratios—both favor men but only one hews to monogamy. And because of that we should expect men to partner differently. If monogamy

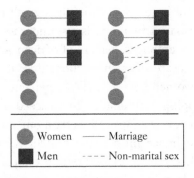

FIGURE 5.4 The effect of non-monogamous sex on the marriage rate, with sex ratio constant

Source: Youm and Paik 2004: 174.

is socially reinforced, as in the model on the left, all three men will marry and two women will go un-partnered. If non-monogamy is permitted, as in the model on the right, only two of the men would marry and one of those will engage a second partner. More of the women in the second scenario will be partnered but fewer will be married. Youm and Paik conclude that non-monogamy directly decreases the marriage rate. It fits the contemporary American mating market experience well.

We asked survey respondents whether they had ever overlapped sexual relationships, meaning they were still in a sexual relationship with one person while having begun a sexual relationship with another person. To be sure, respondents might not think of these relationships as non-monogamous or polyamorous. They may well have considered themselves as "cheating" on someone, or in the process of ending one relationship and beginning another. That is fine—what interests me is less their description of it than how many have experienced it. Analyses of the data reveal that two-thirds of American adults ages 18–60 said they had never been in a sexual relationship that overlapped with another one. An additional 20 percent said they had, but that the overlap was brief—less than a month. Just under 10 percent said they had been in a longer overlapping situation (over one month).[66] If we were searching for genuine polyamory, I think it would be wise to use the more-than-a-month measure rather than likely misrepresent those 20 percent of respondents whose relationships overlapped for a brief period.

Although race/ethnicity is not a central theme in this book, the sex-ratio imbalance in African American communities should lead us to hypothesize that African American men are more likely to report longer term overlapping sexual partnerships, due to their optimal ability to navigate their local sexual economies as they please (given the presence of more women than men). Is that the case? Yes. While the overall experience of longer term overlapping sexual partnerships is just under 10 percent of American adults, it was the case among 17 percent of African Americans. And since women may be unaware of such relationships, it pays to distinguish between men and women here as well: 22 percent of African American men report overlapping partnerships that exceed a month in duration (while 28 percent report overlaps of less than one month). Moreover, the most educated (and hence most marriageable) African American men were also the most likely to report long-term overlaps, at 31 percent among those with post-graduate education, compared with 18 percent of high-school dropouts, a phenomenon Youm and Paik noted as well in their study of Chicago neighborhoods.

Yes, monogamy is still preferred, but it's more preferred by older than younger Americans, and by the religious more than the irreligious. But most of all it's more preferred by women than men; that is, it's more preferred by those in a weaker position in the mating market.[67] Women are less apt to get what they want in that market, so of course it is reasonable to perceive that expectations of monogamy, too, have receded some as well.

Perhaps, then, Americans are on a trajectory to get over their hang-ups about poly and instead display what some call "compersion," or appreciating the sexual pleasure that a spouse (or primary partner) receives when with someone else. *Huffington Post* writer "Gracie X," who advocates for the socialization of compersion, realizes the challenge it represents:

> Feeling all warm and gooey because your spouse had a great time banging someone else is not something we're socialized to feel. We can be thrilled for our partner if they get a raise or promotion or receive some kind of unexpected windfall, but why can't we be happy for our partners who find joy in bed with someone else?[68]

Compersion, however, faces long odds. Antagonism toward marital infidelity remains very high in the population—72 percent versus 7.5 percent (who think it is permissible), but the share of respondents who are not sure is notable, at 17.5 percent.[69] Social change concerning the permissibility of polyamorous (and extramarital) relationships will begin with them, no doubt.

The authors of *Sex at Dawn* welcome the idea, suggesting that trying to rise "above our nature" is problematic. It is an "exhausting endeavor," they caution, "often resulting in spectacular collapse." But to believe that loosening sexual standards, like monogamy, means that everyone will be free to do as they please is flat wrong, as I just detailed. Groups and communities do not work like that. There will always be rules—with resulting winners and losers—in any sexual system.

A monogamous system, however, allows for more winners. That is, more men and women are in successful relationships. How so? A team featuring an economist, an anthropologist, and an environmental scientist set out to solve what they called the "puzzle" of monogamous marriage. That is, why monogamous arrangements comprise a historical minority of the globe's societies, but the vast majority of the more successful and flourishing ones. Monogamous marriage, they detail, fosters savings and economic output, and reduces competition among men for women, which functions to reduce the pool of low-status, risk-oriented, unmarried men. (It reduces competition not through sex-ratio manipulation but through normative expectations of one partner.) And that, in turn, lowers multiple types of crime, abuse, household conflict, and fosters greater paternal investment in both their work and in their children, who are more apt to enjoy their attention and exhibit notably lower stress levels than in households display-ing all manner of outsiders.[70] Speaking of outsiders, a review of data from 69 polygamous societies from around the world failed to reveal a single case where the relationships between a man's partners or wives could be described as consistently harmonious. Sexual-economics expert Marina Adshade jokes that "if I had to live in a household where my husband had more than one wife, there would have to be alcohol involved."[71]

Monogamy also means confidence in the biological link between mother, father, and child, a combination long known to reduce the threat of abuse, violence, and homicide in the household.[72] And monogamy means greater equality—more men and women have the opportunity to meet, marry, save, and invest for the long term, instead of competing (and spending resources, etc.) for others' available attention. This is why monogamous marriage systems preceded the emergence of democratic institutions in Europe, and the rise of notions like human rights and equality between the sexes. This "package of norms and institutions that constitute modern monogamous marriage systems spread across Europe, and then the globe," precisely because it competed well.[73] Monogamy, after all, is disciplined—by definition. No other form of organizing rela-tionships between the sexes does a better job of fostering a fair exchange between the distinctive interests of men and women. Societies that disre-gard monogamous norms undermine their own long-term interests.

So men win. Women win. Children win. Entire societies benefit. Sounds good. What's not to like? Not so fast, modern polyamorist skep-tics say. That is not the kind of relationship system we're talking about, they claim. We are not pushing polygamy, but rather supporting "open" relationships, not closed ones between one man and several women. And women are free to be poly, too. It's "ethical" polyamory, after all.

It is true—modern polyamory does not look or feel like old-school polygamy. Poly men and women typically do not share spouses and chil-dren and homes, but rather just sex and dinner dates. It sounds simple. But the reality of it gets complicated—the specter of envy is never far away, and the "over-sharing" of information and renegotiations that are coun-seled in order to avoid drama can unwittingly stoke it instead.[74]

At bottom, polyamory means a great deal of trust is constantly required of people who openly resist the idea of fidelity. It is pretty ironic, and it's also why such relationships almost never last. Unlike with marriage, most of which involve childbearing and rearing, there is little incentive to continue polyamorous relationships. Moreover, a polyamorous life is only conceivable when no one actually conceives. Paternity concerns and jealousy, especially among primary partners, would abound. Working hard at one relationship—not many—historically paves the way for a father's investment in his children. Few popular accounts of polyamory ever discuss what happens when poly meets fertility. It is there that non-monogamy contributes to no shortage of anxiety, misery, and agonizing decisions—especially for women.

A child is not the only thing polyamory can leave one with. Overlapping partners is the single biggest factor accelerating the spread of sexually transmitted infections in a network of partners. In sub-Saharan Africa, concern about "multiple partners" is the focus of a major public health effort.[75] But among trend-setters in the United States, it's part of the attraction. Unsurprisingly, white Americans in the *Relationships in America* survey who have had at least two STIs are 52 percent more likely than those who've never had an STI to agree with the statement "It is OK for three or more consenting adults to live together in a sexual/romantic relationship."

Is Non-Monogamy a Free Rider Problem?

Is it possible that the West is living off the social capital accrued by generations of monogamy—albeit imperfectly lived out—only to watch those it has benefited turn on it, oblivious to the social hazards that will accompany undermining a monogamous system? A poly society will require a more vigilant public health system, a more active security state to protect its citizens—especially women—and a more aggressive social welfare system, since invested fathers will continue to recede. Misogyny is embedded in polyamory, too, however "ethical" it claims to be. That's because sexual objectification—the treatment of persons as objects—is unavoidable in a non-monogamous system, especially a modern one characterized less by plural marriage than by the serial circulation of multiple, overlapping sex partners. A non-monogamous future, were it to occur—and I have my doubts that it will—would decidedly rest on a very undemocratic approach to relationships. Sociologist Catherine Hakim notes that monogamy remains popular, especially among women, precisely because

it offers sexual democracy.[76] A non-monogamous sexual system, meanwhile, would undoubtedly be Darwinian, hierarchical, and patriarchal.
The New Polyamory masquerades as egalitarian at present. It can afford
to for the moment because of the "free rider problem." That is, polyamorists can be a minority who flout (but still benefit from the fruits of) the
trust, fidelity, and stability exhibited by the vast majority of couples. But
it cannot become a majority system while retaining the benefits that only
monogamy consistently delivers.

Historically, getting (monogamously) married meant "getting serious."
It meant higher expectations of one's proper behavior.[77] The social ties
of marriage create interdependent systems of obligation, mutual support, and restraint. Marriage meant having someone to care for and having someone to take care of you—yes, being interdependent—and these
responsibilities and obligations only grew stronger when children entered
the family. Non-monogamy flouts such norms, exhibits little constraint,
a great deal of "checking in," and invites partner jealousy and pernicious
bugs, all in the pursuit of genital pleasures and perceived "needs." Some
things may just be more important than that. And some facets of marriage
will endure, like the link between the wish to have children and the desire
for monogamous commitment. No one actively hopes to have children
by multiple men or women. Individuals may elect not to form marriages
or families—and they may openly resist the forms of both presented to
them—but they are not capable of socially constructing monogamy out
of existence. We are simply not free to write off fertility's debt to love, its
desire for exclusivity, and its idealization of marital union. It will resist and
reemerge, if even only in wounded form.

Secularization and Support for Confluent Love

There have always been forces that have pulled marriages apart. But it
is the forces that push people together that were once common but are
now increasingly rare. For example, although 21 states retain adultery laws
on their books, they are largely historical curiosities today. Legal cases of
"alienation of affections" are uncommon now and very difficult to win.
The US military, long trusted to help safeguard the sexual behavior of husbands away on deployment, is following suit. The military's recognition
of same-sex marriage in spite of its definition of adultery as penile-vaginal
penetration means that enforcing its own adultery codes would first
require considerable revision before new prosecutions can move forward.

I cannot imagine that occurring. Hence the armed forces' recession from actively supporting marriage and generously benefiting married spouses leaves organized religion as the only obvious, active institutional supporter of marriage.

Religious Americans clearly continue to idealize and exhibit marriage the most.[78] That is not surprising, since religion and family are institutions that look to each other, figuratively speaking, for mutual support. Social reinforcement of marriage elsewhere—from sources such as the workplace, the law, entertainment, the school system—is fading rapidly or has completely collapsed. But Americans are still comparatively more religious than the rest of the West, and the way our citizens couple, split, and recouple is distinctive as well.[79]

Figure 5.5 displays the share of Americans ages 24–35 who are married or cohabiting, sorted by their religious service attendance patterns. It reinforces the claim that organized religion is still a friend of marriage: one in three married young adults report weekly (or greater) religious service attendance. The same is true of less than 7 percent of currently cohabiting young adults, who are far more likely to never attend religious services at all (74 percent, compared with 44 percent of married persons). If we reverse the axis (results not shown), we learn comparable things. Married persons comprise 68 percent of all weekly attenders between ages 24 and 35. Sociologist Jeremy Uecker, assessing longitudinal data from the Add Health study, comes to the same conclusion about cohabitation: it is toxic to religious behavior. His study assessed religious "returns," that is, people

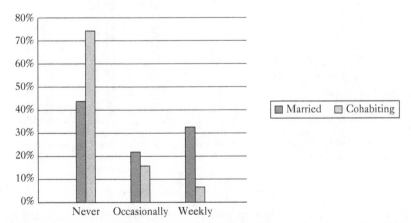

FIGURE 5.5 Frequency of religious service attendance, by current relationship status

Source: Relationships in America, Ages 24–35.

who drift away from religious participation in early adulthood and return later (most commonly after marriage and children), a phenomenon that was predictable for generations. Not so much anymore as marriage lags. Cohabiters without children are far and away less likely to return either to regular or even sporadic attendance when compared with unmarried (but uncoupled) adults, to say nothing of married adults with children.[80]

Religious Americans are not only more likely to be married, at any age, they are also the most likely to balk at the idea of many of the sexual behaviors discussed earlier in this book. Assessing religious influence on such behavior is not my intention, so I spent little time on the subject in the interviews.[81] But it deserves some discussion if I am to make claims about the coming primacy of confluent love, for it is this group that should be the last holdouts. Are they?

To begin, keep in mind that among this age group (24- to 35-year-olds) about 23 percent of Americans claim to attend religious services weekly. Another 22 percent say they do occasionally, and 52 percent say they never do.[82] Does that matter for what they think about marriage, cohabitation, pornography, no-strings-attached sex, extramarital sex, and polyamory?

It absolutely does, but there are clear cracks beginning to show in the foundation. Figure 5.6 displays the share of 24- to 35-year-olds who either "disagree" or "strongly disagree" with a set of statements they were asked about. I will not detail every estimate here; you can get the big picture

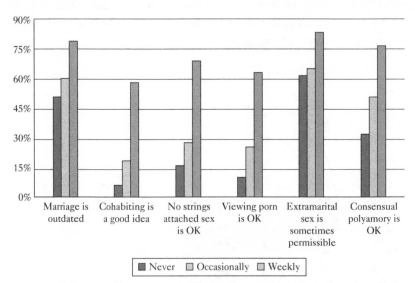

FIGURE 5.6 Percent disagreement with statements on sex/marriage, by religious attendance

Source: *Relationships in America*, Ages 24–35.

just by glancing at the graph. Except on extramarital sex, where occasional and weekly attenders hang very closely together, attendance habits are a linear predictor of what young Americans think about various sexual practices and relational arrangements. The weekly attenders are consistently more skeptical of confluent love ideas and practices than those who never attend, by a long shot. Since "nevers" make up half of the American population at this age, this graph also demonstrates just how much sexual permissiveness and secularization go hand-in-hand. It is not just that religiously proscribed sexual activity promotes religious guilt. (I am sure it does.) Rather, it is often an expression of religious distancing. Cheap sex has a way of deadening religious impulses. We overestimate how effective scientific arguments are at secularizing people. Narratives about science don't secularize. Technology secularizes. And sex-related technology does so particularly efficiently.

Perhaps the "moralistic therapeutic deism" of which sociologist Christian Smith has written is partly a result or unintended consequence of trends in non-marital sexual behavior among American Christians.[83] Perhaps the New Atheism has arisen—now of all times—in the wake of the expansion of pornography and other tech-enhanced sexual behaviors. The pure relationship model has prompted plenty of soul searching over the purpose, definition, and hallmarks of marriage. It may be doing the same with religious belief.

While it is common to display the extent of agreement in graphs like that in Figure 5.6, I elected to reveal disagreement with those six statements because it reveals just how much cohabitation, pornography, and no-strings-attached sex are barely contested by half of the population of American young adults (that is, those who never attend religious services). While in one breath Figure 5.6 can reassure many religious Americans that they are far more restrictive when it comes to sex and marital matters, the glass could just as easily be perceived as half-empty. The graph serves to highlight how far south of 100 percent the most religious of Americans are on these subjects. Only about extramarital sex is there over 80 percent firm disagreement. Uncertainty—that is, neither agreeing nor disagreeing—about such practices and attitudes dominates much of the remaining portion of the faithful. Among weekly attenders:

- 14 percent are unsure about marriage being outdated.
- 23 percent are unsure about the wisdom of cohabiting before marriage.
- 21 percent don't know what they think about no-strings-attached sex.

- 25 percent don't know if viewing pornography is okay or not.
- 10 percent are unsure about whether extramarital sex might ever be permissible.
- 17 percent don't know if consensual polyamorous unions are okay.

One can interpret "fence sitters" as movable—open to being convinced. But when it comes to sexual matters, most who claim neutrality eventually drift toward the more permissive position. Expect that to become true here as well, not because sexual attitudes evolve in a more permissive direction. (They don't.) Expect it because American religion as it is practiced tends to foster it. Andrew Cherlin, author of *The Marriage-Go-Round*, holds that America's version of Christian culture exacerbates rather than relieves our elevated divorce rate and our predilection to serial partnering. How so? In several ways, he asserts. America's Christian culture, tilted toward a generic evangelical Protestantism:

- Exemplifies a therapeutic expressive individualism
- Becomes a site for self-development or "personal growth"
- Fosters a spirituality of "seeking" rather than "dwelling"
- Emphasizes the importance of meeting people "where they're at"
- Encourages the creation of personal religious styles rather than shared traditions
- Emphasizes general social support rather than religious social control

While these traits may be most visible in evangelical Protestantism, they do not stop there. (And to be fair, it is much less true of devoutly observant evangelicals.) It is "in the water" here, so to speak, in ways not seen in other Western (and certainly non-Western) nations. Annulments granted to Catholics in the United States dwarf the number approved elsewhere, Cherlin notes.[84] Before the Second Vatican Council (1962–1965), about 400 annulments were granted annually. After it, but not likely because of it, the rate surged, peaking in 1991 at 63,000. The United States accounts for only 6 percent of the world's Catholic population but makes up 60 percent of all annulments granted. Americans may be more religious than Europeans, Cherlin observes, but we are not more traditional, at least when it comes to marriage and family. The six traits noted above spill over into relationship development and conduct, making us more likely to get into romantic and sexual relationships earlier, sacralize them, grow dissatisfied with them, exit, and try again with others who have done the same. Twenty-one percent of Americans between the ages of 18 and 60 have either been divorced before (13.5 percent) or are divorced presently (7.2 percent). Not half, as the typical American often misperceives. And, curiously, weekly attendance habits are more evident among divorcees the more times they have been divorced. I think Cherlin is on to something.

The Religious Consequences of a Bifurcated, Gender-Imbalanced Mating Market

Martin is a 28-year-old property inspector in Austin. He's also a de facto organizer of the singles ministry at a large evangelical church, where he is very active. While he anticipated a vibrant dating scene there, given how evangelicals typically esteem marriage, it has oddly not materialized. It has been a disappointment because he's a big fan. Marriage, he holds, is:

> Just a real beautiful thing. I have gotten to see it done well with my parents and just creating that covenant with someone and the intimacy that's there and having a family you know. Sharing your life with somebody rather than living it by yourself.

This is the kind of talk we expect of devout Christians in America. They remain friends of marriage. But they too have been affected by the mating market dynamics around them. Martin has pursued online dating (on Match.com, not something more traditionally religious like eHarmony), even though he told us there are at least 80 women in the single's group. Martin and his last girlfriend were sexually active in their relationship, even though he said it made him feel like a hypocrite. They managed to stop, but in keeping with Duke economist Peter Arcidiacano's research on "habit persistence," young relationships that cease sex seldom survive, and Martin's was no different.[85] It was over within five months. She was his first and only sexual partner. Martin has struggled with pornography at times, though less so in the present. Like most, he perceives the "economic" effect of porn on sex—that it raises men's (real) sexual expectations and lowers women's.

It is not the case that there are separate mating markets for evangelicals like Martin, as there tends to be for some American religious minorities (such as ultraorthodox Jews or Mormons). Hence what happens among many religious Americans in their later twenties and thirties is seldom radically different from that which other Americans narrate except by degree. They want love, like nearly everyone else. They couple. Sex often follows after a (longer) period of time, a pattern which confuses them more than most, since premarital sex remains proscribed—meaning it is actively discouraged, but impossible to effectively prevent—among them. Moreover, plenty of religious Americans have taken breaks from the faith for periods of time, been burned, returned, and then struggle to navigate relationships in a manner distinctive from their previous mating-market experiences (which have established price points for sex, patterned expectations for behavior, etc.). To be sure, there are "ideal types" among them who hew to a more orthodox path—that is, dating without sex, "courtship," marriage in a timely fashion, etc. They are just becoming rarer by the year.

We ought to expect all this to take a toll on marriage rates among religious Americans, and it may already be occurring. Whereas only 37 percent of the most irreligious of never-married adults in the *Relationships in America* survey said they would prefer instead to be married, 56 percent of the most religious never-married adults said the same. But 56 percent is a far cry from, say, 80 or 90 percent. What is happening in the wider mating market is affecting religious Americans, too, as well as their congregations and denominations.

Sociologist Justin Farrell assessed the sexual and marital attitudes of evangelicals and found consistent age differences—younger evangelicals (below age 30) were notably more permissive on nearly all outcomes (especially on pornography).[86] Critics might claim that this is nothing more than the standard age effect on sex visible from time immemorial—that older Americans have always been less permissive about sex than younger ones. However, exceptions to Farrell's age effect were apparent among married evangelicals, meaning that under-30 evangelicals who were already married were notably less permissive. But the age at first marriage of evangelicals is climbing, in step with (but a little over a year behind) the median age of other marrying Americans. The same challenge is now facing the LDS Church. Mormon age-at-marriage is climbing as well. Hence, current mating market dynamics are affecting how the faithful think and act.

This puts added market pressure on denominations and congregations, operating as they are in a free religious market in the United States. How so? Because it signals that the predictable "return" to organized religious life of late twenty-somethings after they marry and begin having children is receding because the return is either delayed (among many) or may not occur at all if Steven Ruggles's prediction that one in three twenty-somethings will never marry proves true.

It's not only in diminished numbers of returnees that mating-market dynamics are affecting congregations. Long-standing Christian sexual ethics are making less and less sense to the unchurched—a key niche market for evangelicals—giving church leadership fits over just how "orthodox" they can be or should be on matters of sex and sexuality.[87] "Meeting people where they're at" becomes more challenging when where they're at has become the population norm rather than the exception. Congregations are coming face to face with questions of just how central sexual ethics are to their religious life and message. The issue is a live and very poignant tension, exacerbated by the fact that Protestant churches operate in a free market, meaning that positions on sexual matters are more sensitive to the wishes of the faithful.

American Catholics, meanwhile, have access to more robust and developed (and less democratic) conservative teachings on sexuality and marriage than do Protestants, but suffer from a profound "supply chain" problem. Average Catholics are unaware of their Church's own teachings or are insufficiently trained in them, due to Catholicism's historically poor theological education system.[88] American Catholics also tend to approach religious life with a spirit of independence and an anti-authoritarian streak, out of step with the hierarchical nature of the Magisterium. As a result, the average Catholic's sexual behavior looks (and is) more permissive than the average evangelical Protestant's.

Conclusion

Young Americans are taking flight from marriage—by avoiding it, delaying it, or exiting it. It should not surprise us, either, since this is cultural lag in action: the uptake of contraceptive technology is slowly undermining long-standing reasons for marrying. And yet we still want to marry, but the difference between needing and wanting marriage is a big one. Cheap sex—that is, the wide availability of sexual access—is arguably diminishing men's marriageability, since the quest for sex was long a key motivator for men to marry. No more. Cheap sex has transformed modern men (and women), undermined and stalled the marital impulse, and stimulated critics of monogamy, who fail to recognize the goods historically secured by it and polyamory's reliance on a male-dominated mating market. Despite increasingly unfavorable terms for marriage, men are not going their own way. Once in it, they tend to like marriage. Women, on the other hand, exhibit higher ideals for marriage. They remain far more likely to want out once in. And given their comparative recent economic successes, women are in a better position to leave—and still thrive—than ever before. Marriage has changed, no doubt. Once a staid institution characterized by its functional gain in trade between men and women, it has become a symbol of success shared by two increasingly similar spouses. All of it has thrown organized Christianity—marriage's biggest supporter— for a loop. Cheap sex, it seems, secularizes. The more traditional ways American Christians think about marriage and family remain distinctive from emerging norms of confluent love for now. Cracks in the foundation, however, are visible.

6

The Genital Life

DESPITE SHRINKING DOUBLE standards and growing egalitarianism, something seems amiss with sex these days. Most Americans—left or right, religious or not—can sense it. We have sexualized childhood. We titillate each other online. We're catching more pernicious bugs in bed than ever.[1] Online porn is now standard operating procedure for a near-majority of men. We construct comprehensive identities and communities around sexual attraction in a way unfamiliar to most of the Western world, including Western Europe.[2] Cultural struggles over marriage continue—now out of the political limelight—in households, congregations, and workplaces. Meanwhile, the common date has eroded, now quaint in light of the ubiquitous, unromantic hookup. Programs aimed at "sexual health" proliferate, cost bundles, but seem to meet only modest success in the realm of consent. We medicate low sexual desire and market *Fifty Shades*. We can't seem to get enough of sex—so we focus on technique—but what we get is leaving us hungering for still more or longing for some emotion or transcendent satisfaction that cheap sex seems to promise but seldom delivers. Social and interpersonal trust erodes; solitude and atomization increase. Mothers and fathers split. In light of these common realities, how many of us would confidently declare that yes, these are the best of times in American sexuality, that we are making progress, that we have modeled a template of more satisfying, fulfilling sexual unions?

Sex is cheap. It is more widely available, at lower cost to all than ever before in human history. What has emerged is not at all unlike the decline of the locally owned boutique shops and the rise of big-box, discount chains. Cheap sex has been mass-produced with the help of two distinctive means that have little to do with each other—the wide uptake of the Pill and mass-produced high-quality pornography—and then made more efficient by communication technologies. They drive the cost of sex down, make real commitment more "expensive" and challenging to navigate, have created a massive slow-down in the development of long-term relationships, especially marriage, put women's fertility at risk—driving up demand for infertility treatments—and have taken a toll on men's marriageability. The "pure relationship" regime, which has flourished alongside the dramatic rise in cheap sex, is not nearly so consonant with other long-standing priorities like childrearing and relational stability. But it is becoming the norm in the West—the template for evaluating relationship development. And it has changed how men and women perceive themselves, their sexuality, each other, and the point of relationships. Cheap sex does not make marriage unappealing; it just makes marriage less urgent and more difficult to accomplish.

I offer no wistful elegies for earlier eras. They all had their problems. My point in writing this book has been more basic, namely to document the expectations of sexual economics in light of new, influential technologies, and to reveal how keeping an eye on the timeless exchange relationship behaviors of men and women helps us better understand the sexual activity patterns we see around us, whether gay or straight.

There is no creating new winners without losers. That should not surprise anyone; every sexual system has inequalities. If a critical mass ever successfully snubs relationship commitment, permanence, and sexual exclusivity—and that is a possibility, given ample time—it will become difficult for a minority to do otherwise.

Who are the winners in this new relational regime? The easiest to spot, of course, are career-minded women, for whom access to the contraception that made sex far cheaper also enabled them to finish education and commence careers in far greater numbers than previously, in so doing fostering new structured patterns (and a culture of expectation) of career building. And the world is no doubt better off for their economic, intellectual, and social contributions.

There are other winners. Sexual minorities have begun to flourish, as Giddens predicted. Sexually opportunistic men have taken wide advantage of the greater access to sex. The wealthy (as always) have found economic opportunities to exploit. For instance, gentrified urban neighborhoods have appealed to childless, dual-income couples, sending central business district and inner core real estate prices skyrocketing and concern about affordable housing surging. And there is short-term corporate profit both in curbing births—expanding disposable income—and, on the backside, medically stimulating faltering fertility. (Assisted reproductive technology is often very expensive.) Indeed, America's late modern capitalist economy now relies upon those technologies that have made sex cheap.

There is no free lunch, however. This grand bargain yielded trouble forming enduring relationships. (Some mislabel it a paradox.) The high "opportunity cost" of having children among women has led them to have fewer children in general. While most of them are just fine with that, plenty of women have fewer children than they had wished to have, and nearly twice as many women today (compared with the mid-1970s) have no children at all. Moreover, half of such women in their mid-30s to early 40s still wish for a child.[3]

And there are obvious losers in this system shift. Working-class Americans—both men and women—would benefit more from the functionality and dual-income possibility of marriage, but are uniting in matrimony at dismally low levels. The marriage prospects of lower SES women have turned sour. Many children, too, are losing out. They thrive in the presence of stable parents and exposure to siblings and intergenerational communities—all arrangements that the pure relationship system erodes. Giddens said precious little about children in *The Transformation of Intimacy*, but what he did say reads like a haunting understatement: "It would certainly not be right to suppose that childhood has remained unaffected by the world of pure relationships."[4] Giddens's expectation of troubled and compulsive male sexuality has come true as well, as Chapter 4 describes. Many men feel powerless to say no to the cheapest of sex, but wish they could. The women who love them lose out on their monogamous attentions. There are other losers, too. Women who prefer a shorter and nobler search for a mate won't likely get their wish. A holistic, person-centered dating service is not just around the corner, either. And those who prefer childrearing to career—they form like-minded communities to counter the cultural disdain they feel from their career-minded counterparts.

We find ourselves in a liminal spot, one between long-taken-for-granted traditional relationships anchored in marriage and the future relationship system characterized more consistently by "confluent love." There will not be two dominant systems. Marriage as it has long been understood is in the throes of deinstitutionalization. Meant to be a "haven in a heartless world," as the late social critic Christopher Lasch described it, marriage is fast becoming a contest, another tenuous social arena in competition with the economic marketplace (for our limited time and energy) and the remarriage market (for second chances and sexual variety). Marriage will not disappear, of course, but it will someday become a minority practice, as Figure 5.1 suggests.

Confluent love may make for compelling films—manipulated narratives, really—but it will not serve persons, families, or communities well. Instead, it will be the source of profound relational inequality and solitude, navigated with aplomb only by the most successful. It will trade the limited but clear benefits of a monogamous marital system for the lure of constant desiring. Social conservatives tend to bemoan these and other developments, but what they really want is what they cannot have—a culture in which marriage is normative and expected, together with all the desired fruit brought about by the pure relationship and confluent love model: greater freedom, flexibility, time, and opportunity.

The Genital Life

For winners and losers alike, sex is different today. Kristin Dombek, while reviewing a trio of books on American sexual behavior for the *New York Times*, hit it on the head: "Sixty years (after Kinsey), many of us have come to regard sex—preferably passionate, hot, transformative sex—as central to our lives."[5] Great (infertile) sex is now a priority, a hallmark of the good life, signaling that our genital and psychosexual life—sexual expression and how we experience it—is close to the heart of being human. Those who do pity those who don't, won't, or can't experience toe-curling orgasms. This is the Genital Life. Its advent coincided with, but was not caused by, a shift in the dominant language around sexuality and its expression from that of sexual desires to that of sexual needs in the service of "well-being," a lingo dominated by public health, psychiatry, and now even law.[6] (Any form of suffering in relationships, on the other hand, is now widely considered an unequivocal signal of an unhealthy state.) Quality sexual experiences are increasingly perceived to be just as pivotal to human flourishing as clean air, potable water, edible food, ample shelter, and antibiotics. And in social theorist Zygmunt Bauman's words, "When the quality lets you down, you seek salvation in quantity," a decidedly male sexual virtue.[7] Giddens predicted the genital life. He just didn't call it that. Others refer to it by different names. "Orgasmic sexuality" is what Illouz dubs it, noting how it has become a form of competence to be developed.[8]

While our most distant ancestors were no doubt acquainted with sexual pleasure, they associated it with babies. They were part of the deal. No more. Today, in the unabashed words of a sexuality educator friend of mine, "it's all about the fucking." Sex is about pleasure, with a side of bonding. About fertility, the pinnacle of natural human creativity and women's unique capacity, Westerners have become ambivalent.[9] The US fertility rate has dropped 10 percent in the past decade alone, and it wasn't very high before that.[10] The very word procreative is typically met with eye-rolling, LOLs, and contempt.[11]

"Sex is, like, a big, big, big, big part of everything now," reported Miguel, whom we first met in Chapter 3. He continues: "I feel like people don't care no more. Nowadays people are so free about their thoughts, their actions, and um, people don't even care ... how they come off to other people." A gay man, Miguel nevertheless conveys ambivalence about the developments Giddens holds made it possible for the flourishing of homosexuality. His words describe unintended consequences:

Forty percent of me is kind of, like, not happy with how things have progressed. I think they should have progressed a little bit differently, but ... the other 60 (percent) I feel like, it's a big step for society, um, to be more comfortable with other things, um, one of those (being) leading up to gay marriage.

While Miguel described at length the patterns described in Chapter 3, what he detects is hardly limited to gay men. Men in general expect a rich, diverse genital life today. And many women are following suit. Numerous men with whom we spoke told of women whose sexual demands and kinky interests exceeded their own.

If this is evolution, the widely respected naturalist writer (and same-sex marriage supporter) Wendell Berry wonders just what sort of higher version of humanity we are evolving toward. "It is odd that simply because of its 'sexual freedom' our time should be considered extraordinarily physical."[12] But physical it is. Berry tags it all with far less optimism than most have, choosing to perceive the shift as constituting an element not of the organic, local, and virtuous life but as a synthetic compound of our Western penchant for bigger, cheaper, better, diverse, and more—an ironic postmodern intersection where Wal-Mart meets Dan Savage. "Industrial sexuality," he calls it, our latest effort to "conquer nature by exploiting it and ignoring the consequences, by denying any connection between nature and spirit or body and soul."[13] And, he holds, there's a significant price to pay for thwarting our ecology:

> The spiritual, physical, and economic costs of this "freedom" are immense, and are characteristically belittled or ignored. The diseases of sexual irresponsibility are regarded as a technological problem and an affront to liberty. Industrial sex, characteristically, establishes its freeness and goodness by an industrial accounting, dutifully toting up numbers of "sexual partners," orgasms, and so on, with the inevitable industrial implication that the body is somehow a limit on the idea of sex, which will be a great deal more abundant as soon as it can be done by robots.[14]

The robots comment would be laughable were it not for genuine, mounting concern about exactly that.[15]

Industrial sex is a fitting term for plenty of what we heard about in our interviews. The personal narratives I detailed in *Premarital Sex in America*, which interviewed emerging adults up to age 23, had nothing on the orgasmic experiences, partner numbers, time in pursuit, exotic accounts, one-night stands, regrets, pain, addictions, infections, abortions, wasted time, and spent relationships we heard about from 24- to 32-year-olds, all in the service of an industrial sex whose promises consistently exceeded its deliveries. That we even felt comfortable asking rather explicit questions of strangers—and expected and received articulate answers—is a testimony to the advancement of the genital life.

This new regime is harder on women than men because the detachment of love from sex has made the establishing of self-worth a great deal more precarious for women. I can readily affirm that women (and men) have inherent dignity, or intrinsic worth, apart from their performance and conduct in relationships. But it is more difficult to convince women of it.[16] They tend to draw a straighter line between success in relationships and self-image than men do and are more apt to blame themselves when things go wrong. They seldom finger the new relationship ecology brought about by the split mating market. Efforts at "self-care" among them prove popular but fleeting, more cliché than anything.

Meanwhile, the "organic" citizens in our midst—those who are skeptical about the boundless promises of the sterile and undisciplined life—are commonly portrayed as restrictive, misogynist, and backward. Among the many ironies that greet us in the domain of human sexuality, this is one of the most profound. But classic sexual restraint, typically more a product of social than personal control, fostered a future orientation that dovetailed well with a productive life.

Even when sex becomes about reproduction, we presume (incorrectly) that we retain complete control over the when, where, and how we have children. Anticipated by Giddens, we are increasingly outsourcing conception and treating assisted reproductive technology (ART) as if it is as plausible and natural (and as inexpensive) as sexual intercourse:

> What used to be "nature" becomes dominated by socially organized systems. Reproduction was once part of nature, and heterosexual activity was inevitably its focal point. ... We have not yet reached a stage in which heterosexuality is accepted as only one taste among others, but such is the implication of the socialization of reproduction.[17]

Live-birth deliveries from ART jumped 60 percent in the decade leading up to 2010, and another 10 percent in the three years after that, issuing in just under 68,000 babies in 2013. It is certainly a growth industry.[18] And yet one of the greatest myths believed by educated persons today is that science can fix infertility. But failures far outstrip successes. The CDC estimates that ART's success rate at age 40 is only 19 percent. At 42, it's down to 10 percent, and by 44, success rates languish under 3 percent.[19]

Let's not get too far ahead of ourselves, though, since 98 percent of human reproduction remains of nature. But it is nevertheless significant that we no longer automatically associate the two, a product of media priming and the reality of a great deal of sterile sexual experience. Even my use of the word "nature" here aggravates many, I suspect. But to assert that what has happened in the domain of sex was anything but a concerted accomplishment of synthetic technology undermining nature in the service of human consumption is to say something that is untrue. Cheap sex was a trade-off. In its wake, human sexuality has become anything but natural and "green." Once something that belonged to the physical world, sexuality is now characterized by a postmodern dualism—the consumptive, malleable body housing the essential self.

It is no surprise that the Genital Life is leaving us lonelier. Its supporters even said it would. Sex educator and relationship therapist Laura Berman, describing a world no doubt dystopian to Berry's, concludes—together with Giddens—that there is a trade-off:

> I suspect for the next decade or so we will be riding a wave, seeking more stimulation in less time, quick transitory couplings, and the

next big thing to make sex more exciting. The good news is that sex will be safer and more exploratory than ever, given the virtual capabilities. The bad news is that we will likely see an uptick in sexual addiction and a decrease in emotional connection with partners. People struggle with the existential depression and loneliness that comes from a lack of rich, authentic connections.[20]

Naomi Wolf is less sanguine than Berman, reflecting on the pornography that was—in 2003—still nascent in its capability of mimicking reality:

> Mostly, when I ask about loneliness, a deep, sad silence descends on audiences of young men and young women alike. They know they are lonely together, even when conjoined, and that this imagery is a big part of that loneliness. What they don't know is how to get out, how to find each other again erotically, face-to-face. Other cultures know this. I am not advocating a return to the days of hiding female sexuality, but I am noting that the power and charge of sex are maintained when there is some sacredness to it, when it is not on tap all the time. In many more traditional cultures, it is not prudery that leads them to discourage men from looking at pornography. It is, rather, because these cultures understand male sexuality and what it takes to keep men and women turned on to one another over time—to help men, in particular, to, as the Old Testament puts it, "rejoice with the wife of thy youth; let her breasts satisfy thee at all times." These cultures urge men not to look at porn because they know that a powerful erotic bond between parents is a key element of a strong family.[21]

It is not often that you hear an avowed, consistent feminist approvingly quoting the Bible—the Old Testament, no less—on sexual norms. Addiction, relationship anxiety, and failed unions. Good times ahead?

Eight Predictions for 2030

In Aldous Huxley's most famous work, his dystopian 1932 novel, *Brave New World*, the civilized elite neither married nor were sexually monogamous, both out of principle and commitment to the "stability" of society. (Like the authors of the nonfiction *Sex at Dawn*, the emotions and suppressed passions of monogamy were thought to be a key source of social instability.) For the sake of social order, polyamory is normative and sex infertile, with birthing outsourced to a lower caste. And yet one of the book's key protagonists (John) objects, preferring the pursuit of a solitary affection. His quest, however, is considered bizarre and unhealthy to a population socialized to believe that sex ought to be easy and cheap, because sex is just sex, and he should not complicate it with thoughts of exclusivity or challenge. He demurs, however, expressing genuine love rather than lust. It won't work, so socialized are the natives in gratification. John concludes, "Nothing costs enough here."[22]

I enjoy a good dystopian novel on occasion—especially older ones like Huxley's—if for no other reason than to see what they get right, what they get wrong, and to discern how the intellectual, economic, and cultural contexts of the era in which they write emerge despite their best efforts to think into a future that is foreign by definition. Most are way off base. But *Brave New World* gets more right than it does wrong. We live in a world where technology has eclipsed fertility, making it voluntary (though still common). We are getting more talented at artificial reproduction. Use of escapist substances or experiences is normative. Some gay men—to the chagrin of most lesbians, I suspect—reference heterosexuals as "breeders," a class referent more visible in the novel *The Wanting Seed* but still perceptible in *Brave New World*. Non-monogamy is creeping up in practice, but surging in attitudinal support. "Dating" technology, like Tinder, emphasizes sex appeal above all other qualities, a trait novelist Gary Shteyngart dubbed "fuckability" in his 2010 dystopian *Super Sad True Love Story*.[23] Extreme individualism is coming into focus as we retreat (rather than recoil, as in the book) from marriage. And cheap sex has become the operative assumption.

Those who balk at such trends today are considered misfits, threatened with social isolation and shaming, a tactic Huxley's characters were well acquainted with. Not every dystopian prediction of his has a shot at becoming reality, but a realist human anthropology and sociology will recognize that technology is increasingly separating sex from love, from fertility, and from meaningful human connection. And the human society that results from wide uptake of this will be filled with orgasms, but will be relationally less pleasant and lonelier. Love is not gone, but it's receding. Think *Fifty Shades of Gray*—the pursuit of pleasure while starving for real connection. We seem unwilling to admit that cheap sex came with strings attached.

As I write this, the year 2030 is 13 years away. A great deal of scrutiny has been given to marriage and family lately, especially in light of political and legal wrangling over same-sex marriage in the West and in the United States in particular. The resulting "quiet" of sorts that emerged in the wake of the Supreme Court's June 2015 decision to recognize a constitutional right to same-sex marriage has created an opportunity to reflect on what has happened and to give attention to what is likely to occur next. In that spirit, I offer eight educated guesses at what we will witness in the realm of sex, relationships, and marriage by the year 2030. Some of these predictions are easy to make, so confident I am in the ingredients necessary for them to emerge. Others are a bit more speculative, but not so much that I lack confidence in them. Some are concrete—about this or that rate or figure—while others are more subjective, concerning latent concepts and trends. Some predictions are of continuity rather than change. Some are about acceleration; others about slowing down. While I am confident in each of them, I am even more confident that they will not all come true. The odds are simply against being right all the time. Here is what I expect.

First, Sex Will Get Even Cheaper

This one is easy. Little evidence points in any direction but this one. Fertility control is getting better. Moves are afoot—including among conservatives—to promote long-acting reversible contraceptives (LARCs) for women.[24] Less risk of pregnancy equals cheaper sex. It is an unintended consequence, I realize, but a certain one. It cannot stimulate stability in relationships. That's not how it works.[25]

Contraception, however, is not the only technology altering sexual behavior. Men's pornography use is high and shows no sign of abating, as Chapter 4 detailed. So long as our economy is oriented toward technology and efficiency, men will harness it toward making erotic experiences more accessible, a pattern which further cheapens the real thing. Pornography, the subject of increased consternation, will have become conventional by 2030. That is, most persons will take it for granted—the new normal. It will be very difficult for mainstream companies to shun advertising there, so great will be the lure of its popularity. Men's actual social skills, once honed to enable them to navigate the complexities of real relationships, will recede apace, creating a cottage industry in social skill development that outpaces the one that has already emerged. If you do not think this will happen, then you do not understand men. Where the ground may give here is not with regard to men's preferences for cheap sex, but women's. The latter will be pressured to increasingly accept such outsourcing as socially and relationally legitimate. Some will not, but many will feel forced to compromise or lose out.

It's not just about men and porn, either. The 2013 film *Her* explored the challenges of a relational world in which men and women—struggling to make their marriages work—turn to form emotional relationships with their computers' operating systems. Understood by most as a dystopian fiction, I'm not so sure, given the way that very many Westerners remain in far closer contact with their smart phone than with their family members, spouses included. Together with the anxiety that many sense when separated from the Internet for several hours, the evidence suggests rather that persons are quite susceptible to such "relationships." Men may be more susceptible to porn than women, but women may be more prone to this—an interactive operating system that not only talks to them but listens and learns. I see no reason why this wouldn't become more popular. (Preferred, however, may be a stretch.) Nor does Laura Berman, who predicts—with seeming approval—an increase in use of sex-related technologies:

> Virtual romantic partners like Samantha in the movie "Her" will be a reality. . . . We will be able to have robust sexual experiences without touching. Talk about disease prevention! Imagine engaging in anything from targeted foreplay to exploring your wildest fantasies by stimulating your partner with a click of a mouse, even when you are across town or in another country. Meanwhile, our understanding of the neurobiology of sex will lead to a new ability to stimulate the brain directly to simulate mind-blowing sex regardless of physical contact. This will not only have endless recreational implications, but will significantly improve the sex lives of people with disabilities, as well.[26]

I cannot imagine any politicization of such "outsourcing" of sex, nor do I perceive any impending curbing of it. Indeed, legal changes around sex—like those I wrote about earlier in this chapter—have historically concerned the space between persons. I am speaking here about the space that persons occupy largely by themselves (and their devices, of course).

Like Giddens, though, Berman recognizes a downside: "We will likely see an uptick in sexual addiction and a decrease in emotional connection with partners." More loneliness. Solitary sexual experiences have a way of doing that, of leaving one hungering for something richer than satiation. Masturbation may be a good teacher (of sexual preferences), as Leslie Bell holds, and sex dolls may come to look, sound, and feel rather life-like, but only real human beings make for good help-mates, confidantes, and comforters.[27] Love cannot be outsourced. And the sex is better, too.[28]

Second, Age of (Sexual) Consent Laws Will Be Enforced Only in the Most Egregious Cases

Consent as a key legal guarantor of sexual freedom from harm is stronger than ever, as recent contests over campus "rape culture" have revealed. But age of consent is quietly up for grabs.[29] Among the many socialized fictions in the domain of sexual expression, age of consent is a big one. That a 16-year-old is unable to consent to sexual activity in New York but a 17-year-old is ready to do so is an obvious social construction. (Remember, just because something is socially constructed does not mean it is arbitrary or meaningless.) Age of consent laws were meant to protect the vulnerable, but instead of age concerns, values like mutuality, positive body image, sexual exploration, and autonomy have begun to emerge as lynchpins of a "healthier" sexuality at the same time as the language of public health and social science have come to dominate discourse in this domain.[30] American parents will not embrace adolescent sex anytime soon.[31] But you should expect less enforcement of the age component of consent laws, especially among those adolescents near the legal age of consent (which vary by state).[32] The "powers-that-be no longer seem interested in drawing the boundary between 'right' and 'perverse' sex," Bauman laments.[33] Indeed, the term "perverse" itself is rapidly receding in use. Prosecutors will not wish to press charges unless the victim is visibly pre-pubescent. Of course, the laws themselves will not be changed. There is not nearly enough political will for that. But they will not be enforced.

Sexual interactions between teachers and minor students—now exploding in number—may soon be decreasingly enforced as well, or dealt with less severely than at present. This will be especially so in the case of female teachers' relationships with male students.

Third, the Rising Age at First Marriage for Women Will Begin to Slow and Might Even Peak, but the Share of Unmarried Americans Will Continue Its Upward March Unabated

For Americans, marriage remains a key value and ideal, and it is cognitively connected with childbearing, especially among those that marry in their late twenties or thirties. Given this connection, the median age at first marriage for women (currently just above 27) will likely rise, but will peak below age 30. There is less of an urgent ceiling for men, but the age-gap difference between marrying men and women is smaller than it has ever been—less than two years—so I anticipate when women's median age at first marriage peaks, men's will soon after. If it does not, it will signal a new pattern—an increasing gap in age between marrying men and women—and with it, predictable power differences (in men's favor, of course).

Meanwhile, the share of Americans who marry will continue to slide, as demographers project. The dominant narrative continues to finger men's fear of commitment. But men are not afraid of commitment. They never have been. Commitment is just not needed to access sex today in the split, gender-imbalanced modern mating pool. Women no longer need men to socially, culturally, and economically succeed in life. In step, there is less motivation for men to "be noble" and respect women's interests. Cheap sex slows down the road to marriage, makes its would-be participants think twice about it, and draws their attention toward consumption rather than production.

In an era wherein marriage has become more of a symbol than a project, it becomes easy to forget that marriage's still-viable functional purpose is for the material protection of its members. Marriage remains powerfully associated with all manner of optimal outcomes in American life—among children, adolescents, and adults. While I empathize with scholars who assert that marriage rates will not recover if men's wages remain low, other policy analysts demur. Moreover, poverty is a long-standing nemesis. Hence, it is unlikely the sole (or even the primary) culprit in the flight from marriage, especially since extreme poverty has recently diminished, not increased.

Marriage involves relationships with other fallible human beings. There is no other way around this, except by generous public assistance policymaking that would unwittingly serve to further atomize us. What governments and communities cannot do, however, is love. And, as social theorist Margaret Archer notes, "Love is something that human beings cannot thrive without, whether giving or receiving it; it is also indispensable to the good society."[34] Such love is best fostered, rooted, and flourishes within the context of a comprehensive stability and social reproduction, whether you label it marriage or something else.

Thus, we will find that as marriage retreats so will enduring love, giving way to the dominance of confluent love. And with it will recede less expensive forms of stable social order. In its place we will attempt to secure some semblance of solidarity by intervention or by virtual communities, but it is just not the same. A nation of partnering singles—a country in which the pure relationship becomes the norm—is ultimately a lonelier and far more vulnerable one than we have been led to believe.[35]

Fourth, after a Brief Period of Pent-Up Demand, Same-Sex Marriage Will Recede

Given Giddens's incisive prophecies, it is difficult to imagine that—as American heterosexual marriage rates continue to decline and the average age at first marriage climbs—marriage will become the preferred relational arrangement of American same-sex couples. Early evidence from England and Wales already hints in this direction.[36] There are several reasons for this. To begin, the success of political and legal challenges to longstanding marriage law constitutes a sign of the deinstitutionalization of marriage and not of a revitalization of the same. Claims to the contrary—that same-sex marriage will give a boost to an institution lagging among the masses by convincing men and women to tie the knot more—make little sense. Another reason to be skeptical of its future is that marriage, however defined, remains more of a conservative arrangement than a cosmopolitan one. It is the stuff of Lubbock, not Chelsea. But some same-sex couples have legally married, and will marry—especially the more traditional among them. The best man in my own wedding came out of the closet about 15 years ago and got married in Massachusetts not long after it became legal to do so. It should not surprise anyone: he and I are both from the same small, rural community in northern Michigan. Marriage is in his cultural script. Less so for many of his peers.

Confluent love, however, strains at the reins that marriage entails. If sexual economics understands men's and women's union formation patterns correctly, on average, then it means we should expect non-monogamy to characterize a significant share of gay men's unions. In that case, I would expect the uptake rate (for same-sex marriage among men) to peak quickly before commencing a slow decline because an institution whose historic trademarks include expectations of monogamy and childbearing will not shed those easily. (Early evidence from Sweden tracks in this manner.)[37] Old narratives are not undone in a decade or by legal fiat. If gay men are able to both successfully integrate non-monogamy into marriage on a wide scale—and enjoy broad social support for doing so—it would signal a cultural accomplishment heretofore unheard of. But the most likely scenario remains that, after pent-up demand is met and the novelty has worn off (about five to seven years), civil marriage will be selected by proportionally far fewer gay couples than heterosexuals or lesbians. This is in part because marriage remains embedded in long-standing expectations about permanence, fidelity, and children—values more tightly held whenever women are involved. In lesbian marriages, children will be comparatively few—the property of the most prosperous because they are expensive to artificially create or adopt. Emotional satisfaction in such unions will remain a key priority, however, lending itself to heightened instability.

In the end, the exchange relationship is heteronormative, and that will not change. While marriage is in the throes of deinstitutionalization, the essence of the union itself will survive. It will not be deconstructed, because it is not a mere social construction, despite convictions and legal moves to the contrary. Given enough time, long-standing (general) male and female preferences will trump sexual identity in marital matters. By 2030, there is a good chance that a look-back at June 2015 will reveal same-sex marriage as a quest for rights and a cultural land grab rather than a product of the genuine desire to access an historic institution.

Fifth, Men's Sexuality (Not Just Women's) Will Become More Evidently Malleable

A significant share of young-adult women have same-sex sexual experiences and self-identify as something besides entirely heterosexual, as Chapter 2 detailed. Men are presently much less likely to report either of these, but scholars are beginning to reveal that men exhibit a degree of sexual malleability as well.[38] While they may not shift across the Kinsey scale, men nevertheless learn to sexualize new things and in new ways. Men were not "born to" have sex with robots, or stare at high-definition porn for hours, or pursue rimming, prostate massage, sadomasochism, or dozens of other emergent sexual practices, but plenty have adopted new practices (to varying degrees). I expect more men will experiment with same-sex sexual behavior as well, short of identification as exclusively gay. Why? Because the evidence suggests so. Even casual observers can note the following four developments: (1) increasing popular emphasis on diverse sexual experiences; (2) tightening secular regulations—not to mention a double standard—on heterosexual but not homosexual events (e.g., verbal consent law, anxiety over subsequent accusations);[39] (3) "omnivorous" pornography delivery that blends straight, lesbian, and multi-partner forms, together with clear interest among straight men in the depiction of male pleasure and ejaculation;[40] and (4) declining stigma of non-heterosexual identities. When men marinate in the Genital Life in a social context that esteems if not promotes sexual diversity, of course more same-sex experimentation will occur. As sociologist Jane Ward describes in her 2015 book *Not Gay: Sex between Straight White Men*, this phenomenon is not uncommon but is likely to be limited to sexual behavior, rather than to the adoption of a (gay) culture or community. So while the share of American men who self-identify as bisexual may increase, it will not grow as much as the share that dabbles, if even temporarily, in bisexual behavior patterns.

Sixth, Polygamy Will Not Make a Comeback, but Polyamory May Emerge as a Minority Norm

Polygamy—that is, plural marriage—may make a formal return appearance, since we have now demonstrated the legal malleability of the structure of marriage. The historic importance of one man and one woman, now dismissed, concerned the tight connection between coupled sex and fertility and the long-standing state interest in protecting women and children. Hence, the significance of a union of two persons is no longer a profound one. Plural marriage, which has a far longer social history and contemporary precedents around the globe, may well make a legal comeback in the United States. But it may not: Canada's high court did not reverse its sentiment on plural marriage in a 2011 case, which is a signal that the US Supreme Court may not pay it much attention, either. Even if it does return, Americans are fleeing legal marriage. They certainly are not interested in more than one marriage, at least not on any notable scale. Moreover, the long-term legal shift in family law is toward privileging individuals, not the unions they form. I cannot imagine a political environment in America wherein the people's representatives (local, state, or federal) come to agree upon showering more benefits on those unions that have more members. Given that unlikelihood, legalized polygamy would thus come with a penalty (that is, three or four spouses would receive the same legal benefits as one pair). Moreover, polygamy is profoundly anti-feminist and historically hinges on the dependence of multiple women on one man. But won't "new" polygamy also feature one woman marrying two or three men? No. That is not how men roll, nor how the exchange model of relationships works. But leave it to the mass media to feature the handful they would no doubt uncover.

What about "open" marriages and polyamorous unions? The first has no future, but the second one may. Few people claim to be in (stable) open marriages in the first place, but the odds are against any "second genera-tion" of open marriages. We could witness non-monogamy among parents and then among their children, but only the parents' generation would think to pass it off as a type of marriage. Remember, marriage is in the throes of deinstitutionalization.

Far more likely is the rise of polyamory, given it has achieved an ele-ment of (modest) popularity among younger Americans and cultural elites (e.g., positive coverage in media). So yes, I think polyamory will have its day and may well emerge as a minority norm. Given it is, at bot-tom, a reflection of male power in the mating market—more sex with more women without the responsibilities of plural marriage—polyamory will certainly be tolerated. Since unlike polygamy it is not currently illegal, states will pay it no attention. And since it is already a de facto arrange-ment among a significant minority of gay couples, consensual overlap-ping unions have a future in America. It also has numerous enemies, including many feminists, most Christians, relationship traditionalists, and more women than men. Again, polyamory will emerge insofar as men hold the upper hand in the mating market. But as the Pareto prin-ciple discussed in Chapter 3 suggests, only a small fraction of men will experience it.

Seventh, the Retreat from Marriage in the United States Will Not Be Stemmed by Organized Christianity

The share of nonreligious Americans is rising. While some hold that secularization has brought about a more tolerant sexual era in the West, I think the causal order runs best in the other direction.[41] Most religious disaffiliation occurs not because of a deliberate move away from Christian belief but because of passive alignment of religious behavior with secular (sexual) practice. Cohabitation, now rocketing in popularity, is prompting sustained disaffiliation, a break from the once-normal pattern of return to active participation after marriage and childbearing.[42]

Even among those that return—or who never left—there is a retreat from marriage. American Christians still value lifelong, monogamous matrimony. But many have an aversion to actually doing what it takes to accomplish it. This is due in part to the same thing that makes American religion popular yet institutionally weak—its sensitivity to the free market. The free market in religion encourages competition among congregations for adherents, a system which has made for vibrant worship communities. But this same system radically decentralizes Christianity. How does that undermine marriage? By fostering profound diversity of thought, teaching, and practice, hamstringing the ability of any particular Christian denomination or organization to speak and act with authority widely recognized as legitimate. Nobody speaks for American Christianity because there is no center. For every congregation, pastor, or public persona that presses young adults toward chastity and marriage, there is another that yawns at both. Denominational schism—a legacy of the Reformation—remains visible, disabling the ability to effect institutional accomplishments. Since matters of sexuality and marriage tend to be navigated locally or through denominations, any cooperative efforts among Christians here tend to be half-hearted, and always subject to the boundary maintenance concerns of their respective bases. This is why America can be considered a religious country—with weekly church attendance around 21–23 percent—and yet any joint efforts among them almost certainly fail.

Additionally, congregational competition tacitly encourages a turn away from social control, which can drive away "customers," and toward social support, which woos them. Princeton sociologist of religion Robert Wuthnow sees this in action:

> The meaning of divine guidance shifted subtly away from behavioral norms and focused instead on reassurance. People talked about receiving divine guidance, but what they meant, when pressed to explain, was that they felt better about what they already were doing.[43]

Enforcing behavior in a truly free market in religion is rather difficult. What of value can be denied those who are openly thwarting congregational sexual and marital standards? In an evangelical mega-church, nothing except perhaps leadership roles. The Catholic Church, on the other hand, counsels such persons to refrain from receiving the Eucharist, the highlight of the Catholic Mass. That they continue to counsel this multiplies accusations of meanness (that is, an absence of social support).[44]

The free market in religion, however, has been a hallmark of America since the Bill of Rights and the collapse of established state churches. (Massachusetts was the last to give it up, in 1833.) Why haven't these problems materialized before now? While the seeds of revolution were always present, a shared sexual matrix managed to prevail within the various strands of Christianity, according to sociologist Philip Rieff.[45] There was a "sacred canopy" of sorts over the erotic instinct, to borrow Peter Berger's term. Since the time of St. Paul's missionary venture to Corinth, "renouncing the sexual autonomy and sensuality of pagan culture was at the core of Christian culture."[46] And Christianity did so, embedding the sexual instinct within a community. Is sex the linchpin of Christian cultural order, the source of its power as a social force? That's what conservative columnist Rod Dreher wonders.[47] It might be.

That cosmology is suffering today, having taken a big hit with the advent and uptake of contraception. Today only a small number of American Catholics consistently avoids artificial birth control, and among evangelicals there is now talk about whether it's more moral for sexually active unmarried Christians to be on birth control than not.[48] By the time the same-sex marriage movement gained momentum, the old order had already been rent asunder.

In its place, the new American Christian cosmology privileges individual rights and the pursuit of happiness—wherever it may lead—over notions of solidarity and the common good. Marriage is typically considered a private matter, not the public foundation of societal order. Any "return" to a robust familism—that is, the esteeming of marriage and family over the individual—will not originate in the United States, a nation with deeply atomistic tendencies. Some hold that given enough time, demographic change will favor higher Christian birthrates. But it's hardly enough to suggest any demographic shift could be in sight by 2030. Moreover, much of this elevated birthrate is confined to Latino immigrants who, while above average in religiosity, are prone to secularization patterns by the second or third generation.[49]

Eighth, Efforts to De-gender Society and Relationships
Will Fall Short

To be sure, women no longer need men's resources so much, and men have unparalleled means of accessing sexual experiences today. But the exchange relationship has not disappeared. The assumptions behind sexual exchange are robust, readily discernable in popular media consumption, online dating behavior, campus sexual assault debates, and men's propositions of marriage. Men and women still pursue each other, and often want each other to stay. Men still appreciate the feminine genius, and women are still attracted to masculinity. They pair off because each wants something the other has. Many still commit because each has something the other wishes not to live without.

Yes, I realize the idea of "complementarity" is not a popular one, falsely pitted as it often is against visions of a utopian egalitarianism. But like it or not, complementarity remains obvious in the social and natural world. In fact, egalitarianism depends upon the complementarity of men and women; that is, it perceives sex distinctions that it then actively seeks to minimize. But even same-sex relationships seldom exhibit such blunt egalitarianism, and instead often recreate the roles common among opposite-sex unions. Difference, after all, attracts. And it works.

Some passionately object to this sort of talk, especially in the United States. This is partly because the intellectual and political movements to "de-gender" society largely originated here. The successful movement to de-gender civil marriage in the West has reinvigorated efforts aimed at the general dismantling of gender and the male–female distinction (dubbed "gender theory" elsewhere). Influential feminist law scholar Susan Moller Okin held that a "just future would be one without gender. In its social structures and practices, one's sex would have no more relevance than one's eye color or the length of one's toes."[50] Expect such efforts to have a modicum of success, well short of its hopes. Why? Because while the globe's inhabitants may exhibit sympathy for the equal treatment of its citizens, and perhaps efforts to ensure equal economic access, they have much less patience for efforts aimed at obliterating all sexual difference— that is, eradicating the truth of sexual dimorphism.

Being male or female is different than matters of sexual orientation, as I have repeatedly asserted in this book. The former is more powerful, more robust, more evident, and more resistant to malleability. There is certainly more to it than just social, legal, or linguistic construction. Chromosomes do not care what you think of them, and sex is observed, not "assigned," at birth. Bauman notes with profound irony that culture is now perceived as the inherited part of identity that should not be tinkered with, while what we long understood as "nature" (the stuff of genetic inheritance) is "ever more presented as amenable to human manipulation and [thus] open to choice."[51]

Back in 2000, Dick Udry, a demographer at the University of North Carolina at Chapel Hill (my graduate alma mater) and co-founder of the Add Health project, wrote about the biological limits of gender construction in the *American Sociological Review*. It drew sharp barbs from the feminist community in sociology, which constitutes the obvious scholarly nucleus of the discipline. Udry's crime was an intellectual one. He wondered whether gender may not be simply or solely socially constructed, as many of us sociologists-in-training were taught to believe:

> Traditional social science models of gender begin with the postulate that in humans, males and females are born neutral with respect to sex-dimorphic behavior predispositions. These models assume that behavioral differences between the sexes emerge as a consequence of socialization and social structure.[52]

But the empirical evidence to support this model, he showed, just wasn't there.[53] He is not alone, either. In fact—and in what amounts to a great irony—a recent review of 21 sources of data revealed that most sex differences are actually larger in magnitude and variability in cultures with more egalitarian sex role socialization and greater gender equity.[54] The notion that males and females have evolved to be the same is not just untrue, it's nonsensical.

This does not amount to dismissing the effects of socialization and social structure. Hardly. It's about recognizing that boys and girls are not blank slates to begin with, and that limitations are often paired with strengths, and interests with disinterests. Biology, Udry concluded, sets limits on the construction of gender and the effectiveness of gender socialization. We can push against those limits, but only draconian efforts, he concluded, will get anywhere:

> Humans form their social structures around gender because males and females have different and biologically influenced behavioral predispositions. Gendered social structure is a universal

accommodation to this biological fact. Societies demonstrate wide latitude in this accommodation—they can accentuate gender, minimize it, or leave it alone. If they ignore it, it doesn't go away. If they depart too far from the underlying sex-dimorphism of biological predispositions, they will generate social malaise and social pressures to drift back toward closer alignment with biology. A social engineering program to de-gender society would require a Maoist approach: continuous renewal of revolutionary resolve and a tolerance for conflict.[55]

Maoist approaches. Social engineering. Revolutionary resolve. Heavy words from a man who explicitly asserted that he was "certainly willing to mess with Mother Nature" and took no position on the morality of it all. Even an empathetic Pope Francis recognizes this isn't about rights. It's about ideological colonization. And since it builds upon a theory of sex differences that is empirically groundless, it won't work.

Conclusion

Professor Udry survived his professional pillorying over the sex differences study by not overreacting, not apologizing, not being intimidated, but instead by continuing to pursue the uncomfortable empirical truths as best he could discern them. I seek to do the same. I wrote this book not to make a personal case for social change but a professional case for better understanding the social change that has already come about in the sexual relationships of men and women. Our contemporary sexual and relational realities are far more the accomplishment of technology than of human quests for a more expansive social justice or a return to our "primal roots."

Women are learning to have sex like men. But peel back the layers, and it becomes obvious that this transition is not a reflection of their power but of their subjugation to men's interests. If women were more in charge of how their relationships transpired—more in charge of the "pricing" negotiations around sex—we would be seeing, on average, more impressive wooing efforts by men, fewer hookups, fewer premarital sexual partners, shorter cohabitations, and more marrying going on (and perhaps even at a slightly earlier age, too). In other words, the "price" of sex would be higher: it would cost men more to access it. Instead, none of these things are occurring. Not one.[56] The route to marriage, something the majority of young Americans still assert as a key goal, is more fraught with years and failed relationships than in the past. Once-familiar narratives about romance and marriage—how to date, falling in love, whom to marry, why, and when—are no longer widely affirmed, creating a great deal of consternation among young adults about how to move forward. They ask me for advice, but since this is a social problem, not a personal one, I have little to offer other than to counsel them to perceive the realities of the mating market early rather than fail to see it until it has duped them.

We are now a quarter-century removed from Giddens's prophecies in *The Transformation of Intimacy.* He got a great deal right. Change in sexual behavior patterns continues apace, further stimulated by yet more technology making sex and sexual experiences even cheaper and more widely available. Giddens, like Udry on gender, was keen not to object. I am not so reticent, having become convinced that the Genital Life we are adopting is misanthropic, ultimately anti-woman, and not sustainable. The exchange relationship, on the other hand, is old. It is deeply human. It fosters love when navigated judiciously. And it remains the historic heartbeat, and the very grammar, of human community and social reproduction.

Regression Models

Table A3.1 Estimated coefficients from OLS regression model predicting frequency of sex in past two weeks

	24- to 35-year-olds	18- to 60-year-olds
Demographics		
Age	−0.04*	−0.03***
Female	−0.21*	−0.27***
Hispanic	0.24	0.57***
Black	0.32	0.45***
Other race	−0.02	0.11
Educational attainment	−0.27***	−0.08**
Relationship status		
Cohabiting	0.22	0.44***
Never married	−1.56***	−1.57***
Divorced	−1.24***	−0.85***
Separated	−0.83	−0.85***
Widowed	−0.73	−0.94***
Other controls		
Heterosexual	−0.10	−0.04
Self-reported health	0.22***	0.16***
Number of biological children	0.21***	0.13***
Religious service attendance	0.00	0.01
N	3,192	14,264
R-Square	0.18	0.17

Notes: Reference groups are white, married, and non-heterosexual.

* $p < .10$.

** $p < .05$.

*** $p < .01$.

Source: Relationships in America.

**Table A3.2 Estimated odds ratios from logistic regression models
predicting wanting more sex, women ages 24–35**

Political liberalism	1.39***	1.24*	1.24
Demographics			
Age	1.00	1.01	1.02
White	1.05	0.94	0.96
Educational attainment	1.20*	1.17	1.16
Married	0.63**	1.10	1.11
Sexual Behavior			
Masturbated in past week		2.89***	2.89***
Pornography in past week		0.75	0.76
Lifetime N of male sex partners		1.10*	1.10*
Heterosexual		0.74	0.73
Frequency of sex in past 2 weeks		0.77***	0.77***
Emotional Well-being			
CESD (depression)		0.98	0.97
Self-rated happiness		0.75**	0.75**
Religion			
Importance of religion			0.99
Less religious than 10 years ago			1.68**
Religious service attendance			1.03
N	1,387	1,387	1,387
Constant	0.13*	0.47	0.27

Notes: Dependent variable comparison group (0 = respondent is content with sex or wants less sex).

* $p < .10$.

** $p < .05$.

*** $p < .01$.

Source: Relationships in America.

Table A3.3 Estimated odds ratios from logistic regression models predicting no sex (with current partner) until married

Demographics		
Age	1.00	0.99
Black	0.19***	0.37***
Hispanic	1.43**	1.49**
Other race	2.64***	2.49***
Female	0.74**	0.67***
Educational attainment	1.18***	0.94
Religion		
Importance of religion	1.45***	1.01
Religious service attendance	1.48***	1.30***
Evangelical self-identification	1.40**	1.05
Other controls		
Political conservatism		1.37***
Heterosexual		1.23
Higher age at first sex		2.17***
No-strings-attached sex is OK		0.50***
Considers self attractive		1.00
Self-rated happiness		1.26***
Parents are still married		1.32*
Family-of-origin positive experience		0.93
N	12,688	12,688
Constant	0.00***	0.00***

* p < .10.

** p < .05.

*** p < .01.

Source: Relationships in America.

Table A3.4 Estimated coefficients from OLS regression model predicting relational happiness (on a scale from 1–10)

Frequency of sex in past two weeks	0.16***
Key controls	
Self-rated happiness	0.86***
Currently/recently in therapy	−0.29*
Last pornography use (0 = most recent)	0.04**
Social media use frequency	0.01
Demographics	
Female	−0.30***
Age	−0.10***
Age-squared	0.00***
Educational attainment	−0.02
Black	−0.68***
Hispanic	−0.33***
Other race	−0.14
Household income	0.02*
Household size	−0.03
Relationship status	
Cohabiting	−0.33***
Never married	−0.64***
Divorced	−0.68***
Separated	−1.31***
Widowed	−0.72*
Other controls	
Political liberalism	−0.08*
Importance of religion	0.07***
N	10,884
R-Square	0.26

Note: Relationship status categories are compared to "currently married" respondents.

* $p < .10$.

** $p < .05$.

*** $p < .01$.

Source: Relationships in America.

Table A4.1 Estimated coefficients from OLS regression model predicting
support for same-sex marriage among men

Last pornography use (behavior, 0 = most recent)	−0.03***
Pornography is OK (attitude)	0.42***
Key controls	
Heterosexual	−0.45***
Political liberalism	0.27***
Thinks government regulations protect consumers	0.07***
Demographics	
Age	−0.01***
Educational attainment	0.09***
Black	−0.25***
Hispanic	0.03
Other race	−0.07
Household income	0.02***
Relationship status	
Cohabiting	0.07
Never married	0.01
Divorced	−0.08
Separated	−0.25
Widowed	−0.06
Other controls	
Social media use frequency	0.04**
Religious service attendance	−0.01
Importance of religion	−0.21***
N	6,904
R-Square	0.42

* p < .10.

** p < .05.

*** p < .01.

Source: Relationships in America.

Notes

CHAPTER 1

1. Anthony Giddens, *The Transformation of Intimacy* (Stanford, CA: Stanford University Press, 1992). The quote is from page 27.
2. Ibid., 29.
3. Ibid., 28.
4. Ibid., 29.
5. James Davison Hunter, *To Change the World* (New York: Oxford University Press, 2010).
6. Giddens, *The Transformation of Intimacy*, 28.
7. Ibid., 58.
8. Eva Illouz, *Why Love Hurts: A Sociological Explanation* (London: Polity, 2013). The quote is from page 12.
9. Giddens, *The Transformation of Intimacy*, 61.
10. Zygmunt Bauman, *Liquid Love* (Cambridge: Polity Press, 2003).
11. Bauman, *Liquid Love*, 47.
12. Emily Alpert Reyes, "Fewer Men are Paying for Sex, Survey Suggests," *Los Angeles Times*, November 2, 2013, http://www.latimes.com/nation/la-na-paying-for-sex-20131102-story.html.
13. Susan Aud, William Hussar, Grace Kena, Kevin Bianco, Lauren Frohlich, Jana Kemp, and Kim Tahan, *The Condition of Education 2011* (NCES 2011-033), US Department of Education, National Center for Education Statistics (Washington, DC: US Government Printing Office, 2011).
14. Knowledge Networks recruited the first online research panel that is representative of the US population. Dubbed the KnowledgePanel®, members are randomly recruited by telephone and mail surveys, and households are provided with access to the Internet and computer hardware if needed. Unlike other Internet research panels sampling only individuals with Internet access who

volunteer for research, the KnowledgePanel® is based on a sampling frame which includes both listed and unlisted numbers as well as those without a landline telephone, is not limited to current Internet users or computer owners, and does not accept self-selected volunteers. As a result, it is a random, nationally representative sample of the American population. At last count, over 350 working papers, conference presentations, published articles, and books have used Knowledge Networks' panels, including the 2009 National Survey of Sexual Health and Behavior, whose extensive results were featured in an entire volume of the *Journal of Sexual Medicine*—and prominently in the media—in 2010. The same is true of the longitudinal data collection project entitled *How Couples Meet and Stay Together*, collected by Stanford demographer Michael Rosenfeld. More information about KN and the KnowledgePanel®, including panel recruitment, connection, retention, completion, and total response rates, are available from KN's website.

15. Here are some additional details about the sample: 77 percent of our sample identified as White/Non-Hispanic, 7 percent as Hispanic, 11 percent as Black/Non-Hispanic, 3 percent as Asian American, and 2 percent as Mixed-Race. Forty-three percent of the participants were single, and 57 percent were in a relationship. Of the partnered men and women, 21 percent were cohabiting at the time of the interview. In terms of education, 7 percent had no more than a high-school degree; 13 percent were either currently enrolled in college (or community college) or had some college education but were not currently working on finishing their degree; 47 percent finished either a four-year college degree or a community college education, and 33 percent had earned or were working toward an advanced degree.

16. For example, there are very many scholars of sexuality who read *The Transformation of Intimacy* and not only agree with Giddens's empirical and conceptual assertions—which I certainly do—but are ideologically committed to carrying out the developments he predicts. (I'm less interested in that.) The social scientists that tend to study sex, sexuality, and relationship formation and development tend themselves to hold fairly permissive perspectives about sexuality and human freedom. Indeed, there is no American Sociological Association "section" or network of scholars who study straightforward sexual behavior. But there is a very active section on "sexualities," which signals that sociologists who study sexual behavior are vastly outnumbered by those who prefer research on sexual identity.

17. Lawrence S. Mayer and Paul R. McHugh, "Sexuality and Gender: Findings from the Biological, Psychological, and Social Sciences," *The New Atlantis* 50 (2016): 10–143.

18. Chris C. Martin, "How Ideology has Hindered Sociological Insight," *The American Sociologist* 47 (2016): 115–130.

19. In his 2005 study on the poor validity of most published research findings, John Ioannidis highlighted how diversity in measurement, research design, ways of analyzing data, and the surge in popularity of a particular research topic like sex and sexuality are all apt to elevate the risk of scientific missteps and weaken confidence in published research findings, making it harder to develop broad confidence in conclusions across studies. See John P. A. Ioannidis, "Why Most Published Research Findings Are False," *PLoS Medicine* 2 (2005): e124.

20. Duncan J. Watts, *Everything Is Obvious: How Common Sense Fails Us* (New York: Crown Business). The quote is from page 42.

21. Christian Smith, *What Is a Person? Rethinking Humanity, Social Life, and the Moral Good from the Person Up* (Chicago: University of Chicago Press, 2010).

22. Neil Gross and Solon Simmons, "Intimacy as a Double-Edged Phenomenon? An Empirical Test of Giddens," *Social Forces* 81 (2002): 531–555. The authors measure "pure love" by asking survey respondents whether their partners understand how they feel, the degree to which they can talk about their worries with their partners, and how often they talk to them about important matters. These seem far more like the makings of a "relational closeness" variable than constituting a plausible measure of the postmodern love system upon which Giddens elaborates.

23. Anthony Giddens, *Social Theory and Modern Sociology* (Cambridge: Polity Press, 1987).

24. Illouz, *Why Love Hurts*, 21.

CHAPTER 2

1. Portions of this chapter first appeared in "Contemporary Mating Market Dynamics, Sex-Ratio Imbalances, and their Consequences," *Society* 49 (2012): 500–505.

2. Roy Baumeister and Kathleen Vohs, "Sexual Economics: Sex as Female Resource for Social Exchange in Heterosexual Interactions," *Personality and Social Psychology Review* 8 (2004): 339–363.

3. See, for example, the following: Roy F. Baumeister, Kathleen R. Catanese, and Kathleen D. Vohs, "Is There a Gender Difference in Strength of Sex Drive? Theoretical Views, Conceptual Distinctions, and a Review of Relevant Evidence," *Personality and Social Psychology Review* 5 (2001): 242–273; E. Sandra Byers and Adrienne Wang, "Understanding Sexuality in Close Relationships from the Social Exchange Perspective," in *The Handbook of Sexuality in Close Relationships*, ed. John H. Harvey, Amy Wenzel, and Susan Sprecher (Mahwah, NJ: Lawrence Erlbaum, 2004), 203–234; Letitia Anne Peplau, "Human Sexuality: How Do Men and Women Differ?" *Current Directions in Psychological Science* 12 (2003): 37–40;

Pamela C. Regan and Leah Atkins, "Sex Differences and Similarities in Frequency and Intensity of Sexual Desire," *Social Behavior and Personality: An International Journal* 34 (2006): 95–102.

4. Andrew Galperin, Martie G. Haselton, David A. Frederick, Joshua Poore, William von Hippel, David M. Buss, and Gian C. Gonzaga, "Sexual Regret: Evidence for Evolved Sex Differences," *Archives of Sexual Behavior* 42 (2013): 1145–1161.

5. Catherine Hakim, "The Male Sexual Deficit: A Social Fact of the 21st Century," *International Sociology* 30 (2015): 314–335.

6. Paula England and Jonathan Bearak, "The Sexual Double Standard and Gender Differences in Attitudes toward Casual Sex among U.S. University Students," *Demographic Research* 30 (2014): 1327–1338.

7. Illouz, *Why Love Hurts.*

8. Catherine Hakim, "Supply and Desire: Sexuality and the Sex Industry in the 21st Century," IEA Discussion Paper No. 61 (2015), Institute of Economic Affairs, London.

9. Deborah A. Prentice and Dale T. Miller, "When Small Effects are Impressive," *Psychological Bulletin* 112 (1992): 160–164.

10. J. Richard Udry, "Biological Limits of Gender Construction," *American Sociological Review* 65 (2000): 443–457. The quote is from page 453.

11. David M. Buss, *The Evolution of Desire: Strategies of Human Mating* (New York: Basic Books, 2003).

12. Baumeister and Vos, "Sexual Economics."

13. None of the 1,219 women in the Chicago Health and Social Life Survey (CHSLS) reported paying someone for sex in the past year. See Martha Van Haitsma, Anthony Paik, and Edward O. Laumann, "The Chicago Health and Social Life Survey Design," in *The Sexual Organization of the City*, ed. Edward O. Laumann, Stephen Ellingson, Jenna Mahay, Anthony Paik, and Yoosik Youm (Chicago: University of Chicago Press, 2004), 39–65. An August 2015 YouGov survey similarly found no women (out of 523 surveyed) reported ever having paid for sex. Fourteen percent of men said they had. https://d25d2506s-fb94s.cloudfront.net/cumulus_uploads/document/7w1vgkkwdn/tabs_OPI_Prostitution_20150828.pdf. A recent article from the United Kingdom turned out to be anything but convincing. Its claim is based on the accounts of male escorts, not women. Efforts to interview women who actually paid for sex were not successful. See Rose Troup Buchanan, "Women Are Buying Sex More Than Ever, Research Claims," *Independent*, May 23, 2015, http://www.independent. co.uk/life-style/love-sex/women-are-buying-more-sex-than-ever-before-new-research-claims-10272103.html.

14. Stephen Ellingson, Edward O. Laumann, Anthony Paik, and Jenna Mahay, "The Theory of Sex Markets," in *The Sexual Organization of the City*, ed. Edward O. Laumann, Stephen Ellingson, Jenna Mahay, Anthony Paik, and Yoosik Youm (Chicago: University of Chicago Press, 2004), 3–38.

15. Laurie L. Cohen and R. Lance Shotland, "Timing of First Sexual Intercourse in a Relationship: Expectations, Experiences, and Perceptions of Others," *Journal of Sex Research* 33 (1996): 291–299.

16. Baumeister and Vohs, "Sexual Economics."

17. Colleen C. Hoff and Sean C. Beougher, "Sexual Agreements among Gay Male Couples," *Archives of Sexual Behavior* 39 (2010): 774–787.

18. In her 2013 book, sociologist and psychotherapist Leslie Bell relays this anecdote and truism: "Sophia, though currently in a relationship with a woman, 'felt confident initiating sex with male partners because she knew they would be receptive.'" See Leslie C. Bell, *Hard to Get: Twenty-Something Women and the Paradox of Sexual Freedom* (Berkeley: University of California Press, 2013). The quote is from page 155.

19. Hanna Rosin, *The End of Men: And the Rise of Women* (New York: Riverhead, 2012). The quote is from page 19.

20. Illouz, *Why Love Hurts.*

21. Giddens, *The Transformation of Intimacy,* 11.

22. Roy F. Baumeister and Kathleen D. Vohs, "Sexual Economics, Culture, Men, and Modern Sexual Trends," *Society* 49 (2012): 520–524. The quote is from page 521.

23. Pierre Bourdieu, *The Logic of Practice* (Stanford, CA: Stanford University Press, 1990).

24. See, for example, Andrew Cherlin, *The Marriage-Go-Round: The State of Marriage and the Family in America Today* (New York: Vintage, 2010); Kathryn Edin and Maria J. Kefalas, *Promises I Can Keep: Why Poor Women Put Motherhood before Marriage* (Berkeley: University of California Press, 2007).

25. To be sure, it is also in part due to the reduced significance of a non-marital pregnancy in the lives of many of those Edin interviewed.

26. Christopher Ryan and Cacilda Jethá, *Sex at Dawn: The Prehistoric Origins of Modern Sexuality* (New York: HarperCollins, 2010). The quote is from page 302.

27. Jean M. Twenge, Ryne A. Sherman, and Brooke E. Wells, "Changes in American Adults' Sexual Behavior and Attitudes, 1972–2012," *Archives of Sexual Behavior* 44 (2015): 2273–2285; Tom W. Smith and Jaesok Son, "Trends in Public Attitudes about Sexual Morality" Final report presented by National Opinion Research Center, April 2013.

28. Ryan and Jethá, *Sex at Dawn,* 304.

29. Sex columnist Dan Savage is a key ally and promoter. A book-length anthropological critique was self-published in 2012 by Lynn Saxon, entitled *Sex at Dusk: Lifting the Shiny Wrapping from Sex at Dawn* (CreateSpace Independent Publishing, 2012).

30. Portions of this section originally appeared in a 2012 article by the author entitled "Mating Market Dynamics, Sex-Ratio Imbalances, and their Consequences," *Society* 49 (2012): 500–505.

31. Others agree. The president of the National Institute for Reproductive Health went so far as to suggest the Pill created the most profound change in human

history. See Vanessa Grigoriadis, "Waking Up from the Pill," *New York Magazine*, November 28, 2010, http://nymag.com/news/features/69789.

32. Danielle Haynes, "Ethan Hawke: Society has 'Childish View of Monogamy,'" UPI, December 1, 2013, http://www.upi.com/blog/2013/12/01/Ethan-Hawke-Society-has-childish-view-of-monogamy/3401385924484/.

33. Jesús Fernández-Villaverde, Jeremy Greenwood, and Nezih Guner, "From Shame to Game in One Hundred Years: An Economic Model of the Rise in Premarital Sex and Its De-stigmatization," *Journal of the European Economic Association* 12 (2014): 25–61.

34. See Table 2 of Claudia Goldin and Lawrence F. Katz, "The Power of the Pill: Oral Contraceptives and Women's Career and Marriage Decisions," *Journal of Political Economy* 110 (2002): 730–770.

35. Claudia Goldin and Lawrence F. Katz, "Career and Marriage in the Age of the Pill," *American Economic Review* 90 (2000): 461–465.

36. Ibid., 464.

37. I occasionally refer to these components or "corners" of the mating market as markets themselves, too, since they function like distinctive markets even while they overlap.

38. Repeated use of the term "deregulation" is the closest Eva Illouz gets to identifying the role of contraception in altering the mating market.

39. While the real gender gap in historical sexual behavior was not likely as profound as it appears—given strong social desirability concerns—it is a safe assumption that in the era of the Pill a far greater share of 18-year-old women are sexually active today than 50 or 100 years ago. See Albert D. Klassen, Colin J. Williams, Eugene E. Levitt, Laura Rudkin-Miniot, Heather G. Miller, and Sushama Gunjal, "Trends in Premarital Sexual Behavior," in *AIDS: Sexual Behaviors and Intravenous Drug Use*, ed. Charles F. Turner, Heather G. Miller, and Lincoln E. Moses (Washington, DC: National Academy Press, 1989). Data from the National Longitudinal Study of Adolescent Health estimates that—by the mid-1990s—around two-thirds of 18-year-old women had already had sex. See Mark Regnerus, *Forbidden Fruit: Sex and Religion in the Lives of American Teenagers* (New York: Oxford, 2007).

40. For a more extensive and economics-intensive explanation of this, see Timothy Reichert, "Bitter Pill," *First Things*, May 2010.

41. Anonymous, "I'm a PTA Mom Who Spent a Year on Ashley Madison, and I Have No Regrets," Scary Mommy, July 2015, http://www.scarymommy.com/im-a-pta-mom-who-spent-a-year-on-ashley-madison-and-i-have-no-regrets/.

42. Lisa Taddeo, "I Went Undercover on America's Cheating Website," *Redbook*, March 30, 2011, http://www.redbookmag.com/love-sex/relationships/advice/a11620/cheating-websites.

43. Buss, *The Evolution of Desire*, 71.

44. Ibid.; Marina Adshade, *Dollars and Sex: How Economics Influences Sex and Love* (San Francisco: Chronicle Books, 2013); David P. Schmitt, "Short- and Long-term Mating Strategies: Additional Evolutionary Systems Relevant to Adolescent Sexuality," in *Romance and Sex in Adolescence and Emerging Adulthood: Risks and Opportunities*, ed. Ann C. Crouter and Alan Booth (Mahwah, NJ: Lawrence Erlbaum, 2006), 41–47.

45. Karen Cook, Coye Cheshire, and Alexandra Gerbasi, "Power, Dependence, and Social Exchange," in *Contemporary Social Psychological Theories*, ed. Peter J. Burke (Stanford, CA: Stanford University Press, 2006), 194–216. The quote is from page 194.

46. Ibid., 196.

47. Baumeister and Vohs, "Sexual Economics."

48. Thomas Anderson and Hans-Peter Kohler, "Low Fertility, Socioeconomic Development, and Gender Equity," *Population and Development Review* 41 (2015): 381–407. See also Paula England and Elizabeth Aura McClintock, "The Gendered Double Standard of Aging in US Marriage Markets," *Population and Development Review* 35 (2009): 797–816.

49. Illouz, *Why Love Hurts*, 96.

50. Ibid., 78.

51. Reichert, "Bitter Pill." The popular blogosphere is filled with articles on this subject. For a pair of examples, see Laura Jane Williams, "Single, Imperfect Women Here's the Truth: Men Are Not a Scarce Resource," *Thought Catalog*, May 11, 2015, http://thoughtcatalog.com/laura-jane-williams/2015/05/single-imperfect-women-heres-the-truth; see also Lori Gottlieb, "Marry Him!," *The Atlantic Monthly*, March 2008, http://www.theatlantic.com/magazine/archive/2008/03/marry-him/306651.

52. Catherine Hakim sees it too: "The traditional distinction between marriage markets and sexual markets . . . eroded and seems to be vanishing in the 21st century," and "Sexual markets now overlap with marriage markets." See Hakim, "Supply and Desire," 8 and 10. Eva Illouz distinguishes the two corners differently than I wish to by emphasizing how the "sexual field" emerged from the marriage market. See Illouz, *How Love Hurts*.

53. Hephzibah Anderson, *Chastened: The Unexpected Story of My Year Without Sex* (New York: Viking, 2010).

54. Aylin Zafar, "The Year Without Sex," *The Atlantic Monthly*, June 23, 2010, paragraphs 34 and 36, http://www.theatlantic.com/entertainment/archive/2010/06/the-year-without-sex/58592.

55. Unfortunately, all this talk about the emergence of love and commitment must remain largely conceptual here, since this is primarily a study of unmarried young adults.

56. Scott M. Stanley, Galena K. Rhoades, and Sarah W. Whitton, "Commitment: Functions, Formation, and the Securing of Romantic Attachment,"

Journal of Family Theory Review 2 (2010): 243–257. Recent research on sexual objectification even reveals that women don't mind if their husbands objectify them sexually—but only in the presence of clear signals of commitment. Without it, objectification predicted marital dissatisfaction. See Andrea L. Meltzer, James K. McNulty, and Jon K. Maner, "Women Like Being Valued for Sex, as Long as it is by a Committed Partner," *Archives of Sexual Behavior* 46 (2015): 475–488, doi:10.1007/s10508-015-0622-1.

57. Stanley et al., "Commitment," 244.

58. Philip S. Gorski, "The Matter of Emergence: Material Artifacts and Social Structure," *Qualitative Sociology* 39 (2016): 211–215.

59. Buss, *The Evolution of Desire.* Additionally, women often struggle to decode and discern commitment, and tend to display it in ways different from men.

60. Susan Sprecher, Maria Schmeeckle, and Diane Felmlee, "The Principle of Least Interest: Inequality in Emotional Involvement in Romantic Relationships," *Journal of Family Issues* 27 (2006): 1255–1280.

61. Peter M. Blau, *Exchange and Power in Social Life* (New York: Wiley, 1964). The quote is from page 84.

62. University of San Francisco economist Bruce Wydick labels such entanglements as socially unjust, asserting that a monogamous commitment—at its pinnacle in marriage—is the most just toward women and their distinctive biological interests. See Bruce Wydick, "Why Married Sex Is Social Justice," *Christianity Today*, June 23, 2016, http://www.christianitytoday.com/ct/2016/julaug/why-married-sex-is-social-justice.html.

63. Scott M. Stanley, Galena K. Rhoades, and Howard J. Markham, "Sliding vs. Deciding: Inertia and the Premarital Cohabitation Effect," *Family Relations* 55 (2006): 499–509.

64. Illouz, *Why Love Hurts*, 19.

65. Yuval Harari, *Sapiens: A Brief History of Humankind* (New York: Harper, 2015). The quote is from page 361.

66. Illouz, *Why Love Hurts*, 41.

67. Roy F. Baumeister and Jean M. Twenge, "Cultural Suppression of Female Sexuality," *Review of General Psychology* 6 (2002): 166–203; Baumeister and Vohs, "Sexual Economics."

68. Illouz, *Why Love Hurts.*

69. Roy F. Baumeister and Kathleen D. Vohs, "Sexual Economics, Culture, Men, and Modern Sexual Trends," *Society* 49 (2012): 520–524. The quote is from page 521.

70. E. L. James, *Fifty Shades of Gray* (New York: Vintage, 2012).

71. Sabino Kornrich, Julie Brines, and Katrina Leupp, "Egalitarianism, Housework, and Sexual Frequency in Marriage," *American Sociological Review* 78 (2012): 26–50.

72. Kornrich, Brines, and Leupp, ""Egalitarianism, Housework, and Sexual Frequency," 26.

73. Bell, *Hard to Get*, 8.

74. Ibid., 7.

75. Giddens, *The Transformation of Intimacy*, 39.

76. Illouz, *Why Love Hurts*, 184.

77. Glenn Kessler, "One in Five Women in College Sexually Assaulted: An Update on This Statistic," *Washington Post*, December 17, 2014, https://www.washingtonpost.com/news/fact-checker/wp/2014/12/17/one-in-five-women-in-college-sexually-assaulted-an-update.

78. An earlier version of this argument appeared in "Naked Consent: Why Personal Speech Codes Won't Curb a Social Problem Like Sexual Assault," *Public Discourse*, September 8, 2014, http://www.thepublicdiscourse.com/2014/09/13769.

79. Michael Kimmel and Gloria Steinem, " 'Yes' is Better than 'No,' " *New York Times*, September 4, 2014, http://www.nytimes.com/2014/09/05/opinion/michael-kimmel-and-gloria-steinem-on-consensual-sex-on-campus.html.

80. Jacob Gersen and Jeannie Suk, "The Sex Bureaucracy," *California Law Review* 104 (2016): 881–948.

81. Cathy Young, "Feminists Want Us to Define These Ugly Encounters as Rape. Don't Let Them," *Washington Post*, May 20, 2015, https://www.washingtonpost.com/posteverything/wp/2015/05/20/feminists-want-us-to-define-these-ugly-sexual-encounters-as-rape-dont-let-them.

82. Yes, men can be sexually assaulted by women. But the reason that statement almost always raises eyebrows (and unasked and unanswered questions) is because people perceive sexual violence through the lens of sexual exchange. It is the default cognitive model.

83. Elizabeth A. Armstrong, Laura Hamilton, and Brian Sweeney, "Sexual Assault on Campus: A Multilevel, Integrative Approach to Party Rape," *Social Problems* 53 (2006): 483–499. This is actually a very fine study of the dynamics that contribute to what has come to be called "rape culture" on campus. My only beef with it is the suggestion that men's pursuit of sex and women's gatekeeping role are artifacts of a malleable social script. As should be obvious by now, I think they are more robust realities than that. Other dynamics, like women's reticence to complain and expectations that they will defer to men in interactions, seem more obviously scripted.

84. Illouz, *Why Love Hurts*, 192.

85. This approach is consonant with a broken political culture fixated on rights, not goods. See Aleksandr I. Solzhenitsyn, *A World Split Apart* (New York: HarperCollins, 1978).

86. Giddens, *The Transformation of Intimacy*. The various quotes appearing here are from pages 27–28.

87. Jean M. Twenge, Ryne A. Sherman, and Brooke E. Wells, "Changes in American Adults' Reported Same-Sex Sexual Experiences and Attitudes, 1973–2014," *Archives of Sexual Behavior* 45 (2016): 1713–1730.

88. Giddens, *The Transformation of Intimacy*, 15.

89. Jane Ward, "No One Is Born Gay (or Straight): Here Are 5 Reasons Why," *Social (In)Queery*, March 18, 2013, paragraph 12, http://socialinqueery.com/2013/03/18/no-one-is-born-gay-or-straight-here-are-5-reasons-why.

90. Roy F. Baumeister, "Gender Differences in Erotic Plasticity: The Female Sex Drive as Socially Flexible and Responsive," *Psychological Bulletin* 126 (2000): 347–374; Lisa M. Diamond, *Sexual Fluidity: Understanding Women's Love and Desire* (Cambridge, MA: Harvard University Press, 2008); Lisa M. Diamond, "Was It a Phase? Young Women's Relinquishment of Lesbian/Bisexual Identities over a 5-Year Period," *Journal of Personality and Social Psychology* 84 (2003): 352–364; Lisa Diamond, "Development of Sexual Orientation among Adolescent and Young Adult Women," *Developmental Psychology* 34 (1998): 1085–1095; Illouz, *Why Love Hurts*; Letitia Anne Peplau and Linda D. Garnets, "A New Paradigm for Understanding Women's Sexuality and Sexual Orientation," *Journal of Social Issues* 56 (2000): 329–350.

91. J. Michael Bailey, "What Is Sexual Orientation, and Do Women Have One?," in *Contemporary Perspectives on Lesbian, Gay, and Bisexual Identities*, ed. Debra A. Hope (New York: Springer, 2009), 43–64. The quote is from page 60.

92. Bell, *Hard to Get*.

93. A similar u-shaped curve is visible for women's same-sex behavior in the National Survey of Sexual Health and Behavior. See Debby Herbenick, Michael Reece, Vanessa Schick, Stephanie A. Sanders, Brian Dodge, and J. Dennis Fortenberry, "Sexual Behavior in the United States: Results from a National Probability Sample of Men and Women Ages 14–94," *Journal of Sexual Medicine* 7, Suppl. 5 (2010): 255–265.

94. By shift I am commonly referring to incremental moves on the Kinsey scale, not typically large leaps across the spectrum.

95. Sociologist Paula England's recent assessment of NSFG data concluded similarly, noting "increases across cohorts in the proportion of women who report a bisexual identity, who report ever having had sex with both sexes, or who report having had sex with women only." By contrast, they found no such cohort trends among men. See Paula England, Emma Mishel, and Mónica L. Caudillo, "Increases in Sex with Same-Sex Partners and Bisexual Identity across Cohorts of Women (But Not Men)," paper presented at the 2016 annual meeting of the Population Association of America, Washington, DC.

96. Illouz, *Why Love Hurts*. Writer Anna Mussmann captures this idea when she admits, "We may talk about the need to pursue 'fitness,' but we really mean that everyone should be as sexually attractive as possible because attractiveness is now the most universal ranking method within society." See Anna Mussmann, "Death Doesn't Care If You're Sexy," *The Federalist*, October 18, 2013, http://thefederalist.com/2013/10/18/death-doesnt-care-about-sexy. The quote appears in paragraph 6.

97. Giddens, *The Transformation of Intimacy*, 34.

98. Sociologist Paula England, in her 2015 presidential address to the American Sociological Association, stakes the territory a bit differently. In her social explanation for the more common experience of female (rather than male) same-sex relationships, England holds that "both sexes face pressures to conform to gender norms, and thus to be straight, but I believe that men's gender nonconformity is more controversial precisely because the male gender is more valued. As a result, being a gay man is more stigmatized than being a lesbian." This is why, she holds, "women feel freer than men to have sexual partners of the same sex." See Paula England, "Sometimes the Social Becomes Personal: Gender, Class, and Sexualities," *American Sociological Review* 81 (2016): 4–28.

CHAPTER 3

1. Nancy Jo Sales, "Tinder and the Dawn of the Dating Apocalypse," *Vanity Fair*, August 31, 2015, http://www.vanityfair.com/culture/2015/08/tinder-hook-up-culture-end-of-dating.

2. Some scholars dispute this. British sociologist Catherine Hakim holds that male sexual demand is so consistently higher than women's (a point on which I agree with her) that it prompts the flourishing of paid sexual services. It's there that I disagree. To be sure, sex remains for sale, but when you can text your way into a woman's bed with little more than a pretty picture of yourself—and sometimes less than that—I do not see how paid sexual services will thrive unless the two markets attract different customers (e.g., age, SES, etc.).

3. Sales, "Tinder and the Dawn of the Dating Apocalypse," paragraph 22.

4. Ibid., paragraph 23.

5. Ibid., paragraph 77.

6. Ibid., paragraph 73.

7. Paula England's review of *Premarital Sex in America* appears in *Contemporary Sociology* 40 (2011): 613–614.

8. Illouz, *Why Love Hurts*, 25.

9. Watts, *Everything is Obvious*, 48.

10. Jonathan Chew, "Here's Why Tinder Flipped Out on Twitter Last Night," *Fortune*, August 12, 2015, http://fortune.com/2015/08/12/tinder-twitter.

11. Dan Slater, *Love in the Time of Algorithms: What Technology Does to Meeting and Mating* (New York: Current, 2013). The quote is from page 8.

12. Charles Horton Cooley, *Human Nature and the Social Order* (New York: Scribner's, 1902).

13. Michael Rosenfeld and Reuben J. Thomas, "Searching for a Mate: The Rise of the Internet as a Social Intermediary," *American Sociological Review* 77 (2012): 523–547.

14. Ibid., 532.

15. Amanda Hess, "The Women! They're Using Gadgets and Having Sex!," *Slate*, August 18, 2015, http://www.slate.com/articles/technology/users/2015/08/tinder_and_the_moral_panic_over_women_using_technology_to_meet_men_and_have.html; "In Twitter Rant, Tinder Blasts 'Vanity Fair' Article on New York Dating Culture," NPR, http://www.npr.org/2015/08/13/432122588/in-twitter-rant-tinder-blasts-vanity-fair-article-on-new-york-dating-culture.

16. Cynthia Feliciano, Rennie Lee, and Belinda Robnett, "Racial Boundaries among Latinos: Evidence from Internet Daters' Racial Preferences," *Social Problems* 58 (2011): 189–212; Belinda Robnett and Cynthia Feliciano, "Patterns of Racial-Ethnic Exclusion by Internet Daters," *Social Forces* 89 (2011): 807–828.

17. Sebastián Valenzuela, Daniel Halpern, and James E. Katz, "Social Network Sites, Marriage Well-Being and Divorce: Survey and State-Level Evidence from the United States," *Computers in Human Behavior* 36 (2014): 94–101.

18. Slater, *Love in the Time of Algorithms*, 11.

19. Dan Slater, "A Million First Dates," *The Atlantic Monthly*, January/February 2013, paragraph 11, http://www.theatlantic.com/magazine/archive/2013/01/a-million-first-dates/309195/.

20. Zygmunt Bauman, *Consuming Life* (London: Polity, 2007). The quote here is from page 21.

21. Slater, *Love in the Time of Algorithms*, 121.

22. Illouz, *Why Love Hurts*.

23. Slater, *Love in the Time of Algorithms*, 126.

24. Yoosik Youm and Anthony Paik, "The Sex Market and Its Implications for Family Formation," in *The Sexual Organization of the City*, ed. Edward O. Laumann, Stephen Ellingson, Jenna Mahay, Anthony Paik, and Yoosik Youm (Chicago: University of Chicago Press, 2004), 165–193.

25. How did I calculate this? Using the *Relationships in America* survey, which asked respondents how many times in the past two weeks they've had sex, divide the number of times (0–14) in the past two weeks respondents reported having sex by the number of days (14) to get the probability that the respondent had sex on any given day in the past two weeks. So someone who reported having sex twice in the past two weeks has a .1428571 (2/14) probability of having sex on any given day. Then take the mean to get the percentage, on average, that are having sex on any given day. It's a rough estimate, to be sure.

26. The World Health Organization articulates a right to sexual health, which "requires a positive and respectful approach to sexuality and sexual relationships, as well as the possibility of having pleasurable and safe sexual experiences, free of coercion, discrimination and violence." The key term here is "possibility." It does not, however, articulate any sort of obligatory claims upon another person, save for their responsibility to resist coercive or violent action. WHO, "Sexual Health," http://www.who.int/topics/sexual_health/en/.

27. Jean M. Twenge, Ryne A. Sherman, and Brooke E. Wells, "Sexual Inactivity during Young Adulthood is More Common among U.S. Millennials and iGen: Age, Period, and Cohort Effects on Having No Sexual Partners after Age 18," *Archives of Sexual Behavior* 46 (2017): 433–440.

28. Anthony D'Ambrosio, "5 Reasons Marriage Doesn't Work Anymore," *USA Today*, April 13, 2015, http://www.usatoday.com/story/news/nation/2015/04/07/sex-columnist-5-reasons-marriage-doesnt-work-anymore/25398635/.

29. A portion of this section first appeared in the Austin Institute for the Study of Family and Culture's Fall 2014 report on the *Relationships in America* survey. https://www.relationshipsinamerica.com.

30. "Modern Marriage," *Pew Research Social & Demographic Trends*, July 18, 2007, http://www.pewsocialtrends.org/2007/07/18/modern-marriage.

31. Roy F. Baumeister, *Is There Anything Good about Men? How Cultures Flourish by Exploiting Men* (New York: Oxford University Press, 2010).

32. Bettina Arndt, *The Sex Diaries: Why Women Go Off Sex and Other Bedroom Battles* (London: Octopus Books, 2009).

33. Laumann et al., *The Social Organization of Sexuality*; Denise A. Donnelly, "Sexually Inactive Marriages," *Journal of Sex Research* 30 (1993): 171–179.

34. The entire sample of 15,738 respondents in the *Relationships in America* survey was asked how many times in the past two weeks they had had sex. If a respondent was married or cohabiting and reported zero instances of sex in that period of time, they were asked a follow-up question: "How long has it been since you last had sex with your spouse/partner?"

35. Among such couples age 18–23, the sexless rate is only 3.5 percent. Among 40- to 49-year-olds and 50- to 60-year-olds, the sexless (in the past three months) rates are 10 and 21 percent, respectively.

36. Karla Mason Bergen, Erika Kirby, and M. Chad McBride, " 'How Do You Get Two Houses Cleaned?': Accomplishing Family Caregiving in Commuter Marriages," *Journal of Family Communication* 7 (2007): 287–307.

37. Denise A. Donnelly and Elisabeth O. Burgess, "The Decision to Remain in an Involuntarily Celibate Relationship," *Journal of Marriage and Family* 70 (2008): 519–535; Donnelly, "Sexually Inactive Marriages."

38. Meghan Laslocky, "Face it: Monogamy is Unnatural," *CNN*, June 21, 2013, http://www.cnn.com/2013/06/21/opinion/laslocky-monogamy-marriage.

39. Cathy S. Greenblat, "The Salience of Sexuality in the Early Years of Marriage," *Journal of Marriage and the Family* 45 (1983): 277–288.

40. It is important to remember, though, that sexually inactive couples are more likely than sexually active couples to get divorced (and so remove themselves from eligibility for these analyses), deflating the sexual inactivity rates for those who remain married. It is not clear if having a longer marriage decreases rates of sexual inactivity or if sexually active marriages are simply more likely to last, or both.

41. The survey question appeared as follows: "In terms of politics, do you consider yourself very conservative, conservative, middle-of-the-road, liberal, or very liberal?"

42. Bell, *Hard to Get*.

43. Katherine G. Kusner, Annette Mahoney, Kenneth I. Pargament, and Alfred DeMaris, "Sanctification of Marriage and Spiritual Intimacy Predicting Observed Marital Interactions across the Transition to Parenthood," *Journal of Family Psychology* 28 (2014): 604–614; Alfred DeMaris, Annette Mahoney, and Kenneth I. Pargament, "Sanctification of Marriage and General Religiousness as Buffers of the Effects of Marital Inequity," *Journal of Family Issues* 31 (2010): 1255–1278.

44. Giddens, *The Transformation of Intimacy*, 203. Giddens qualifies this assertion, however, noting that "when directly bound up with reproduction, sexuality was a medium of transcendence."

45. Shannon Ethridge, "Searching for God, Settling for Sex," CNN, November 24, 2012, http://religion.blogs.cnn.com/2012/11/24/my-take-searching-for-god-settling-for-sex; Steve Taylor, "Transcendent Sex: How Sex Can Generate Higher States of Consciousness," *Psychology Today*, January 29, 2012, https://www.psychologyto-day.com/blog/out-the-darkness/201201/transcendent-sex.

46. Baumeister and Vohs, "Sexual Economics, Culture, Men, and Modern Sexual Trends."

47. Anna Mussmann, "Death Doesn't Care If You're Sexy." The quotes here are from paragraphs 3 and 7.

48. Philip Blumstein and Pepper Schwartz, *American Couples: Money, Work, Sex* (New York: William Morrow, 1983).

49. Leticia A. Peplau and Adam Fingerhut, "The Close Relationships of Lesbians and Gay Men," *Annual Review of Psychology* 58 (2007): 405–424.

50. An example of this is Jacqueline N. Cohen and E. Sandra Byers thorough evaluation of the sexual desire and behavior patterns of lesbian women in their article entitled "Beyond Lesbian Bed Death: Enhancing our Understanding of the Sexuality of Sexual-Minority Women in Relationships," *Journal of Sex Research* 51 (2014): 893–903. While it is a fascinating read, it is also undermined—at least in its ability to understand what is going on among *populations*—by the fact that its sample was recruited, in a method not unlike the influential National Longitudinal Lesbian Family Study (which is not national in its scope), "by means of an e-mail announcement that was posted on social and academic lesbian- and bisexual-related electronic mailing lists, as well as through announcements posted in community-based bookstores and community centers, placed in community newspapers and magazines, and distributed at community events." Hence, as the NLLFS is, their data set is overwhelmingly white (87 percent) and educated (70 percent finished college or a more advanced degree).

51. While statistically fewer coupled lesbians reported recent sexual activity, it bears noting that the sample size of currently coupled lesbians is modest (N = 84),

well below the 142 coupled gay male respondents and the far more numerous heterosexually coupled men and women in the data set. Statistical power, however, is not so low as to prevent an apparent between-group difference from appearing.

52. David Hurlbert reported lower desire for sexual activity among lesbians when compared with women in opposite-sex relationships. David F. Hurlbert, "Female Sexuality: A Comparative Study between Women in Homosexual and Heterosexual Relationships," *Journal of Sex and Marital Therapy* 19 (1993): 315–327.

53. Cohen and Byers, "Beyond Lesbian Bed Death," 893–903; Diane Holmberg and Karen L. Blair, "Sexual Desire, Communication, Satisfaction, and Preferences of Men and Women in Same-Sex versus Mixed-Sex Relationships," *Journal of Sex Research* 46 (2009): 57–66. Cohen and Byers assert, on page 894 of their study, "The term having sex is phallocentric, in that most people do not include genital touching or oral-genital activity, let alone nongenital sexual activities, in their definition."

54. Dietrich Klusmann, "Sperm Competition and Female Procurement of Male Resources," *Human Nature* 17 (2006): 283–300; Dietrich Klusmann and Wolfgang Berner, "Sexual Motivation in Mateships and Sexual Conflict," in *The Oxford Handbook of Sexual Conflict in Humans*, ed. Todd K. Shackelford and Aaron T. Goetz (New York: Oxford University Press, 2012), 233–256.

55. Cohen and Byers, "Beyond Lesbian Bed Death," 894.

56. Giddens, *The Transformation of Intimacy*, 28.

57. If sexual reticence in opposite-sex relationships was long due to elevated risk of pregnancy—now often reduced or eliminated—one might reasonably expect lesbian relationships to exhibit more, rather than less, sex. But they do not.

58. Sales, "Tinder and the Dawn of the Dating Apocalypse."

59. Bell, *Hard to Get*.

60. Ibid., 148.

61. Gladys Martinez and Joyce C. Abma, "Sexual Activity, Contraceptive Use, and Childbearing of Teenagers aged 15–19 in the United States," NCHS data brief, no. 209 (Hyattsville, MD: National Center for Health Statistics, 2015).

62. Giddens, *The Transformation of Intimacy*, 58.

63. Since the survey groups together numbers of sexual partners (e.g., 10–15) rather than asking respondents to volunteer a specific number, I took the midpoint of each range and assigned it to each respondent. For those men reporting 100 or more partners, I assigned them to 100. This elicits an estimate of the top 20 percent of men reporting 69 percent of the partners. When I assign the top category (100+) 150 partners, the share of all partners only rises to 71 percent.

64. Susan Walsh, "Sex and the Pareto Principle," *Hooking Up Smart*, September 14, 2010, http://www.hookingupsmart.com/2010/09/14/hookinguprealities/sex-and-the-pareto-principle.

65. In the *Relationships in America* data, 10 percent of men and 9 percent of women report having ever had overlapping sexual relationships. Men who have ever overlapped reported a median of 10 to 15 lifetime partners. Those men who never overlapped report a median of two lifetime partners. Looking at it a different way, only 18 percent of men with 16 or more partners in their lifetime had never overlapped, and 31 percent of those reported long-term overlap (defined as lasting one month or longer). Women report similarly.

66. Michael Carey, "Is Polyamory a Choice?," *Slate*, October 16, 2013, paragraph 3, http://www.slate.com/blogs/outward/2013/10/16/is_polyamory_a_choice. html.

67. Mark Oppenheimer, "Married, with Infidelities," *New York Times*, June 30, 2011, http://www.nytimes.com/2011/07/03/magazine/infidelity-will-keep-us-together.html.

68. Helen Fisher, "Casual Sex May Be Improving America's Marriages," Nautilus, March 5, 2015, http://nautil.us/issue/22/slow/casual-sex-is-improving-americas-marriages; Ann E. Tweedy, "Polyamory as a Sexual Orientation," *University of Cincinnati Law Review* 79 (2011): 1461–1515.

69. Nico Lang, "Gay Open Marriages Need to Come Out of the Closet," *The Daily Beast*, January 1, 2016, http://www.thedailybeast.com/articles/2016/01/01/gay-open-marriages-need-to-come-out-of-the-closet.html.

70. Ogas and Gaddam, *A Billion Wicked Thoughts* (New York: Penguin, 2012), 149.

71. Randy Shilts, *And the Band Played On: Politics, People, and the AIDS Epidemic* (New York: St. Martin's, 1987). The quotes here are from page 89.

72. Oppenheimer, "Married with Infidelities," paragraph 41.

73. Debra Umberson, Mieke Beth Thomeer, and Amy C. Lodge, "Intimacy and Emotion Work in Lesbian, Gay, and Heterosexual Relationships," *Journal of Marriage and Family* 77 (2015): 542–556. The quote here is from page 551.

74. Technically, the estimate among bisexual women is statistically indistinguishable from that reported by gay men.

75. Peter Arcidiacano, Ahmed Khwaja, and Lijing Ouyang, "Habit Persistence and Teen Sex: Could Increased Access to Contraception have Unintended Consequences for Teen Pregnancies?" *Journal of Business and Economic Statistics* 30 (2012): 312–325.

76. The survey asked respondents the question, "Think about your current (or most recent) sexual relationship (it may be a spouse). When did you first begin having sex with that person?"

77. It should be qualified that this sample does not include uncoupled adults—plenty of whom have already had sex, while some have not.

78. Lawrence B. Finer, "Trends in Premarital Sex in the United States, 1954–2003," *Public Health Reports* 122 (2007): 73–78.

79. Mark Regnerus, *Forbidden Fruit: Sex and Religion in the Lives of American Teenagers* (New York: Oxford University Press, 2007).

80. María del Mar Sánchez-Fuentes, Pablo Santos-Iglesias, and Juan Carlos Sierra, "A Systematic Review of Sexual Satisfaction," *International Journal of Clinical and Health Psychology* 14 (2014): 67–75.

81. See, among many recent study examples, the following: Holly N. Thomas, Rachel Hess, and Rebecca C. Thurston, "Correlates of Sexual Activity and Satisfaction in Midlife and Older Women," *Annals of Family Medicine* 13 (July/August 2015): 336–342; Elizabeth A. Schoenfeld, Timothy J. Loving, Mark T. Pope, Ted L. Huston, and Aleksandar Štulhofer, "Does Sex Really Matter? Examining the Connections between Spouses' Nonsexual Behaviors, Sexual Frequency, Sexual Satisfaction, and Marital Satisfaction," *Archives of Sexual Behavior* 46 (2016): 489–501.

82. Kathleen Bogle, *Hooking Up: Sex, Dating, and Relationships on Campus* (New York: NYU Press, 2008); Norval Glenn and Elizabeth Marquardt, *Hooking Up, Hanging Out, and Hoping for Mr. Right: College Women on Dating and Mating Today* (New York: Institute for American Values, 2001); Regnerus and Uecker, *Premarital Sex in America*.

83. Stuart Brody and Rui Miguel Costa, "Satisfaction (Sexual, Life, Relationship, and Mental Health) is Associated Directly with Penile-Vaginal Intercourse, but Inversely with Other Sexual Behavior Frequencies," *Journal of Sexual Medicine* 6 (2009): 1947–1954. See also Niklas Langstrom and R. K. Hanson, "High Rates of Sexual Behavior in the General Population: Correlates and Predictors," *Archives of Sexual Behavior* 35 (2006): 37–52.

84. Stuart Brody and Rui Miguel Costa, "Sexual Satisfaction and Health are Positively Associated with Penile-Vaginal Intercourse but Not Other Sexual Activities," *American Journal of Public Health* 102 (2012): 6.

85. Some of these other factors deserve brief mention as well. Married respondents report the greatest relational happiness, women less than men, and liberals (slightly) less than conservatives. Greater religiosity spells slightly better relational happiness, while more recent pornography use spells less. The standard U-shaped age curve appears as well. For a more focused evaluation of marital happiness, see Shawn Grover and John F. Helliwell, "How's Life at Home? New Evidence on Marriage and the Set Point for Happiness," National Bureau of Economic Research Working Paper 20794, December 2014, http:www.nber.org/papers/w20794.

86. Elizabeth A. Armstrong, Paula England, and Alison C. K. Fogarty, "Accounting for Women's Orgasm and Sexual Enjoyment in College Hookups and Relationships." *American Sociological Review* 77 (2012): 435–462.

87. Ibid., 455.

CHAPTER 4

1. Baumeister, *Is There Anything Good about Men?*

2. Hakim, "The Male Sexual Deficit"; Illouz, *Why Love Hurts*. The quote is from page 91.

3. Giddens, *The Transformation of Intimacy*, 120.

4. Baumeister, *Is There Anything Good about Men?*, 223.

5. Naomi Wolf, "The Porn Myth," *New York Magazine*, October 20, 2003, http://nymag.com/nymetro/news/trends/n_9437. The quotation in the section heading appeared in paragraph 8.

6. Ibid., paragraph 7.

7. Ibid., paragraph 11.

8. "Jennifer Lawrence Calls Photo Hacking a 'Sex Crime,'" *Vanity Fair*, November 2014, http://www.vanityfair.com/hollywood/2014/10/jennifer-lawrence-cover.

9. Carlos's commentary about Theresa and about her sexual and physical ideals reinforce Eva Illouz's assertion that "sexual attractiveness is made into an independent criterion by which to classify and hierarchize people," and into a criterion for mate selection well apart from long-standing concerns about social status, class, and other traditional forms of homogamy. See Illouz, *Why Love Hurts*, 54.

10. Wolf, "The Porn Myth," paragraph 10.

11. Illouz, *Why Love Hurts*, 9.

12. Ibid., 60. Strikingly, this is the only reference—and a passing one at that—which Illouz makes to pornography in what is otherwise a very illustrative study of the modern mating market dynamics.

13. Sales, "Tinder and the Dawn of the 'Dating Apocalypse,'" paragraph 121.

14. Giddens, *The Transformation of Intimacy*, 111.

15. Ibid., 120.

16. Darren E. Sherkat and Christopher G. Ellison, "The Cognitive Structure of a Moral Crusade: Conservative Protestantism and Opposition to Pornography," *Social Forces* 75 (1997): 957–980.

17. Jonathan Haidt, *The Righteous Mind: Why Good People Are Divided by Politics and Religion* (New York: Vintage Books, 2012).

18. If anything, porn is finding support in the academy. Publications in the new journal *Porn Studies*, for example, seem far more concerned with documenting industry inequality (such as differential treatment among porn actors) than with assessing the relationship consequences of porn in normal people's lives. See Marleen J. E. Klaasen and Jochen Peter, "Gender (In)equality in Internet Pornography: A Content Analysis of Popular Pornographic Internet Videos," *Journal of Sex Research* 52 (2015): 721–735.

19. Ann Friedman, "Too Much or Too Little: DSM-V's Gray Area on Sex Addiction," *New York Magazine*, May 23, 2013, http://nymag.com/thecut/2013/05/too-much-or-too-little-dsm-vs-gray-area-on-sex.html#.

20. Alexandra Katehakis, "Sex Addiction Beyond the DSM-V," *Psychology Today*, December 21, 2012, https://www.psychologytoday.com/blog/sex-lies-trauma/201212/sex-addiction-beyond-the-dsm-v.

21. Donald L. Hilton Jr. and Clark Watts, "Pornography Addiction: A Neuroscience Perspective," *Surgical Neurology International* 2 (2011): 19.

22. Why only ask about annual use? Because that is how the GSS asked about it starting back in 1972, when pornography use came via magazines in the back of the drugstore or by attendance at X-rated films. To preserve reliability—the ability to track answers to the same question over time, hence documenting trends—they still ask the same question at each iteration.

23. An expanded version of this section appears in Mark Regnerus, Joseph Price, and David Gordon, "Documenting Pornography Use in America: A Comparative Analysis of Methodological Approaches," *Journal of Sex Research* 53 (2016): 873–881.

24. Cynthia A. Graham, Joseph A. Catania, Richard Brand, Tu Duong, and Jesse A. Canchola, "Recalling Sexual Behavior: A Methodological Analysis of Memory Recall Bias via Interview Using the Diary as the Gold Standard," *Journal of Sex Research* 40 (2003): 325–332; Sharon R. A. Huttly, Fernando C. Barros, Cesar G. Victoria, Jorge U. Beria, and J. Patrick Vaughan, "Do Mothers Overestimate Breast Feeding Duration? An Example of Recall Bias from a Study in Southern Brazil," *American Journal of Epidemiology* 132 (1990): 572–575.

25. The answer choices offered were: today, yesterday, 2–4 days ago, 3–5 days ago, 1 to 2 weeks ago, 3–4 weeks ago, over one month ago, over six months ago, over a year ago, and "I've never intentionally looked at pornography."

26. Tom W. Smith and Jaesok Son, "Trends in Public Attitudes about Sexual Morality: Final Report," National Opinion Research Center, University of Chicago, April 2013. In the *Relationships in America* survey, 63 percent of respondents who reported pornography in the past six days agreed with the statement "Viewing pornographic material is OK." An additional 25 percent were unsure, and a little over 10 percent disagreed.

27. Smith and Son, "Trends in Public Attitudes about Sexual Morality."

28. Ogas and Gaddam, *A Billion Wicked Thoughts*. Additionally, the Chicago Health and Social Life Survey (CHSLS), collected in 1995 and 1997, hinted at greater porn use among gay men; its "Shoreland" neighborhood, which is overrepresented by gay and lesbian respondents, displayed past-year porn use rates (65 percent among men and 25 percent among women) that dwarfed—typically doubled—those male and female residents of other Chicago neighborhoods. See Van Haitsma, Paik, and Laumann, "The Chicago Health and Social Life Survey Design."

29. I draw little attention to the self-identity category "mostly homosexual," since the fewest number of women occupy it.

30. Gert Martin Hald and Aleksandar Štulhofer, "What Types of Pornography Do People Use and Do They Cluster? Assessing Types and Categories of Pornography Consumption in a Large-Scale Online Sample," *Journal of Sex Research* 53 (2016): 849–859.

31. Jane Ward, *Not Gay: Sex between Straight White Men* (New York: NYU Press, 2015).

32. Those who are unsure—they neither agree nor disagree that viewing pornography is OK—also tell a story. Forty-one percent of young moderates were not sure what they believed about porn, but only 22 percent of very conservative and very liberal young adults were similarly unsure.

33. Benjamin Edelmann, "Red Light States: Who Buys Online Adult Entertainment?," *Journal of Economic Perspectives* 23 (2009): 209–220. Edelmann's study lists many conservative states as the biggest buyers of adult entertainment, but the study has significant limitations. It uses data from only a single online adult entertainment provider, while no attempt is made to ensure that this single provider is representative of the entire market for adult entertainment. The analysis is also troublesome because much pornography is accessible for free (hence this provider may not be representative of the market for all adult entertainment both paid and free). Additionally, the percentage of broadband users who subscribe to the service is only one-half of 1 percent in the state with the highest percentage of broadband subscribers (Utah). This figure is far below the percent of adults who report viewing pornography recently, as the analyses herein document, and hence a single service can only represent a tiny fraction of the pornographic market, representing less than 1.5 percent of viewers in the past month.

34. An earlier version of this section, "Porn Use and Supporting Same-Sex Marriage," first appeared in *Public Discourse*, December 20, 2012, http://www.thepublicdiscourse.com/2012/12/7048/. While I realize that 8 of the top 10 states in terms of online porn consumption voted Republican in the 2008 presidential election, I am analyzing individuals' survey responses, not state-level data, which prevents me from falling into the trap of the ecological fallacy, or deducing things about individuals from the groups of which they are a part.

35. The gender effect on support for same-sex marriage is not profound but is robust, and has appeared in most Gallup polls in the past decade, has been true of the GSS since 1988, and is apparent in the NFSS and the *Relationships in America* surveys. As late as 2012, the GSS reported a gender gap in the moral approval of homosexual sex of 16 percentage points (35 percent of men and 51 percent of women).

36. Ogas and Gaddam, *A Billion Wicked Thoughts.*

37. Paul J. Wright and Ashley K. Randall, "Pornography Consumption, Education, and Support for Same-Sex Marriage among Adult U.S. Males," *Communication Research* 41 (2014): 665–689.

38. Paul Bedard, "Study: Watching Porn Boosts Support for Same-Sex Marriage," *Washington Times*, February 4, 2013, paragraphs 4–5, http://www.washingtonexaminer.com/study-watching-porn-boosts-support-for-same-sex-marriage/article/2520461.

39. Taylor Kohut, Jodie L. Baer, and Brendan Watts, "Is Pornography Really about 'Making Hate to Women'? Pornography Users Hold More Gender Egalitarian

Attitudes than Nonusers in a Representative American Sample," *Journal of Sex Research* 53 (2016): 1–11.

40. Giddens, *The Transformation of Intimacy*, 117.

41. Wolf, "The Porn Myth," paragraph 4.

42. Christopher J. Ferguson and Richard D. Hartley, "The Pleasure is Momentary . . . the Expense Damnable? The Influence of Pornography on Rape and Sexual Assault," *Aggression and Violent Behavior* 14 (2009): 323–329.

43. Even with virtual (that is, pornographic) violence, evidence is limited. To be sure, violent pornography exists in spades. Its popularity or uptake, however, appears limited. See Hald and Štulhofer, "What Types of Pornography Do People Use and Do They Cluster?"

44. George Gilder, *Men and Marriage* (Gretna, LA: Pelican, 1992).

45. Reinhard Hütter, "Pornography and Acedia," *First Things*, April 2012, http://www.firstthings.com/article/2012/04/pornography-and-acedia.

46. Samuel L. Perry, "Does Viewing Pornography Diminish Religiosity over Time? Evidence from Two-Wave Panel Data," *Journal of Sex Research* 54 (2017): 214–226.

47. Caroline Rigo, Filip Uzarevic, and Vassilis Saroglou, "Make Love and Lose Your Religion and Virtue: Recalling Sexual Experiences Undermines Spiritual Intentions and Moral Behavior," *Journal for the Scientific Study of Religion* 55 (2016): 23–39.

48. Milo Yiannopoulos, "The Sexodus, Part 1: The Men Giving Up on Women and Checking out of Society," *Breitbart London*, December 4, 2014, paragraphs 9 and 33, http://www.breitbart.com/london/2014/12/04/the- sexodus-part-1-the-men-giving-up-on-women-and-checking-out-of-society.

49. An earlier version of this section, "The Pornographic Double Bind," appeared in *First Things*, November 11, 2014, http://www.firstthings.com/web-exclusives/2014/11/the-pornographic-double-bind.

50. Porn use is seldom, however, a primary reason for seeking divorce, as some popular sources assert. See, for example, Amy Sohn, "A Laptop Never Says No: Online Porn is Changing (Read 'Destroying') Relationships," *New York Magazine*, n.d., http://nymag.com/nymetro/nightlife/sex/columns/mating/12044.

51. Giddens, *The Transformation of Intimacy*, 15.

52. Aniruddha Das, "Masturbation in the United States," *Journal of Sex & Marital Therapy* 33 (2007): 301–317.

53. In its large national data set of 16- to 59-year-olds, the Australian Study of Health and Relationships (ASHR) found that 65 percent of men and 35 percent of women masturbated in the past year; see Juliet Richters, Andrew Grulich, Richard O. de Vissen, Anthony M. A. Smith, and Chris Rissel, "Sex in Australia: Autoerotic, Esoteric and Other Sexual Practices Engaged in by a Representative Sample of Adults," *Australian and New Zealand Journal of Public Health* 27 (2003): 180–190. In Britain's National Survey of Sexual Attitudes and Lifestyles II, 86 percent of men and 57 percent of women reported masturbating

within the past year; see Makeda Gerressu, Catherine H. Mercer, Cynthia A. Graham, Kaye Wellings, and Anne M. Johnson, "Prevalence of Masturbation and Associated Factors in a British National Probability Survey," *Archives of Sexual Behavior* 37 (2008): 266–278. A large, nationally representative study of Swedish sexual life reports that for adults who have masturbated in the past 30 days, men masturbated an average of 4.5 times, and women an average of 1.5 times; see Brody and Costa, "Satisfaction (Sexual, Life, Relationship, and Mental Health) is Associated Directly with Penile-Vaginal Intercourse." Some may assert that any reports of low frequency of masturbation must be false, the product of social desirability bias, and that the real numbers—if they could be known—would be both high in frequency and comparable across social categories. While I concur that this behavior is subject to greater-than-average response bias, there seems to be no valid reason for questioning the assertion that some types of persons masturbate less than others, and that some exhibit little interest in the behavior.

54. Gert M. Hald, "Gender Differences in Pornography Consumption among Young Heterosexual Danish Adults," *Archives of Sexual Behavior* 35 (2006) 577–585; Mary B. Oliver and Janet S. Hyde, "Gender Differences in Sexuality: A Meta-Analysis," *Psychological Bulletin* 114 (1993): 29–51; Jennifer L. Petersen and Janet Shibley Hyde, "A Meta-Analytic Review of Research on Gender Differences in Sexuality: 1993 to 2007," *Psychological Bulletin* 136 (2010): 21–23.

55. Michael Reece, Debby Herbenick, Vanessa Schick, Stephanie A. Sanders, Brian Dodge, and J. Dennis Fortenberry, "Sexual Behaviors, Relationships, and Perceived Health Status among Adult Men in the United States: Results from a National Probability Sample," *Journal of Sexual Medicine* 7 (2010): 291–304; Debby Herbenick, Michael Reece, Vanessa Schick, Stephanie A. Sanders, Brian Dodge, and J. Dennis Fortenberry, "Sexual Behavior in the United States: Results from a National Probability Sample of Men and Women Ages 14–94," *Journal of Sexual Medicine* 7 (2010): 255–265.

56. Harold Leitenberg, Mark J. Detzer, and Debra Srebnik, "Gender Differences in Masturbation and the Relation of Masturbation Experience in Preadolescence and/or Early Adolescence to Sexual Behavior and Sexual Adjustment in Young Adulthood," *Archives of Sexual Behavior* 22 (1993): 87–98; Naomi N. McCormick, "Sexual Salvation: Affirming Women's Sexual Rights and Pleasures" (Westport, CT: Praeger, 1994); Julie L. Shulman and Sharon G. Horne, "The Use of Self-Pleasure: Masturbation and Body Image among African American and European American Women," *Psychology of Women Quarterly* 27 (2003): 262–269; Baumeister, Catanese, and Vohs, "Is There a Gender Difference in Strength of Sex Drive?"

57. Answer options were: today, yesterday, 2–4 days ago, 5–6 days ago, 1 to 2 weeks ago, 3–4 weeks ago, over one month ago, over six months ago, or over a year ago. Respondents were first screened beforehand by a question that asked whether they had ever masturbated.

58. It is possible, however, for more women than men to interpret the question about masturbation as concerning either a solo activity or an experience during paired sexual intercourse. The two cannot be distinguished here.

59. The estimates for "mostly homosexual" men and women are the least stable here, subject to modest sample sizes.

60. Laumann et al., *The Social Organization of Sexuality.*

61. A look nearby "off-diagonal" is equally illustrative. For example, only 10.3 percent of 24- to 35-year-old men who reported last looking at porn "today" reported last masturbation "yesterday."

62. Ian Kerner, "How Porn is Changing Our Sex Lives," *CNN* Health, January 20, 2011, paragraph 3, http://thechart.blogs.cnn.com/2011/01/20/how-porn-is-changing-our-sex-lives.

63. And yet for the same reason sex addictions can be notoriously difficult to break because people can readily recall sexualized memories and hence create pornographic scenarios in their mind.

64. A longer explication of this argument is found in Mark Regnerus, Joseph Price, and David Gordon, "Masturbation and Partnered Sex: Substitutes or Complements?" Forthcoming (2017), *Archives of Sexual Behavior.*

65. Osmo Kontula and Elina Haavio-Mannila, "Masturbation in a Generational Perspective," *Journal of Psychology and Human Sexuality* 14 (2002): 49–83; Steven D. Pinkerton, Laura M. Bogart, Heather Cecil, and Paul R. Abramson, "Factors Associated with Masturbation in a Collegiate Sample," *Journal of Psychology and Human Sexuality* 14 (2002): 103–121.

66. Laumann et al., *The Social Organization of Sexuality*; Pinkerton et al., "Factors Associated with Masturbation in a Collegiate Sample."

CHAPTER 5

1. Giddens, *The Transformation of Intimacy,* 58.

2. The flight from marriage in America is not a random process, however. Marriage rates in Rhode Island, Connecticut, New York, Massachusetts, New Jersey, and Florida in 2014 were less than half of those in Utah, Alaska, and Wyoming. In other words, some Americans are avoiding or delaying marriage more systematically than others. See US Census Bureau, American Community Survey, 2014. What is also worth noting here is how little the "shock" of the Great Recession affected the marriage rate. That is, it seems neither to have stimulated marriage—which would have surprised everyone—nor accelerated the retreat from it. It did, however, provoke a temporary leap in cohabitation and decline in divorce, neither of which would be reflected in this graph.

3. William Fielding Ogburn, ed., *Social Change with Respect to Culture and Original Nature* (New York: BW Huebsch, 1922).

4. Uptake of the Pill also reduced the need for parents to socialize their children about sex and fertility because the physical costs of sex to women have dropped

so dramatically. Prescribing birth control, many parents found, replaces that awkwardness. See Fernández-Villaverde, Greenwood, and Guner, "From Shame to Game in One Hundred Years."

5. Jennifer Johnson-Hanks, Christine Bachrach, S. Philip Morgan, and Hans-Peter Kohler, *Understanding Family Change and Variation: Toward a Theory of Conjunctural Action* (Berlin: Springer Verlag, 2011).

6. William Julius Wilson, *The Truly Disadvantaged: The Inner City, the Underclass, and Public Policy* (Chicago: University of Chicago Press, 1990).

7. Isabel Sawhill and Joanna Venator, "Is There a Shortage of Marriageable Men?" CCF Brief #56, Center on Children and Families at Brookings, September 2015, http://www.brookings.edu/~/media/research/files/papers/2015/09/ccf-policy-breif/56-shortage-of-marriageable-men.pdf.

8. Binyamin Appelbaum, "Study of Men's Falling Income Cites Single Parents," *New York Times*, March 20, 2013, paragraph 8, http://www.nytimes.com/2013/03/21/business/economy/as-men-lose-economic-ground-clues-in-the-family.html.

9. Baumeister and Vohs, "Sexual Economics," 523.

10. Neil Irwin, "We're in a Low-Growth World: How Did We Get Here?," *New York Times*, August 6, 2016, http://www.nytimes.com/2016/08/07/upshot/were-in-a-low-growth-world-how-did-we-get-here.html. See also Ian Hathaway and Robert E. Litan, "Declining Business Dynamism in the United States: A Look at States and Metros," Brookings Institution; Ryan A. Decker, John Haltiwanger, Ron S. Jarmin, and Javier Miranda, "The Role of Entrepreneurship in US Job Creation and Economic Dynamism," *Journal of Economic Perspectives* 28 (2014): 3–24.

11. Nicholas Eberstadt, *Men without Work: America's Invisible Crisis* (West Conshohocken, PA: Templeton Press, 2016).

12. Rosin, *The End of Men*, 21.

13. Adshade, *Dollars and Sex*, 85.

14. Baumeister and Vohs, "Sexual Economics," 521.

15. Other unrelated phenomena slow down marriage as well, including burgeoning educational loan debt. See, for example, Fenaba Addo, "Debt, Cohabitation, and Marriage in Young Adulthood," *Demography* 51 (2014): 1688–1701.

16. David Autor, David Dorn, and Gordon Hanson, "When Work Disappears: Manufacturing Decline and the Falling Marriage-Market Value of Men," NBER Working Paper No. 23173, February 2017; Steven Ruggles, "Patriarchy, Power, and Pay: The Transformation of American Families, 1800–2015," *Demography* 52 (2015): 1797–1823; Harari, *Sapiens*. Men with "craft occupations" have long been historically more apt to marry, but those jobs have declined considerably in the past 50 years, while the share of unemployed or underemployed young men has risen.

17. Ruggles, "Patriarchy, Power, and Pay," 1819.

18. Giddens, *The Transformation of Intimacy*, 59.

19. Ibid., 74.

20. Ibid., 77.

21. Margaret Archer, "*'Caritas in Veritate'* and Social Love," *International Journal of Public Theology* 5 (2011): 273–295. The quote is from pages 279–280.

22. Ibid., 281.

23. Illouz, *Why Love Hurts*, 13.

24. Anne Case and Angus Deaton, "Rising Morbidity and Mortality in Midlife among White Non-Hispanic Americans in the 21st Century," *Proceedings of the National Academy of Sciences of the United States of America* 112 (2015): 15078–15083.

25. Archer claims that "solidarity is one of the most pressing problems today," given how many people live alone. "Yet institutional interventions into relations, especially by social services, will fail . . . if they are undertaken according to bureaucratic protocols for 'cases', rather than as others entering into a human relationship with particular people in a spirit of friendship" (Archer, "*Caritas in Veritate*," 290).

26. Ibid. Dignity comes in rival forms today. Historically understood, dignity is about inherent worth and has much less to do with autonomy or independence than it does with the ability to flourish. Moreover, dignity cannot be created by social arrangement or policy. The postmodern conception of dignity entrusts individuals to determine their own standards and senses the diminution of dignity when they cannot.

27. Sociologist Steven Seidman notes that "a culture of sexual identities seems to have taken shape primarily in the United Kingdom and her former colonies: the United States, Canada, and Australia. ... Whether this social fact is related to British political culture, its free market individualism, or Protestantism, I cannot say. In any event, in these societies sexuality has functioned as a basis for claiming a core sense of self-identity and community." See Steven Seidman, *The Social Construction of Sexuality*, 3d ed. (New York: W. W. Norton, 2015).

28. Eli J. Finkel, Elaine O. Cheung, Lydia F. Emery, Kathleen L. Carswell, and Grace M. Larson, "The Suffocation Model: Why Marriage in America is Becoming an All-or-Nothing Institution," *Current Directions in Psychological Science* 24 (2015): 238–244.

29. Michael J. Rosenfeld, "Couple Longevity in the Era of Same-Sex Marriage in the United States," *Journal of Marriage and Family* 76 (2014): 905–918. See in particular Table 2 on page 914. An earlier version of this paper, presented at the 2012 annual meeting of the American Sociological Association, documented an interaction effect indicating that same-sex relationships were ironically more apt to break up when the social support of the respondents' parents for their union was greater.

30. Giddens notes the challenges that come from making up the rules as you go along. "Most lesbian women may be in a long-term relationship," he wrote, "but they have difficulty in gaining a sense of security in them." Giddens, *Transformation of Intimacy*, 135.

31. Megan Fulcher, Raymond W. Chan, Barbara Raboy, and Charlotte J. Patterson, "Contact with Grandparents among Children Conceived via Donor Insemination by Lesbian and Heterosexual Mothers," *Parenting: Science and Practice* 2 (2002): 61–76; Raymond W. Chan, Risa C. Brooks, Barbara Raboy, and Charlotte J. Patterson, "Division of Labor among Lesbian and Heterosexual Parents: Associations with Children's Adjustment," *Journal of Family Psychology* 12 (1998): 402–419; Henny M. W. Bos, Nan K. Gartrell, Frank van Balen, Heidi Peyser, and Theo G. M. Sandfort, "Children in Planned Lesbian Families: A Cross-Cultural Comparison between the United States and the Netherlands," *American Journal of Orthopsychiatry* 78 (2008): 211–219; Anne Brewaeys, Ingrid Ponjaert, Eylard V. van Hall, and Susan Golombok, "Donor Insemination: Child Development and Family Functioning in Lesbian Mother Families," *Human Reproduction* 12 (1997): 1349–1359. I have only located one study, based on British data, that suggested a slightly lower break-up rate for female than male same-sex couples: Charles Q. Lau, "The Stability of Same-Sex Cohabitation, Different-Sex Cohabitation, and Marriage," *Journal of Marriage and Family* 74 (2012): 973–988.

32. Timothy J. Biblarz and Judith Stacey, "How Does the Gender of Parents Matter?," *Journal of Marriage and Family* 72 (2010): 3–22. The quote is from page 17.

33. Judith Stacey and Timothy J. Biblarz, "(How) Does the Sexual Orientation of Parents Matter?," *American Sociological Review* 66 (2001): 159–183. The quote is from page 177.

34. Ibid., 177.

35. Demographic historian Steven Ruggles disagrees: "Except for a temporary spike at the end of World War II, divorce has increased almost continuously for 150 years." See Ruggles, "Patriarchy, Power, and Pay," 1797–1823.

36. Illouz, *Why Love Hurts*.

37. Reichert, "Bitter Pill," 28.

38. Brian J. Willoughby, Chad D. Olson, Jason S. Carroll, Larry J. Nelson, and Richard B. Miller, "Sooner or Later? The Marital Horizons of Parents and their Emerging Adult Children," *Journal of Social and Personal Relationships* 29 (2012): 967–981.

39. Gary S. Becker, "A Theory of Marriage: Part I," *Journal of Political Economy* 81 (1973): 813–846.

40. Reichert, "Bitter Pill," 29.

41. Catherine Hakim holds that "women's increasing economic independence allows them to withdraw from sexual markets and relationships that they perceive to offer unfair bargains, especially if they already have enough children or do not want any." See Hakim, "Supply and Desire," 6.

42. Michael Rosenfeld, "Who Wants a Breakup? Gender and Breakup in Heterosexual Couples." Paper presented at the annual meeting of the American Sociological Association, Chicago, August 2015.

43. Moreover, in contrast to Rosenfeld's expectation, Table 6.1 reveals that women outnumber men in thinking, talking, and deciding to separate.

44. Betsey Stevenson and Justin Wolfers, "The Paradox of Declining Female Happiness," *American Economic Journal: Economic Policy* 1 (2009): 190–225.

45. Ruggles, "Patriarchy, Power, and Pay," 1798.

46. Maria J. Kefalas, Frank F. Furstenberg, Patrick J. Carr, and Laura Napolitano, "Marriage Is More than Being Together: The Meaning of Marriage for Young Adults," *Journal of Family Issues* 32 (2011): 845–875.

47. See Eric Klinenberg, *Going Solo: The Extraordinary Rise and Surprising Appeal of Living Alone* (New York: Penguin, 2013).

48. To explore underlying structure in nonlinear data, I initially used local regression (LOESS), which suggested that simpler polynomial regressions may be appropriate. After fitting several polynomial regressions of order one to five, I found a fourth-order polynomial regression provided the best fit for the data.

49. Interestingly, 62 percent of women who report having been told more than once that they have a sexually transmitted infection said they wish they were married, well above the 47 percent of women who had never been told this.

50. Illouz, *Why Love Hurts.*

51. Wendy Wang, "Record Share of Wives Are More Educated than their Husbands," *Pew Research Center*, February 12, 2014, http://www.pewresearch.org/fact-tank/2014/02/12/record-share-of-wives-are-more-educated-than-their-husbands.

52. Kristina M. Durante, Vladas Griskevicius, Jeffry A. Simpson, Stephanie M. Cantú, and Joshua M. Tybur, "Sex Ratio and Women's Career Choice: Does a Scarcity of Men Lead Women to Choose Briefcase over Baby?" *Journal of Personality and Social Psychology* 103 (2012): 121–134.

53. Archer, "*Caritas in Veritate*," 290.

54. Norval D. Glenn, Jeremy Uecker, and Robert W. B. Love Jr., "Later First Marriage and Marital Success," *Social Science Research* 39 (2010): 787–800.

55. Ruggles, "Transformation of American Families."

56. Ruggles, "Patriarchy, Power, and Pay," 1808.

57. Ibid., 1815.

58. For examples of such credit, see Martha J. Bailey, "More Power to the Pill: The Impact of Contraceptive Freedom on Women's Life Cycle Labor Supply," *Quarterly Journal of Economics* 121 (2006): 289–320; Goldin and Katz, "The Power of the Pill."

59. One underestimated finding in my 2012 study of adult child outcomes is how resilient many adult children are to the deaths of their parents. It was far preferential—from the standpoint of economic, social, and psychological flourishing—to have lost a parent through death than from witnessing and navigating their divorce. See Mark Regnerus, "Parental Same-Sex Relationships, Family Instability, and Subsequent Life Outcomes for Adult Children: Answering Critics of the New Family Structures Study with Additional Analyses," *Social Science Research* 41 (2012): 1367–1377.

60. Terri D. Conley and Amy C. Moors, "More Oxygen Please! How Polyamorous Relationship Strategies Might Oxygenate Marriage," *Psychological Inquiry* 25 (2014): 56–63.

61. Giddens, *The Transformation of Intimacy*, 63.

62. Laurie Segall, "I have a Fiancé, a Girlfriend, and Two Boyfriends," *CNN*, January 28, 2015, http://money.cnn.com/2015/01/25/technology/polyamory-silicon-valley.

63. Dalton Conley, *Elsewhere, U.S.A: How We Got from the Company Man, Family Dinners, and the Affluent Society to the Home Office, BlackBerry Moms, and Economic Anxiety* (New York: Vintage, 2009), 143–144.

64. Laslocky, "Face it: Monogamy is Unnatural."

65. Yoosik Youm and Anthony Paik, "The Sex Market and Its Implications for Family Formation," in *The Sexual Organization of the City*, ed. Edward O. Laumann, Stephen Ellingson, Jenna Mahay, Anthony Paik, and Yoosik Youm (Chicago: University of Chicago Press, 2004), 165–193.

66. An additional 4 percent of respondents elected not to answer the question.

67. The sexual exchange model assumes that women prefer monogamous relationships more than men do, and that men—as a cost of being in a relationship with a woman—agree to monogamy as part of the terms. Among married Americans (people conceivably invested in monogamy), twice as many men as women (8.8 vs. 4.4 percent) agree that "it is sometimes permissible for a married person to have sex with someone other than his/her spouse." An additional 17 percent of married men (vs. 10 percent of married women) aren't sure what they think about that statement—neither agreeing nor disagreeing. And more men than women refused to answer the question (5.1 vs. 3.2 percent, respectively). When monogamy does not happen (for whatever reason), it doesn't mean that the exchange model is fatally flawed; it means that for some the terms of exchange have shifted, typically in a direction favoring men's interests (that is, away from monogamy).

68. Gracie X, "Compersion: A Polyamorous Principle that Can Strengthen Any Relationship," *Huffington Post*, March 6, 2015, paragraph 5, http://www.huffingtonpost.com/gracie-x/compersion-a-polyamorous-principle-that-can-strengthen-any-relationship_b_6803868.html.

69. The gender gap in marital infidelity is narrowing, and in the NFSS it does not appear at all: 19 percent of women report having ever had a sexual relationship with someone else while married or cohabiting, while the same is true of 18 percent of men.

70. Joseph Henrich, Robert Boyd, and Peter J. Richerson, "The Puzzle of Monogamous Marriage," *Philosophical Transactions of the Royal Society (B)* 367 (2012): 657–669.

71. Adshade, *Dollars and Sex*, 130.

72. If the social scientific world seemed to agree upon anything from the furor that erupted after my 2012 article on the adult children of parents who've been in same-sex relationships, it is that stability is a good thing for kids.

73. Henrich, Boyd, and Richerson, "The Puzzle of Monogamous Marriage," 666.

74. Kassia Wosick-Correa, "Agreements, Rules, and Agentic Fidelity in Polyamorous Relationships," *Psychology & Sexuality* 1 (2010): 44–61.

75. Helen Epstein, *The Invisible Cure: Why We Are Losing the Fight against AIDS in Africa* (New York: Picador, 2008); Vinod Mishra and Simona Bignami-Van Assche, "Concurrent Sexual Partnerships and HIV Infection: Evidence from National Population-Based Surveys" (Calverton, MD: Macro International, 2009); Martina Morris and Mirjam Kretzschmar, "Concurrent Partnerships and the Spread of HIV," *AIDS* 11 (1997): 641–648.

76. Hakim, "Supply and Desire."

77. Henrich, Boyd, and Richerson, "The Puzzle of Monogamous Marriage."

78. The associations between different religious groups and their sentiments about marriage, cohabitation, infidelity, no-strings-attached sex, and polyamory are discussed at length in the Austin Institute's summary report on the *Relationships in America* survey, https://www.relationshipsinamerica.com.

79. Pippa Norris and Ronald Inglehart, *Sacred and Secular: Religion and Politics Worldwide* (New York: Cambridge University Press, 2004); Cherlin, *The Marriage-Go-Round.*

80. Jeremy E. Uecker, Damon Mayrl, and Samuel Stroope, "Family Formation and Returning to Institutional Religion in Young Adulthood," Unpublished manuscript, August 10, 2015.

81. This was the central research of Regnerus, *Forbidden Fruit.*

82. Three percent did not answer the attendance question. Hence, the total discussed in this paragraph and Figures 6.5 and 6.6 amount to 97 percent of the population of 24- to 35-year-olds in the data.

83. Christian Smith, *Soul Searching: The Religious and Spiritual Lives of American Teenagers* (New York: Oxford, 2005).

84. Cherlin, *The Marriage-Go-Round.*

85. Arcidiacano, Khwaja, and Ouyang, "Habit Persistence and Teen Sex."

86. Justin Farrell, "The Young and the Restless? The Liberalization of Young Evangelicals," *Journal for the Scientific Study of Religion* 50 (2011): 517–532.

87. David Kinnaman, *Unchristian: What a New Generation Really Thinks about Christianity . . . and Why It Matters* (Grand Rapids, MI: Baker Books, 2012).

88. I attribute this to two things. First, there developed no tradition of Sunday School education among Catholics like there did among Protestants. Second, while Catholic priests are focused on the Mass following a short homily, the evangelical pastor down the street has just launched into a 30-minute sermon that functions as Christian education. Hence, the average Protestant service is far more "educational" in programmatic design than the average Catholic Mass.

CHAPTER 6

1. Centers for Disease Control and Prevention, *Sexually Transmitted Disease Surveillance 2014* (Atlanta, GA: US Department of Health and Human Services, 2015); Lena Sun, "STD Rates Hit Record High in U.S. as Screening Clinics Close," *Washington*

Post, October 20, 2016, https://www.washingtonpost.com/news/to-your-health/wp/2016/10/20/std-rates-hit-record-high-in-u-s-as-screening-clinics-close.

2. Seidman, *The Social Construction of Sexuality*.

3. Sandra M. Florian and Lynne M. Casper, "No Nest? Change in Childlessness in the U.S. 1988 to 2006–2010." Paper presented at the annual meeting of the Population Association of America, New Orleans, April 2013.

4. Giddens, *The Transformation of Intimacy*, 98.

5. Kristin Dombek, "'Date-Onomics,' 'The Sex Myth' and 'Modern Romance,'" *New York Times* Sunday Book Review, September 9, 2015, paragraph 1, http://www.nytimes.com/2015/09/13/books/review/date-onomics-the-sex-myth-and-modern-romance.html.

6. Alain Giami, "Sexual Health: The Emergence, Development, and Diversity of a Concept," *Annual Review of Sex Research* 13 (2002): 1–35; Alain Giami, "Between DSM and ICD: Paraphilias and the Transformation of Sexual Norms," *Archives of Sexual Behavior* 44 (2015): 1127–1138.

7. Bauman, *Liquid Love*, 59.

8. Illouz, *Why Love Hurts*, 46.

9. Lant Pritchett and Martina Viarengo, "Why Demographic Suicide? The Puzzles of European Fertility," *Population and Development Review* 38, Suppl. (2012): 55–71.

10. James Hamblin, "Fewer Women Are Having Babies than Ever Before," *The Atlantic*, August 10, 2015, http://www.theatlantic.com/health/archive/2016/08/not-having-kids-is-the-new-having-kids/495251/.

11. Still others struggle to have it both ways, echoing the words my wife and I heard one physician's assistant utter: "Isn't it strange how we spend our 20s trying our best to avoid pregnancy, only to spend our 30s doing the opposite?"

12. Wendell Berry, "Feminism, the Body, and the Machine," in *What Are People For?* (New York: North Point Press, 1990), 178–196.

13. Ibid.

14. Ibid.

15. Julie Beck, "Who's Sweating the Sexbots?" *The Atlantic Monthly*, September 30, 2015, http://www.theatlantic.com/health/archive/2015/09/the-sex-robots-arent-coming-for-our-relationships/407509; Caitlin Gibson, "The Future of Sex Includes Robots and Holograms: What Does that Mean for Us?," *The Washington Post*, January 14, 2016, https://www.washingtonpost.com/news/soloish/wp/2016/01/14/the-future-of-sex-includes-robots-and-holograms-what-does-that-mean-for-us.

16. Illouz painstakingly documents the (premodern to modern) shift that yielded a world in which women's worth and value are now "performatively generated" by and within romantic relationships, rather than as proceeding from "the social fabric of one's community." Hence "romantic interactions elicit acute anxiety." See Illouz, *Why Love Hurts*, 155, 124.

17. Giddens, *The Transformation of Intimacy*, 34.

18. "ART Success Rates," Centers for Disease Control and Prevention, http://www.cdc.gov/art/reports/index.html.

19. Tanya Selvaratnam, *The Big Lie: Motherhood, Feminism, and the Reality of the Biological Clock* (New York: Random House, 2014).

20. Laura Berman, "The Future of Sex: It Gets Better," *Wall Street Journal*, April 26, 2015, paragraph 12, http://www.wsj.com/articles/the-future- of-sex-it-gets-better-1430104231.

21. Naomi Wolf, "The Porn Myth," paragraph 11.

22. Aldous Huxley, *Brave New World* (New York: Bantam, 1958). The quote is from page 183.

23. Gary Shteyngart, *Super Sad True Love Story: A Novel* (New York: Random House, 2011).

24. Isabel V. Sawhill, "Beyond Marriage," *New York Times*, September 13, 2014, http://www.nytimes.com/2014/09/14/opinion/sunday/beyond-marriage.html.

25. Joseph A. Burke and Catherine Pakaluk, "The Contraceptive Revolution and the Second Demographic Transition: An Economic Model of Sex, Fertility, and Marriage," Department of Economics and Business Working Paper No. 1003, Ave Maria University, http://mysite.avemaria.edu/jburke/working-papers/WP1003-Burke-Pakaluk-Contraceptive-Revolution.pdf; Reichert, "Bitter Pill."

26. Berman, "The Future of Sex: It Gets Better," paragraphs 4–5.

27. Bell, *Hard to Get.*

28. Brody and Costa, "Satisfaction (Sexual, Life, Relationship, and Mental Health) is Associated Directly with Penile-Vaginal Intercourse."

29. Remember Giddens, *The Transformation of Intimacy*, 98: "[i]t would certainly not be right to suppose that childhood has remained unaffected by the world of pure relationships."

30. Joseph J. Fischel, "Per Se or Power? Age and Sexual Consent," *Yale Journal of Law & Feminism* 22 (2010): 279–341.

31. Smith and Son, "Trends in Public Attitudes about Sexual Morality."

32. "Statutory Rape: A Guide to State Laws and Reporting Requirements" (Washington, DC: US Department of Health and Human Services, December 15, 2004), https://aspe.hhs.gov/report/statutory-rape-guide-state-laws-and-reporting-requirements-summary-current-state-laws.

33. Bauman, *Liquid Love*, 57.

34. Archer, "*Caritas in Veritate*," 292.

35. Klinenberg, *Going Solo.*

36. Jessica Elgot, "Most Same-Sex Marriages in England and Wales Began as Civil Partnerships," *The Guardian*, January 13, 2016, https://www.theguardian.com/society/2016/jan/13/most-same-sex-marriages-england-wales-already-civil-partnerships.

37. Martin Kolk and Gunnar Andersson, "Two Decades of Same-sex Marriage in Sweden: A Demographic Account," paper presented at the 2016 Annual Meeting

of the Population Association of America, Washington, DC, http://epc2016. princeton.edu/uploads/160627.

38. In a convenience sample of 300 self-identified homosexual, bisexual, and heterosexual men and women, Lisa Diamond found more malleability among men than she anticipated, noting that 42 percent of lesbian women and 40 percent of gay men reported some attraction to the opposite sex within the past year. Thirty-one percent of gay men reported romantic feelings for women in the same time frame. See Lisa Diamond, "Just How Different Are Female and Male Sexual Orientation?," paper presented at Human Development Outreach and Extension Program, College of Human Ecology, Cornell University, October 17, 2013, http://www.cornell.edu/video/lisa-diamond-on-sexual-fluidity-of-men-and-women. Others see it in their data, too. A recent study of 188 same-gender orientation young adults noted that fluidity in attractions was reported by 63 percent of women and half of the men, and fluidity in orientation identity by 48 percent of women and 34 percent of men. See Sabra L. Katz-Wise and Janet S. Hyde, "Sexual Fluidity and Related Attitudes and Beliefs among Young Adults with a Same-Gender Orientation," *Archives of Sexual Behavior* 44 (2015): 1459–1470. And male sexual malleability, however, need not cut just one way, that is, from gay toward straight; see Ward, *Not Gay*.

39. For one example of the double standard here, sociologist Catherine Hakim notes that male sex work "tends to be ignored by pressure groups and policy-makers, who implicitly treat it as unproblematic." See Hakim, "Supply and Desire," 22. The campus consent debate, too, seldom mentions same-sex relationships.

40. Hald and Štulhofer, "What Types of Pornography Do People Use and Do They Cluster?"

41. See, for example, Mary Eberstadt, *How the West Really Lost God: A New Theory of Secularization* (West Conshohocken, PA: Templeton Press, 2013).

42. Ross Stolzenberg, Mary Blair-Loy, and Linda J. Waite, "Religious Participation in Early Adulthood: Age and Family Life Cycle Effects on Church Membership," *American Sociological Review* 60 (1995): 84–103; Jeremy E. Uecker, Damon Mayrl, and Samuel Stroope, "Family Formation and Returning to Institutional Religion in Young Adulthood," Unpublished manuscript, August 10, 2015.

43. Robert Wuthnow, *After Heaven: Spirituality in America since the 1950s* (Berkeley: University of California Press, 1998). The quote is from page 101.

44. Dan McQuade, "Kenney: It's not Christian for Chaput to Deny Communion to Gay Couples," *Philadelphia Magazine*, July 6, 2016, http://www.phillymag.com/citified/2016/07/06/jim-kenney-archbishop-chaput-gay-couples-communion.

45. Philip Rieff, *The Triumph of the Therapeutic: Uses of Faith after Freud* (New York: Harper & Row, 1965).

46. Rod Dreher, "Sex after Christianity," *The American Conservative*, April 11, 2013, http://www.theamericanconservative.com/articles/sex-after-christianity.

47. Ibid.

48. Adelle Banks, "Evangelicals Say It's Time for a Frank Conversation about Sex," *Washington Post*, April 19, 2012, https://www.washingtonpost.com/national/ on-faith/evangelicals-say-its-time-for-frank-talk-about-sex/2012/04/19/gIQA-QeuwTT_story.html.

49. Laurie Goodstein, "For Some Hispanics, Coming to America Also Means Abandoning Religion," *New York Times*, April 25, 2007, http://www.nytimes.com/2007/04/15/us/15hispanic.html.

50. Susan Moller Okin, *Justice, Gender, and the Family* (New York: Basic Books, 1991), 171.

51. Bauman, *Liquid Love*, 54.

52. J. Richard Udry, "Biological Limits of Gender Construction," *American Sociological Review* 65 (2000): 443–457. The quote here is from page 445.

53. The study in particular that Udry draws upon features a unique sample of 351 young women and their mothers (since pregnancy), from whom blood samples (for testosterone) were drawn and social surveys administered over the course of multiple decades.

54. David P. Schmitt, "The Evolution of Culturally-Variable Sex Differences: Men and Women are Not Always Different, But When They Are . . . It Appears Not to Result from Patriarchy or Sex Role Socialization," in *The Evolution of Sexuality*, ed. Viviana Weekes-Shackelford and Todd K. Shackelford (New York: Springer, 2015), 221–256.

55. Udry, "Biological Limits of Gender Construction," 454.

56. This paragraph first appeared in my article entitled "Sex is Cheap," *Slate*, February 25, 2011, http://www.slate.com/articles/double_x/doublex/2011/02/ sex_is_ cheap.html.

Index